New Orleans

Space Center

Popping Up Across America

A Travelogue and How To Guide

by

Arlene Trainor Corby

Bloomington, IN  Milton Keynes, UK

AuthorHouse™
1663 Liberty Drive, Suite 200
Bloomington, IN 47403
www.authorhouse.com
Phone: 1-800-839-8640

AuthorHouse™ UK Ltd.
500 Avebury Boulevard
Central Milton Keynes, MK9 2BE
www.authorhouse.co.uk
Phone: 08001974150

First published by AuthorHouse 5/31/2006

ISBN: 1-4259-4172-9 (sc)

Printed in the United States of America
Bloomington, Indiana

This book is printed on acid-free paper.

Table of Contents

Preface

If you are planning to purchase an RV (recreational vehicle) and head off into the wide blue yonder, I suggest that you consider starting in a pop-up camper. Our pop-up is very economical and easy to tow with our Ford F150. We get 18 MPG and have to keep looking back to make sure it is there. Also, a pop-up is virtually maintenance free. Our pop-up allowed us to test several scenarios. Our first fantasy was to purchase a Class A (shaped like a bus). Once we visited several campers who had them, we found it claustrophobic and very expensive to operate. Our next dream was to purchase a fifth wheel camper. These attach to the bed of the truck thus taking away valuable storage space. After living with that dream and talking to campers that had them, we were not comfortable with all the space we would loose in the back of the truck. A trailer was appealing, but it too had a high profile and could be difficult to maneuver. What ever your decision, do give yourself time to make the right one.

In "Popping Up Across America", I would like to take you on our journey which started on March 10, 2003 when Charles, my husband (age 63) and I (age 55) retired. Actually, I retired early in December to plan for a cross-country camping trip. In my mind's eye, I didn't want Charles to get too comfortable on the sofa with the remote control.

The last year I worked, every penny earned went into a separate savings account to fund our first year. For the past twenty-six years, Charles dedicated his working life to a career with an aviation association. His last position was that of Telecom Manager. This position was eliminated after he installed a state-of-the-art phone system. Fortunately, he was able to maximize the company's contribution to the 401K. That, along with Social Security and a pension, was how we planned to finance our retirement.

In our previous life, we liked to sail and chartered mid-size sailboats. That led us to buy a 45-foot ketch rig sailboat. The whole boat ownership experience proved to be a hardship and not the dream we had envisioned. For example, the labor involved refinishing the teak trim was arduous. Imagine, 45 feet of teak railing on the starboard side and 45 feet on the port side that needed sanding and varnishing. In addition, the cap rails, rub rails and numerous handrails needed the same kind of attention. It seemed like the process took forever. In addition to that stress, every time Charles went down into the engine room, he came up with a defunct part in hand that cost big bucks to replace. The dream of sailing off into the sunset was replaced with the nightmare of reality. So, after three years of ownership, we sold the boat. Sailing had been a big part of my life that started years before I met Charles. With a group of friends, we sailed extensively in the Chesapeake Bay and chartered sailboats in the Caribbean. I was even fortunate to be part of a crew that sailed up and down the eastern seaboard. They say that the happiest days in a sailor's life is the day he buys a boat and the day he sells it. This is true. An era in my life came to an end when we sold the boat.

A three-week tour of Europe compensated for my depression. The mission was to rediscover our land legs. Walking the streets and back alleyways of London and Paris was just the right medicine. Going off on our own, as much as a being part of the tour, was exciting and fun. Our imaginations soared with each explanation of the area's historical facts. I found myself taking notes and wrote stories about our adventures when we got home. I shared these stories with family and friends who enjoyed reading them.

The travel bug had bitten. Upon returning home, a new idea began to form. The events of 9/11 helped us decide to travel in the United States. The theory of driving and camping was tested with a ten day trip through New York State. From the Allegheny Mountains, up through the Hudson River Valley and across the Finger Lakes region, we traveled in our sedan (a 1992 Park Avenue) with a new, two-room Eureka tent and camping gear in the trunk. Our final destination was Charles' sister's home in Hamburg, NY. Some nights we slept in the tent, other nights we stayed with friends. There was one memorable night spent in the restored Belleview Bed and Breakfast Mansion on the Hudson River. This occurred when the campsite we were hoping to stay in was washed out as it had been raining heavily that day. Our luck prevailed when a nice lady at the Rhinebeck Visitor's Center said she could get us a room at the Mansion. This trip prepared us to venture forth in discovering America.

Having proved that tenting was the most economical way to travel and being fearful of our finances, we reasoned all we needed was a truck to carry all the gear. On a cold winter's night in January, we bought a truck from a private owner. It was a 1995 Ford F150. The color was an iridescent bluish/deep purple and it had comfortable, custom conversion style seats. The man made us sign a paper that said, "as is" although we shook hands with the understanding that our mechanic was to inspect it. The result of that inspection was being advised against the purchase. When we went to return the keys, the man said "too bad". We had bought the truck. As I followed Charles home, I saw a hubcap fly into a ravine as he went over a bridge. This was not a good sign. The truck cost $6,000 but cost another $3,000 to fix up. One area where we were able to save money was with the hydraulics. Our mechanic's Maryland inspection failed the hydraulics although the owner's paper said it passed. With his help, I took pictures of the problem areas and got in touch with the Motor Vehicle Department to challenge the owner's inspection paper. It turned out that my mechanic was right and the previous owner had to replace all the hydraulics. So, it was with great trepidation that we left on our trip wondering when the first breakdown was going to be. Fortunately, the truck held up very well.

We designed a cap to fit on the truck bed that cost $2,000. It was five feet high so we could stand up in it and the front was aerodynamically designed so as not to create drag. The back of the truck was then filled with lots of plastic bins that held everything we thought we needed and then some. A girlfriend commented that we had taken too much and offered her place to send the overflow once we had a chance to get organized. I had a feeling we would be taking her up on the offer.

A shelf in the back of the cap carried our travel books and the compartment in the front held bulk goods like paper plates, bowls and napkins. To complete the interior, we added a carpeted bed liner with a thick pad. On top of that went an egg carton mattress, and then our sleeping bag. Our plans were to move the bins to the front of the truck and sleep in the back when the weather got bad or if we didn't want to bother putting up the tent. We heard that you could stay in Wal Mart parking lots for free, if you asked the manager nicely.

So with money and map in hand, we set out to discover America, as cheaply as possible.

Acknowledgements

This book couldn't have been written without the shared vision of my wonderful husband. Charles drove most of the time and proved to be excellent, especially in high stress situations like when the road narrowed and a sign read 12% down hill grade. His patience really balances my zest for life. Through our travels, we have truly become soul mates, where I can be me and he can be himself. Recognizing his love for golf, we made sure that golf was an integral part of our agenda and to that end he played courses of varying terrain. It's tough living together 24/7, but it is worth it to be traveling, eating healthy and sharing each day's adventure. Thank you, honey for being so supportive.

The thought of writing this book came about through the encouragement of friends. It was hard leaving them behind in the working world. I hoped my stories of adventure would spark their imagination so that they felt they were along for the ride. Excited about what I was learning and seeing inspired me to e-mail my stories to them. The plan worked. It seemed they looked forward to reading my e-mails and made their thoughts known through returned e-mails of thanks. I was happy to know that they were traveling with us.

Old friends were rediscovered the first year of travel. They opened their homes and hearts to us and made us feel welcome. Thank you to The Jennings, Bill, Julia, Mary, Doug, Michael, Susan, the Grants, Marty and Carol and Sharon and Max. After traveling for days, we were so appreciative to be able to be at home with friends.

Before we left on our trip, my son and his lovely wife took us out to dinner. They made us promise to call every Sunday morning, around 10 a.m., so they could be sure to be home. Their concern was touching. They also agreed to receive and forward our mail to the post office at our next location. Their love and support made our travels that much more enjoyable. Thank you.

I want to thank the East Lake Library Writer's Workshop, especially the workshop leader Deanna Bennett. At my first meeting, I was asked to read a chapter out loud. It was so embarrassing that I wanted to crawl under the table. When it was over, their positive reactions surprised me. It was very educational to listen to their comments as well as hearing other inspiring writers read their work. I learned a lot about grammar, story flow and publishing.

A very special thank you goes out to our friend Janine, who accepted and stored our overflow boxes and answered numerous domestic questions from the road. They say you should have a friend read your book as part of the editing process and she agreed. Her comments were very valuable and encouraging.

Also credit must be given to Tracy Bozzonetti for designing the cover.

Sharon and Marshall, our friends from Frederick, opened their home to us on numerous occasions. Their warm hospitality has made our move to Florida an easier transition. In our last visit they were instrumental in helping us resolve final issues before going to press. They let us spend hours on their computer, fed us, and lent us their minds for numerous last minutes questions. For this we are very grateful.

Lastly, I would like to express a special thanks to you, the reader. I hope you find the stories tickling your funny bone and the information useful. Being a traveler, every day is new and exciting. There is a spring to our step and wonder in our eyes. So come with us and join the trail, like our forefathers before us.

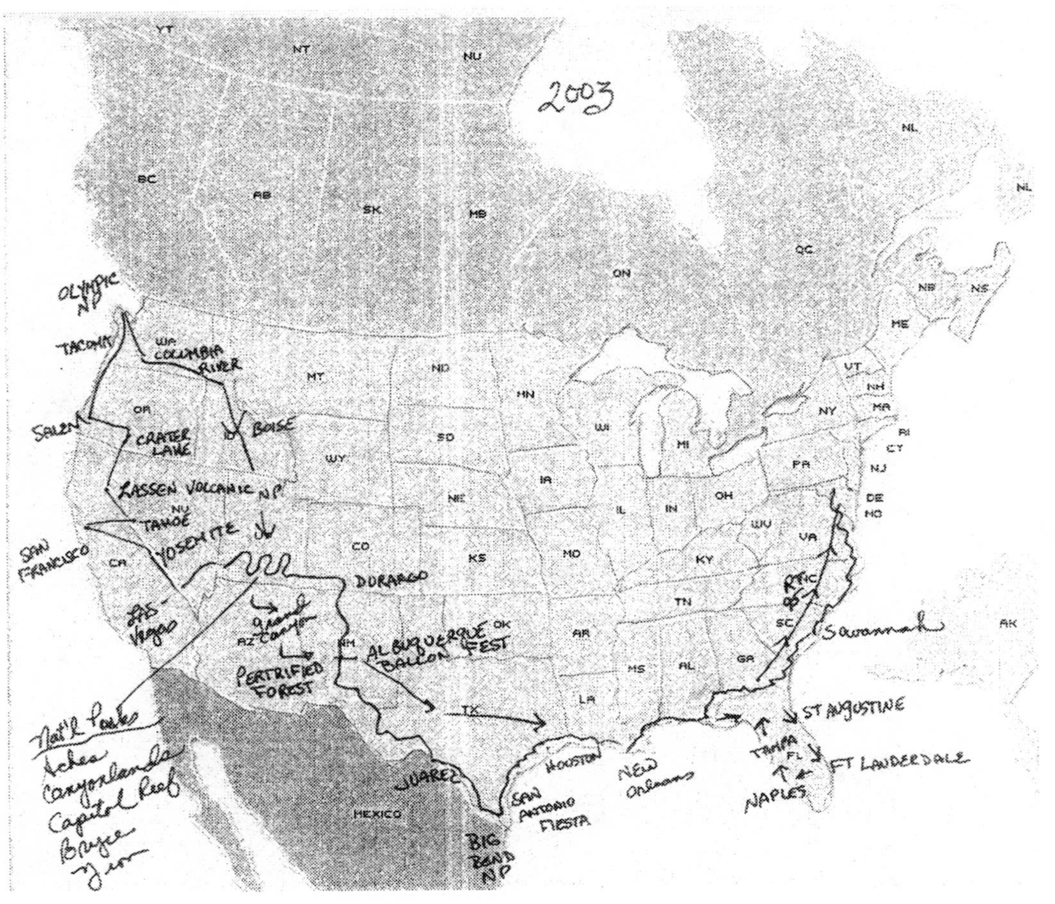

2003
OLYMPIC NP
TACOMA
SALEM
COLUMBIA RIVER
CRATER LAKE
BOISE
LASSEN VOLCANIC NP
TAHOE
YOSEMITE
SAN FRANCISCO
LAS Vegas
Grand Canyon
PETRIFIED FOREST
DURANGO
ALBUQUERQUE BALLON FEST
Nat'l Parks
Arches
Canyonlands
Capitol Reef
Bryce
Zion
JUAREZ
BIG BEND NP
SAN ANTONIO FIESTA
HOUSTON
NEW Orleans
Savannah
ST AUGUSTINE
TAMPA
NAPLES
FT LAUDERDALE

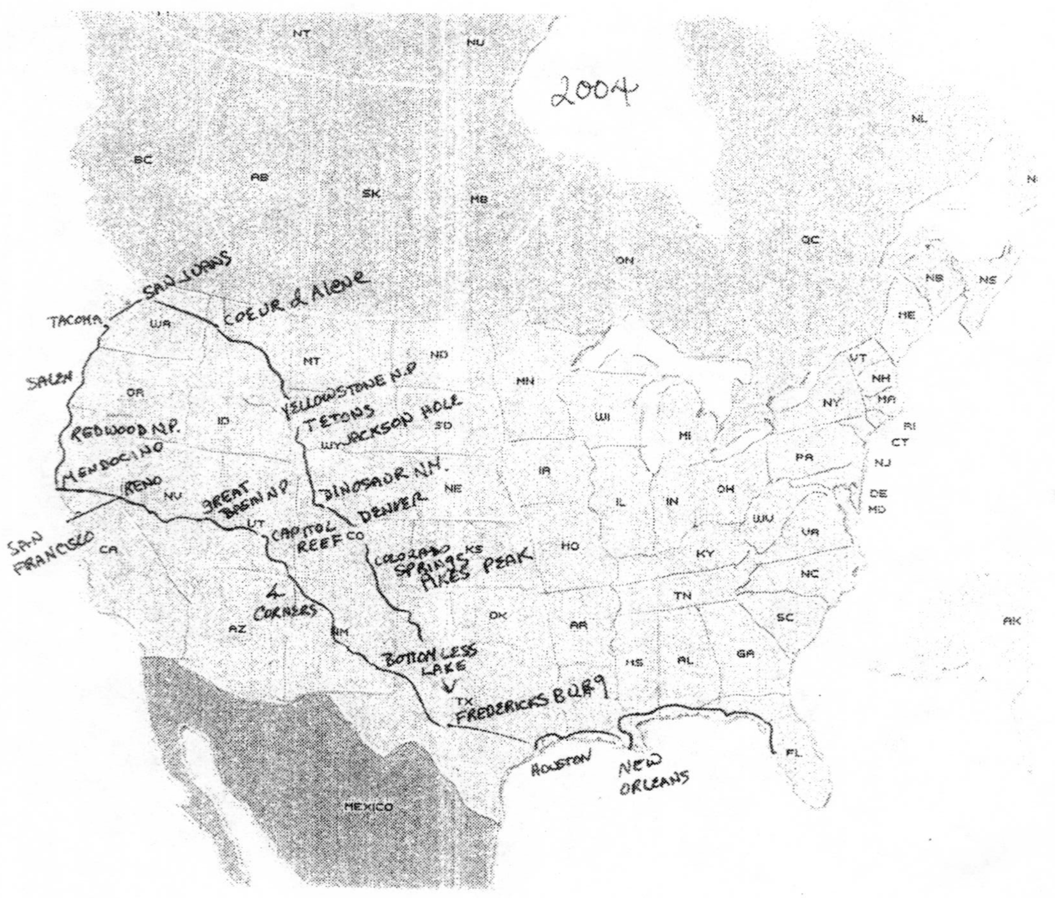

2004
SAN JUANS
TACOMA
SALEM
SAN FRANCISCO
REDWOOD N.P.
MENDOCINO
RENO
GREAT BASIN N.P.
CAPITOL REEF
4 CORNERS
COEUR d ALENE
YELLOWSTONE N.P.
TETONS
JACKSON HOLE
DINOSAUR N.M.
DENVER
COLORADO SPRINGS
PIKES PEAK
BOTTOMLESS LAKE
FREDERICKSBURG
HOUSTON
NEW ORLEANS
MEXICO

Year One
On the Road

Chapter One

A New Beginning

Leaving Frederick, Maryland, our first stop was Richmond, Virginia. One of our interests is visiting old hotels and the Jefferson Hotel, located in downtown Richmond, is a grand dame. Built in 1895, it was modeled after the Villa Medici in Rome and was to be the first of many magnificent hotels we would visit. A large marble statue of Thomas Jefferson greets visitors as they walk into the hotel. He stands under a Tiffany stained glass rotunda, which incorporates geometric designs of seashells and waves done in soft blues, pinks and sparkling crystals. The 5-diamond restaurant "Lemaire" is named after Thomas Jefferson's White House chef. Lemaire was noted for introducing French cuisine to the newly formed Americas, especially cooking with wine. For our first meal as traveling retirees, we lunched on a tasty French onion soup, in honor of Lemaire and for a sweet beginning, had a heavenly rich, chocolate mousse cake for dessert. As we discovered throughout our travels, history can be found in many places.

Leaving the hotel, we headed southeast taking back roads and discovered many colonial mansions. A friend had given us a book called "The Blue Highway*" and that set the tone for our trip. The name "Blue Highway" describes old roads that were in existence long before our spaghetti-like modern highways. On this particular road, we found plantations dating as far back as the early 1600's that survived the Revolutionary War and the War Between the States. Located between the colonial capitals of Jamestown and Williamsburg, and at a bend in the James River, this area was an ideal location for commerce. The main crop that brought top dollar to the early plantation owners was indigo, from which a valuable blue dye was extracted. Visiting the Berkeley Plantation, we were surprised to find out that on December 4, 1619, the first Thanksgiving was held there.

To ease our transition into retirement, we spent the first two nights with friends in Virginia Beach. It was a shock not to have to be on a schedule or get up and go to work. The weather was warm and we were excited. There we unpacked the truck and laid everything out on their lawn. A passerby thought we were having a garage sale. After assessing the situation, we sent three large boxes back home, mostly of winter clothes. It was spring and lots of good weather was ahead of us. We thought it would be fun to see how long we could stay in shorts. Looking into the cavern that was the back of the truck, we decided to build two side shelves, one on each side, to hold camping gear such as a lantern, blankets and pillows. From the space in between the rungs, we were able to hang clothes.

Our plans were to seek out large street party events like the French Quarter Festival in New Orleans, Fiesta in San Antonio and St. Paddy's Day in Savannah. I know some of you might be confused about why we chose Savannah to celebrate St. Patrick's Day, but a few years ago, I read in the Washington Post that next to New York City, Savannah had the biggest St. Paddy's Day street party in the United States. Now we had the time to see for ourselves. We left Virginia Beach with the truck repacked and charted our course to Savannah.

---

* Blue Highways, A Journey Into America by William Least Heat Moon, © 1982

Our first day on the road was a long one, but the scenery was breathtaking. Coastal North Carolina crosses many rivers, bays and estuaries and signs beckon the traveler to take "free" ferry rides to cross its waters. Being former sailors, how could we resist? From the delightful town of Currituck, we boarded a ferry and crossed the Albemarle Sound. It was a chilly, sunny day and we watched a few brave sailors heading south along the ICW (Inter Coastal Waterway) to warmer climes. We saw a man wearing the familiar bright yellow foul weather gear and our thoughts turned to the sailor's life of adjusting sails, navigation, weather predicting and maintenance and wondered if we missed that life. Surprisingly, the answer was no. Land navigation was a lot easier than plotting a course on the water. Assessing ourselves, we found we were warm and dry and in shorts.

We spent our first night in the primitive campground of Goose Creek State Park, located on the Pamlico River. Since the stay was only for one night, we decided to sleep in the truck instead of putting up the tent. A beautiful sunset capped the day and the night was filled with lots of stars. Lying on the dock, we could clearly see the Milky Way as it twinkled across the sky. It was hard to remember the last time we saw the Milky Way given the pollution and lights that surround most of our cities.

Beaufort (pronounced BOW'-fort), North Carolina was a place I wanted to visit for several years and now we had the time to stop and explore. High on my list was a visit to the Maritime Museum. There we saw exhibits describing the survival of the early watermen and their communities. One of the more impressive displays contained artifacts recovered from the 18th Century shipwreck believed to be from Blackbeard's flagship, the *Queen Anne's Revenge*. Another reason to visit the Maritime Museum was for its fantastic nautical library. Walking through town, we saw lots of well maintained historic homes, dating from the 1600's. Many of these homes were B&B's on tree-canopied streets. I must confess that the inns tempted us with nice accommodations, but we were on a different mission. St. Paddy's Day was fast approaching and Savannah beckoned us.

Continuing on, the rolling countryside announced the coming of spring. It was early April and the forsythias and daffodils were starting to bloom. It was nice not seeing fast food chains or endless construction projects. The Cypress trees and moss confirmed that we were in the south. A roadside sign that advertised shrimp for $3.99 a pound welcomed us. In comparison, up north it would be $5.99 a pound.

Chapter Two

In Search of St. Paddy

Skidaway State Park in Savannah, Georgia, was to be our home for a week as we celebrated its famous St. Patrick's Day celebration. Reservations were made months in advance because we knew that the campground would be full. Our arrival at the campsite was greeted by gray skies and we had just enough time to put up our tent and connect to electricity. Then the rains came. Showers, thunderstorms, and drizzle lasted most of the day. We monitored the weather on the truck's CB and the National Oceanic & Atmospheric Administration (NOAA) was predicting possible tornados. It had been a little over a week since we left Frederick, Maryland and the tent situation was proving to be very cramped. Living out of bins was getting old, real fast. On the bright side, we were glad to have made it to our destination.

The historic district of Savannah is made up of 24 park squares. Temple Mickve Israel is located on Montgomery Square and is close to Catholic, Baptist, Presbyterian and Lutheran houses of worship.

Many of these buildings rival their counterparts in Europe. On the first Friday night of our stay, we attended Sabbath services at Temple Mickve Israel. It is the third oldest Jewish congregation in the United States (New York City being first and Charleston, South Carolina being second). Forty-two Jews arrived in Savannah in 1733, fleeing persecution from the Span. Many other religions were experiencing a similar fate and the influx of immigrant boats was too much for New York City's harbor to handle. Many ships were diverted from New York City to Savannah, Georgia and Galveston, Texas.

In preparation for our visit to Savannah, I read the book, "Midnight in the Garden of Good and Evil" written by John Berendt. His book offers a peek inside the characters and culture surrounding a well publicized murder that took place in Savannah on the night of May 2, 1981. After services, I asked an older congregant (four generations in Savannah) how true the book was. She said it was, "pretty much true". Next to us sat a gentleman who looked like the actor, John Lithgow. He and his wife just moved to Savannah from Carlsbad, California, and offered to give us a tour. We got in their car and they graciously pointed out interesting tidbits about the mansions, squares and legends. Large oak trees abound in the squares with some dating back as far as the early 1800's. They told us of public hangings in Johnson's Square and that since its trees bear no moss, superstition is that it is haunted. Johnson's Square was also the place for public gatherings and political rallies. It was here that the Declaration of Independence was read. Each square had a statue to remind us of our young country's history. Benjamin Franklin, Marquis de Lafayette, and the Chippewa Indians are just to name a few.

James Edward Oglethorpe was the founder of the new colony of Georgia and laid out the streets and squares in 1733. Today, houses around the squares are Southern architectural gems. The Moses Eastman house inspired the design of the White House and the Hamilton Turner House inspired Disney's Haunted Mansion. A superstitious story is told about the Telfair House, which was donated to be used as a museum. The donor requested "no music or drinking in the house". On the museum's opening night, her wishes were disobeyed and a cocktail reception was held in the lobby. The next day, the contents of the house were found in disarray and now parties are held in the garden.

After four days of rain, the Sunday before St. Patrick's Day was finally sunny. The campground was in party mode with shamrocks in trees and green lights on campers. As predicted, it was a full camp with no vacancies. Getting an early start, we drove to the wharf and parked in the garage on River Street. It was a short walk to Belford's Restaurant where, from a window seat, we watched the market come alive. Merchants displayed their goods and prepared for another day of St. Paddy festivities. Our waitress said it was wall-to-wall people last night, even in the pouring rain. After breakfast, we put on our green sweaters, shamrock beads and finished our Irish coffee feeling St. Paddified.

Brick warehouses, five stories high, lined River Street and the cobblestone road along the wharf reflected a time when the port was alive with commerce. It was rumored that many a drunken sailor woke up to find himself on a merchant ship, heading for foreign ports. The scene was a perfect backdrop for a street party. Stages were set up along the wharf for music and entertainment. Waterfront bars were open for business and green beer was on tap. The crowd ranged between young and old, and the water in the fountains ran green.

After walking the wharf, we headed off to explore the Squares. We noticed that a crowd was gathering in Madison Square. At the statue honoring Sergeant William Jasper, a memorial ceremony was about to start. He was a local hero, of Irish descent, who fought in the Revolutionary War. All branches of service were there including a four star general that even made my husband stand at attention. Sergeant Jasper was famous for retrieving the Savannah flag at the Siege of Savannah. Just when the British thought they had won, the flag proudly showed their defeat. It was a moving ceremony. Each military service played its anthem and I was surprised to remember them all. The ceremony ended as a wreath was laid at the base of the statue while bagpipes played Amazing Grace.

St. Patrick's Day has been celebrated in Savannah for 179 years. It is an important holiday because it honors the Irish immigrant workers who settled here. Fleeing the potato famine in their homeland, they brought their farming skills to America. These immigrants were a stout and proud people who worked hard and partied hard. In my hometown of Philadelphia, the Italians celebrate their heritage with the January 1st Mummer's Day Parade. This tradition has been going on for over 100 years and is where I developed my love for street parties, parades and history.

As evening approached, live music, beads and beer ruled. The crowd by the wharf sparkled with glitter, bubbles, feathers and lights. Everyone was politely partying.

March 17, St. Paddy's Day. We awoke to horrific downpours and found ourselves surrounded by water. Huge puddles formed around our tent and the weather forecast was not promising. We got out our foul weather gear and boots and sloshed through the water to move the tent to a drier spot. We were pitiful, sitting inside the tent watching the parade on a crate that held the TV. This was not how we envisioned our retirement. A heavy electrical cord was connected to the 30-amp box outside. Although the tent was dry, it sagged from all the water and all around us were large puddles. However, we were not as sad as the marchers who dodged huge puddles on the parade route. One camera was located around the corner from one of these puddles and we could see the surprise of the marchers when they turned the bend. Five men dressed in 1940's military outfits with high, leather boots proudly marched through the puddle to the roar of the crowd. An announcer said that they had never, ever seen so much rain on St. Patrick's Day. To make matters worse, it was high tide and the floats actually began to float as the streets filled with water. It was interesting listening to the commentators describe the people, their floats and memories of yesteryear.

The weather was making it extremely uncomfortable to tent camp. The words of a workmate drifted through my mind, "Tent, cross-country? That's crazy. Do you want to have to live out of bins? Schlepping them in and out of the truck? Do you want to sleep on the ground?" The answer was finally clear. NO! It was time to move to the next level of camping and buy a RV of some sort. The next day was sunny, so we took everything out of the tent and scattered it around the campsite to dry. Then we left. The park ranger had been watching us move the tent numerous times and thought we had given up.

Hastily, we bought the first used pop-up we found. B camping, we wanted to start with the least cumbersome ca liked the tenting aspect but wanted to be up off the ground. R with the pop-up, the park ranger stopped by and congr us on our new purchase. A nearby neighbor brought over a jar of homemade jam for a new, sweet beginning. It felt great to be up off the ground and have amenities such as heat, air conditioning, a refrigerator, a comfortable mattress and cabinets. Best of all, we were dry. We emptied three bins into the camper that quickly disappeared into drawers and donated the empty bins to the park office.

Bonaventure Cemetery played a prominent role in the book of "Midnight in the Garden of Good and Evil" and we had to visit it. Situated high on a bluff, the cemetery overlooks the Savannah River. Some of the statuary dates back to the late 1700's. One of Bonaventure's famous residents is Johnny Mercer, a popular songwriter in the 50's. A white marble bench next to his tombstone remembers all his hit songs such as *Autumn Leaves, Charades*, and *The Days of Wine and Roses.* The hot pink, red and purple colors of the azaleas were in full bloom, and against the white statuary, made the morning serenely beautiful.

The Travel Channel said that Savannah was the most haunted city in the world. York, England was the second and New Orleans, third. Therefore, it seemed appropriate to spend our last night in Savannah on a ghost tour. Our first stop was the 1754 Pirate's Tavern that Robert Lewis Stevenson describes in the beginning of "Treasure Island". Another stop was Jim Williams' house, the main character in "Midnight in the Garden of Good and Evil". He was an antique dealer who lived in a mansion on Montgomery Square and was famous for his Christmas parties. They say that around Christmas, one can hear the sound of partying flow on to the street and Jim can be seen at the upstairs window. Bye Jim. Bye lovely Squares. Bye St. Paddy's Day. It's time to move on.

About seventy-five miles south lay the Okefenokee National Wildlife Refuge. It was here that Charles became an official senior citizen by purchasing the Golden Age Passport. The golden age is 62 and for a one-time fee of $10, the National Parks Service gave him a pass that will allow us to visit national parks for a fraction of the cost and in some cases, free. Eager to explore the swamp, we followed a trail from the Visitor's Center that led to the homestead of W.T. Chesser. Seeing what one man and his family accomplished in the early 1800's in this harsh environment was amazing. What surprised us the most was the lack of grass in the front yard. It was all sand. A Ranger explained that it was so the family could easily spot one of the five poisonous snakes that crawled around in this region. Thankfully, we didn't spot any. At sunset, we climbed a lookout tower and heard the frogs and birds singing their songs welcoming spring.

Charles likes driving at night and I was glad because the road through the swamp went on for 40 miles. A great country radio station played down-home music that amused us along the way. I wished I had remembered where the station was on the dial. Since it was late, we spent the night in the truck, at a Wal Mart. The price was right – free and again, the back of the truck was comfortable to sleep in.

The Okefenokee Swamp borders Florida and it was an easy drive along the panhandle to our next destination, Pensacola and Big Lagoon State Park. Spring breakers were hitting the beaches for Memorial weekend. We were lucky to get a spot, as it was probably the last one in the area. Big Lagoon State Park impressed us with its two beaches, a boardwalk that rose over the Grande Lagoon and connected the beaches. From an overlook, the barrier island of Presidio State Park Beach is visible and at night, the Gulf waters could be heard from our camp site. The bathrooms were immaculate, the trails inviting and the people very friendly. One day we drove to Pensacola and found a jazz concert in a downtown park; another day found us in the tower watching boats traversing the Inter Coastal Waterway (ICW), and the best day was when we sunbathed on a deserted beach. Retirement was starting to feel really good.

Chapter Three

Struttin' Down Bourbon Street

It was the first Monday in April when we got an early start for our drive to Louisiana (pronounced LOOZE'-ē-ana, to the locals). Around 3 p.m., the CB in the truck went off with a loud buzz. This was the first time we heard the warning and wondered where the sound was coming from. Then we figured it out. It was coming from our CB broadcasting an advisory of severe thunderstorms and potential tornadoes. Apparently, the CB has an alert mode that is independent of whether it is turned on or not. The sky had turned black and the wind was picking up. Seventy mile per hour winds were predicted. A few campers were pulling off the road so we followed them to a shopping mall parking lot and awaited the end of the storm. Since we were new to towing a camper, and more bad weather was forecast for the evening, we decided to spend the night, in the truck, at the Louisiana Visitor's Welcome Center. There was so much rain that the Louisiana welcome sign, in front of the center, was covered half way up with water. A few truckers parked in the back of the Visitor's er kept us company but kept their motors running all night, wnich was not conducive to a good nights sleep. In the morning, Charles waded to the welcome center and came back with a fresh cup of hot coffee. The folks there were very helpful in providing information on where, in southern Louisiana, we could hear good music and eat local food.

The highway took us around the perimeter of New Orleans where funnel clouds could be seen hovering above the city. It was a scary sight. Fortunately, Bayou Segnette (pronounced SIN'-yet) State Park wasn't far and the clouds began to disperse as we crossed the Huey P. Long Bridge. The campground is located in a suburb of New Orleans called Westwego. It had clean bathrooms, paved pads and a very helpful staff.

Our main purpose of being in southern Louisiana was to find out more about the Creole and Cajun cultures. The difference being that "Cajun" represents the people expelled from Nova Scotia by the French in the 18th Century. They brought to southern Louisiana language, music, and food. Creoles were descendents of settlers from before the Louisiana Purchase. They were mainly French, Spanish and free men of color and their cuisine was more upscale. From both of these cultures, a unique blend of Spanish and French cooking makes this region a culinary haven.

Our first New Orleans destination was a restaurant called Michaul's. Located in the Garden District, it is famous for its live bands. It was difficult finding the restaurant, because it was located on a one-way street. Getting lost gave us a chance to see the wonderful architecture of the city. Michaul's has a large dance floor where locals and tourists danced to a live Cajun band. Cajun music, traditionally sung in French, is the folk sound of the Arcadians' struggles and love of life. Dance lessons were given and soon a *fais do do (fay' doe doe -Creole for "a party")* commenced. This was our primer for what was to come. Encrusted catfish, meat pies and crawfish gumbo was what we ordered for dinner.

The next morning, we drove north on River Road and stayed close to the levees of the Mississippi River. To see the river, travelers must take a road to the top of a levee. River Road winds around and around and seemed to go on forever. It was surprising to see so many refineries on the shoreline. We passed a very old cemetery and a vacant plantation that had rows of slave cabins close to the road. This scene gave us an unsettling feeling as we peered into the harsh reality of what was once a way of life. Over 400 plantations existed between Baton Rouge and New Orleans. Constructed between the late 1700's and mid 1800's, most were owned and operated by Creole families. Today, only eight plantations exist.

We chose to tour the 1805 Creole Plantation called, "Laura's Plantation". It was the Creole custom to pass on inheritance to the brightest child and Laura was that child. She inherited the plantation at age 13. In later years, she wrote a published diary called, "Memories of the Old Plantation Home". In her book, Laura described what life was like in the upper class of Creole Society. She lived on a successful sugar plantation and her story covers a span of 250 years and includes information about the slaves who worked on the plantation. The family was so wealthy that they also owned a home in the French Quarter. Alcee Fortier worked at Laura's Plantation and was famous for writing the "Tales of Bre'r Rabbit". These were folk stories he collected from the slaves of Senegal from West Africa whose labor built the plantation. The workmanship in the construction of the main house and the brickwork was very exact, especially when using primitive tools and plans. All the pegs were hand hewn and the beams very straight. In the back of the house was a kitchen garden and a few outbuildings. These supported plantation life along with a few slave cabins.

There was much formality in the upper echelon society of Creoles in New Orleans. Two separate entrances to the house segregated the men and women. The women stayed on one side of the house, the men on the other. If a man was caught looking at a woman, a challenge to a duel could end someone's life.

Before leaving this area, we stopped in Vacherie to eat at the B&C Seafood Market and Cajun Deli. The owner was a big man with a heavy Cajun accent and a warm smile. In a deep voice, he welcomed us graciously and answered my questions about pronunciations and food descriptions. The deli case housed such delicacies as alligator balls, crawfish, shrimp, oysters and frog legs. Boudin (pronounced BOO'-dah with the "n" silent) is a sausage popular in southern

Louisiana. Signs for it were all along the road and it is served in gas stations, delis and restaurants like hot dogs are served in gas stations and groceries up north. We had to have some and this was the place to try it! It tasted like sausage with rice in it. The deli brochure described a family of fisherman, where skills were handed down for three generations. The food preparation came from the family's own recipes.

Further down River Road we boarded a ferry in Eduard (pronounced ED'-werd). It crossed the Mississippi where, on the other side, were more refineries and chemical plants. Locals call this area "Cancer Alley" because of the high frequency of illness related to the industry's pollution. Sometimes our explorations took us to unpleasant places, but that wasn't very often.

About twenty miles from our campground was the Algiers Point Ferry. It crosses the mighty Mississippi and delivers passengers right into the heart of the French Quarter. The ride is free but parking costs $5.00. The ferry stays open late and it is exciting to ride across the Mississippi River. Algiers Point was once home to the not-so-famous musicians that lived there during the heyday of Storyville. Sadly, all the buildings that made up Storyville are gone, but stories of the bordellos and the many great musicians that entertained there are legendary. One of the most famous musicians to come out of Storyville was Louis Armstrong.

Also located in Algiers and not far from the ferry is Blaine Kern's, "Mardi Gras World". The majority of Mardi Gras floats are made here. We started in the gift shop, which had a most impressive selection of books on the history of Mardi Gras from its earliest stages (dating back to 1699) to the present. There were books on the costumes, party invitations to the balls and, of course, the parades. We joined the tour that went through the process of how the floats were designed, made and then recycled for next year's parade. One Krewe's (club) float was 240-feet long and was decorated with fiber optics depicting creatures from the sea. It was large enough to hold 225 riders. During Mardi Gras, over a half a million dollars worth of beads, doubloons and trinkets are thrown to the waiting crowds. Faux painters were redesigning backgrounds, and artists were drawing next year's floats. It reminded me of the paint-by-number kits, popular in the 50's.

These floats were being painted for next year's Mardi Gras para... was like the world's largest fun house. Several shelves contained large Styrofoam heads of various characters like the head of an Indian, the head of a pig, the head of a fox and so on. Larger-than-life figures, some 12 feet and higher, lined the walls. Louis Armstrong, Spiderman, Miss Piggy and many famous men, women and gods were there. Whatever the Krewe's theme, the artisans at Blaine Kern's "Mardi Gras World" knew how to bring their designs to life.

At the beginning of the tour, we saw a movie of past parades and then King Cake was served. In 1872, the Krewe of Rex selected the following colors to represent Mardi Gras. Green stood for faith, purple for justice and gold for power. It is these colors that can be found all over New Orleans and is also the sweet icing that is drizzled on top of the King Cake. The King Cake can be traced to medieval times. Inside one particular slice is a small plastic doll. King Cakes start circulating around New Orleans' schools, offices, and churches from January 6 (Epiphany) until Lent. The baby doll is symbolic of the baby Jesus. Whoever finds the baby gets to buy the next year's cake or throw the next year's party. In days of old, the one who found the baby was crowned king or queen of Mardi Gras. In France, where the King Cake originated, a bean was used instead of the baby. Whoever found the bean got to wear a paper crown and was "king" for a day, hence the name "King Cake". Samples were passed out and it was very tasty.

West of the city, we took another ferry that crossed the Mississippi. Parked next to us was a truck driver eager to share places to see. He said we must see "Jean Lafitte National Historic Park" where the "Battle of New Orleans" was fought. In fact, the ferry passed over the very spot where the British tried to mount an attack on New Orleans. The mud ramparts in the battlegrounds are still there, but beyond that was a massive refinery.

We couldn't wait any longer to experience the French Quarter. Driving down Rampart Street, toward the Quarter, we noticed the houses changing from shacks to more ornate buildings with decorative metal railings that lined the second and third floor balconies. After a short drive and a little difficulty finding a parking spot, we hurried to Bourbon Street. A Cajun band performing at Patout's restaurant was warming up. One member of the band came into the audience and challenged a lady to play the washboard. She picked it up, to the cheers of the crowd, and began to strum it. The audience clapped in appreciation. Across the street, the Dopsie Band was playing Zydeco. Zydeco music is a modern, upscale version of the Cajun folk music. The best way to describe Zydeco is a fast paced sound with a driving beat. As is the scene in the French Quarter, music fills the air. People can stand in the middle of street and sway one way and hear jazz and then sway another way to hear Zydeco. All free for the listening.

The "French Quarter Festival" started the next day. The night before the festival, we left the pop-up at the campground and found a parking space for the truck, near the Civic Center. A few other RV's were also parked on the street, so we felt somewhat protected. That night we slept in the truck. Looking back, this was a very stupid thing to do as we didn't know if this was a good neighborhood or bad. All night we slept with our hands on a bat just in case someone tried to break in. Sometimes we do stupid things and this was one of them. We were just too tired from partying in the French Quarter the night before and knew that festivities were going to start early the next day. I wouldn't recommend sleeping in a strange neighborhood to anyone.

Before the sun rose, we drove into the French Quarter and found ample "Early Bird Parking". This got us half-price parking for the day. The festival honored Pete Fountain, the famous jazz clarinet player. Inside the courtyard of Edison Park was a statue of his likeness along with a statue of Al Hirt. We got there just as the celebration was getting started. Pete Fountain was signing autographs and the Hotel Sonesta catered a continental breakfast. The band played Dixieland and speeches by local politicians, friends of Pete's (like Al Hirt's wife) and then Pete himself were made. He proudly unveiled a statue of himself and took clarinet in hand and played with the band. Next to me was a lady from Canada with a decorated umbrella. She was getting ready to march with the band in a style know as the "cake walk". After the unveiling, the band marched down Bourbon Street, with Pete behind a banner announcing the beginning of the "French Quarter Festival". With the sun shining, we marched and danced. Decorated umbrellas of satin and lace bobbed up and down in time to the music. I didn't have an umbrella, but Charles' white hanky did just fine. If I could freeze one moment in time, that afternoon would have been it; struttin' down Bourbon Street, between Pete Fountain and the band. People hung over the ornate iron balconies and threw beads to the revelers. Behind the band was the "second line" where more folks were struttin', all in time with the beat. The parade ended at Jackson Square. Bringing up the rear were more bands and throngs of people dancing in the streets. It was a glorious day. Dining on crepes and bread pudding with whiskey sauce and listening to live music captured the heart and soul of the French Quarter.

Chapter Four

Cajun Nights and Zydeco Mornings

After a wonderful week of exploring southern Louisiana and the city of New Orleans, it was time to move deeper into Cajun Country. The next destination was Breaux Bridge and a famous restaurant called Mulates. Mulates was established in 1980 and is known for live Cajun music, good food and a large dance floor. Families of all ages come here to dance, eat, and socialize.

"Catfish Heaven" was the only campground we could find near Breaux Bridge. It was a private campground, but it was no "heaven". There were no trees and the sites were aligned in a straight row. More importantly, the bathrooms weren't that nice. However, we weren't planning on staying in the camper as our sights were focused on Cajun food, dance and music at Mulates. We quickly set up the camper and headed out. In Mulates, we saw shy teenage boys asking the girls to dance while their families looked on. Dinner was served at large, wooden tables and the etoufee and gumbo were delicious. After a few beers, we got up and joined in. The steps were easy to learn and around the dance floor we went. The band consisted of a violin, an accordion, and drums. Ballads were sung in Cajun French with some English thrown in for good measure. The instrumentals rocked to the beat of the bayou. A *bon temps* (good time) was had by all.

Saturday morning found us at the Tourist Information Bureau in Breaux Bridge to find out more about the area. The volunteer directed us, up the street, to Café Des Amis. As soon as we opened the door, the scene was captivating. A local band was playing live Zydeco music and all kinds of folk were on the dance floor. The music was so real, that I held up my cell phone and called a few friends to share the sounds. The band stopped playing at noon, so we wandered back to the Visitor's Center to thank them for the tip. Sitting in a folding chair, was a Cajun lady who serenaded us with a French ballad. She told us that her family came from Arcadia (now Nova Scotia) and settled here in the early 1800's. She said that the British exiled all French speaking Acadians who were not loyal to the Crown of England and so the Cajuns settled in Southern Louisiana. Being a recipient of Cajun hospitality was very special.

The next day we broke camp and moved north to Chico State Park located in the parish of Ville Platte (pronounced Vill-PLAT'). This is the center of Cajun culture, in the heart of the Cajun Prairie, where Zydeco reigns. Places like McDonalds and Arby's don't exist here. Instead, every gas station has a "Food Market" with a meat counter otherwise known as a Bucherie (French for butcher). Boudin, the local spicy sausage, is popular as is alligator and pork. Local drive-thru stands offered a "to go" option of whatever momma was cooking in the kitchen. The drive-thru daiquiri bars washed all this down.

Stores along the highway had French names like LeBlanc's, Billeaud, and Le Video. South of Ville Platte is the Parish of Eunice and home to the Liberty Theatre. A restored 1924 movie house, this theater has a stage and below the stage is a large, wooden dance floor. "*Rendez Vous des Cajuns*" is a live public broadcasting radio shows (PBS) that broadcasts every Saturday night. The program has been on the air for 16 years and is spoken only in Cajun French. That night, Danny Collet and the Louisiana Tremor and John Wilson & Zydeco House Rockers were playing. We arrived early to get a front row seat and to eavesdrop on local conversation that fluctuated between English and Cajun French. These people were serious about their music and their dancing. A man spread cornmeal on the wooden floor so the dancers would be able to shuffle their feet. As soon as the music started, the crowd was dancing. Their steps were a cross between the two-step and the waltz. Fresh "crackling" (pieces of pork fat, fried with a little meat still attached) was offered by the man who sat next to me. Then he asked me to dance as his wife asked Charles to dance. Round and round we waltzed, blending in to this wonderful scene. It was another unforgettable memory.

Chico State Park was a good home base to venture out and visit the local Parishes. One day, we took a ride to the Parish called Mamou, to find Fred's. On the way there, we passed miles of crawfish ponds and rice fields. It was nice to drive the backcountry roads and feel the slow pace of the country.

Fred's is a legendary bar in Mamou and is only open on Saturday mornings. All they do is serve beer and play Zydeco music. It is so famous, that it is registered as a "Historical Landmark". To fully enjoy Fred's, locals get there by 8:00 a.m. to be able to get in as it gets crowded early. I hear the dancing flows out into the street.

The motto of Cajun country is *Laissez les bon temps rouler!* (let the good times roll) and it does! You only need to drive through this part of the country to find it.

Chapter Five

Carpe Diem

Cajun country was so interesting and diversified, that it was sad to leave. As the miles passed, smoke stacks of chemical refineries replaced the catfish ponds. Miles and miles of refineries belched smoke into the air, as we tried not to breathe too deeply. It amazed us that with all that industry, Louisiana roads weren't smoother and that the standard of living wasn't higher. Highway 10 to Lake Charles, Louisiana was so bumpy that we had to pull over to the side of the road to let our innards rest and to read the map. After several hours of road abuse, our backs ached and we were in need of a Chiropractor. The first one we saw wanted to treat us as new patients and charged in excess of $100 per person, for the initial examination. No way! Further down the road, we stopped in another Chiropractor's office. They were very helpful and for $35 each, we got a great adjustment. The Chiropractor even gave us his home number in case we needed him.

ndred and fifty miles east of Houston is Sam Houston t is the last Louisiana State campground before entering . Our Gold Card entitled us to half price camping in Louisiana, but Texas did not and was therefore more expensive. We arrived on the weekend and found the campground overflowing with campers. The landscape had the flavor of the bayou but the sites were close together and the bathrooms always full. It was nothing like our previous experiences of camping in Southern Louisiana where the sites were further apart and the vegetation around the campsite, much denser.

With Passover approaching, starting on the 16th of April, we searched for a congregation to share the holiday with. It turned out that Temple Sinai was celebrating its 100th anniversary and the congregants welcomed us to celebrate Passover with them. The first night's Sedar was shared with the congregation in their social hall. The second night, we were invited to a family Sedar. It brought back memories of my childhood. The tables and chairs wound through the house to accommodate all the relatives and friends for a Sedar meal. This Sedar sat 22 people. The story of Passover was read and the matzo ball soup was passed around. It was just like I remembered it as a kid and what amazed me was how tradition prevails, probably all over the world.

After two days of celebration, it was time to drive into Texas. The refineries lining the road were very foreboding.

Galveston State Park was the first campground we stayed at in Texas. Our campsite was located behind the dunes and a short distance from the beach. The sites were arranged on a nice grassy area. The spring breakers hadn't arrived yet, so it wasn't crowded. However, the shrimp boats offshore left the beach littered with sea-plants ripped from their trawling with large nets. That made me uneasy, but in contrast, lying in bed at night, listening to the waves ebb and flow was very soothing.

The first morning there, we met our neighbors who were teachers from Beaumont, Texas and we exchanged camping information. One campground they recommended was in New Mexico near the home of the artist, Georgia O'Keefe. They said the campground was operated by the Bureau of Land Management (BLM) and was located on the Abiquiu reservoir. When I hear of a place that sounds interesting, I write it down and add it to my list of "Must See Places" that I keep on the computer.

Later that day, we drove along the coast to the town of Alvin. Miles and miles of undisturbed beach marked our way. Every once in a while, there would be a community that must have just gotten water and sewer rights as the land was selling for $95,000 an acre.

Not wanting to retrace our tracks back to Galveston, we headed to Keymar. We heard that there was a boardwalk with lots of restaurants and interesting shops. What we found looked like a brand new development with very expensive restaurants. We couldn't figure out what all the hype was about. Across the inlet, shrimp boats were off-loading the day's catch. In Galveston, the shrimp was $5.99 a pound. A little high, considering we could see their boats from the beach. Here, shrimp was selling for $2.99 a pound and $4.99 for the extra large ones. Guess what we cooked for dinner?

Down the road, a street sign read "NASA Highway 1" which lead to the entrance of the NASA Johnson Space Center. We were planning on visiting the Space Center the next day, but couldn't resist stopping to see the large Saturn V Rocket displayed on the front lawn. This was the spaceship that successfully carried the first crew to the moon. Its size could cover three football fields and each section had miles and miles of wiring and widgets. At the entrance to the gate was a memorial to the crew of Columbia where people had left flags, dolls and flowers. Spelled out in white plastic cups, in the mesh wiring, was "We love you Columbia".

Back at the campground, we met two young kids in their early twenties. They were traveling cross-country and occupied the site behind us. They told us that their car had been broken into on a recent trip into town and their money stolen. They had a good attitude and were glad that the car wasn't damaged and that they weren't hurt. We invited them in for a cup of tea and cookies, as the weather was getting windy and cold. The boy was from Seoul, South Korea, and his lady friend was from Des Moines, Iowa. They had a little tent and big dreams and reminded us of our camping experiences back in Savannah. The boy told us that he and his brother were adopted and in his earlier life they were street kids in Seoul. They both were very interesting to talk to. Feeling motherly, I invited them to breakfast the next morning. That night, the wind gusted to 40 miles per hour and we wondered how they were doing. Our camper survived the winds admirably. It shook, it rattled, but did not roll. The kids also survived the wind and were grateful for the hot breakfast.

I call this chapter "Carpe Diem" because although we wanted too, we never got back to the Space Center. The weather turned nasty and the forecast called for a low pressure system. This meant high winds and steady rains and we didn't want to be on the coast to welcome such weather. It was prudent to pack it up and head inland.

From Galveston, we drove to Houston and spent the night with a childhood girlfriend and her husband. They graciously let us park the pop-up in their driveway and we had a wonderful time reminiscing. They were amazed at our plans to travel cross-country and invited us to stay with them anytime we were passing through Houston.

Between Houston and San Antonio is the town of Luling and Palmetto State Park. I remembered someone telling me that Luling has great barbeque food. After a quick set-up, we drove into town. The first thing we noticed was the town's quirky sense of humor. The folks of Luling decorated their oil rigs with fanciful cartoon characters. Roadrunner's head kept bobbing up and down with the movement of the rig's arm, and a cow jumped over the moon. Good food and humor made for a nice stop. The campground was very nice but offered no hookups.

San Antonio and "Fiesta" was our next stop.

Chapter Six

Viva Fiesta, Texas Style

Fiesta happens in San Antonio the last weekend in April and lasts nine days. It has over 150 events including a day parade, a night *Flambeau* (lighted) parade, ethnic foods, Mexican music and lots of fun. The first day parade began in 1891 as a tribute to the lives lost at the Alamo, and the battle of San Jacinto and honors such legends as Davey Crockett and Jim Bowie. It was from these battles that Texas gained its independence. The night parade is advertised as the largest parade in the United States.

Guadalupe State Park is located about 30 miles north of downtown San Antonio. This was to be our new home as we participated in the Fiesta celebration. The State Park is located in an area known as "Hill Country" where temperatures can be as much as twenty degrees cooler than San Antonio. The days in the Hill Country are cool and at night a nice breeze cools the temperatures down. In contrast, San Antonio has a more arid climate and is hot and humid.

From Guadeloupe River State Park, it was an easy drive downtown. We arrived on the sixth day of Fiesta. In Mercado Market Square, was a midway with lots of carnival rides and booths selling local crafts including the popular crepe paper flowered headbands. Around big, wok-like pans, local women prepared authentic dishes such as enchiladas, tacos and beans and rice. No McDonalds here! Stages featured live music and families cruised the midway as generations before them had done.

Most businesses are closed on the first Friday of Fiesta. Banks, post offices and libraries were all closed. However, we were in need of a doctor. Charles was losing weight and not looking too good. We stopped in a clinic and was surprised to find that we were the only ones there. You see, no one gets sick during Fiesta. The doctor had blood work done and gave Charles a complete two-hour examination. He was bored and was happy to have a customer. Charles lost six pounds, but it looked like a lot more to me. I think a large part of the weight loss was due to healthy eating and the absence of Charles' daily donut fix. The doctor was very funny, his staff very competent and they were genuinely concerned. A few days later, the doctor pronounced him in good health as nothing out of the ordinary was shown on the tests. Great, now it was time to join the party!

The next day, we shared a shuttle downtown with another couple. The four of us were the only ones on the bus. It was late morning and we thought we missed the parade. The bus driver laughed as he showed us the start of the parade as we crossed an overpass. There were lines of people along the parade route, five deep.

We found a good viewing spot near the Judge's stand. The first float to start the parade was the Liberty Bell. It was like a personal welcome since I am from Philly. Next came King Antonio LXXXI and his court. They preside over all the festivities. On the fourth day of Fiesta, in an elaborate Coronation ceremony, the king is crowned and his court presented. The King is selected from the Texas Cavaliers for being an exemplary citizen. The young, beautiful ladies of his court wear incredible gowns with long, flowing beaded trains. Their gowns carry the theme of Fiesta. This year's theme was honoring queens throughout history. The newspaper that day showed the court posing with their gowns. A description of the Duchess of Norman

Conquest "had a fluid Celtic design swirling around the dress in royal blue and red lame beaded with Austrian crystals". Other gowns commemorated the Queen of Sheba; Mary, Queen of Scots; the warrior Queen Boadicea; and Queen Elizabeth I. The gowns' designer went to a library in Glenstal Abbey, Ireland, to research the crests and coats of armor so that the designs were authentic in color and style. This library is well known for its century-old manuscripts and texts. Seeing the gowns in person was a testament to art and the finite details were amazing. The princesses kept lifting up their dresses and showing off their sneakers. A local told me it was because up until a few years ago, the girls had to wear heels. Now they were allowed to wear sneakers. Marching bands, huge balloon figures and decorative floats with various bands rounded out the parade.

Another parade during Fiesta is called *Corny-ation*. It honors King Anchovy and pokes fun at the politics of the day. Eight drag queens complement the entourage.

Night In Old San Antonio (NIOSA) was the party after the parade. Again, booths with food and souvenirs, stages for entertainment, and beer gardens were set up in a recreated Mexican village. Upon entering, partygoers were given a pair of maracas so they could make music with the bands. The $10 entrance fee was to discourage people from attending because in previous years, the turnout reached the capacity limit. On that advice, we got there early and were glad we did because within an hour, it was so packed, we couldn't move. A surprise antic of the festival is called *Cascarones*. It is the breaking of confetti-filled eggs over each other's head. Viva Fiesta!

The King William's Fair and Parade started early on Saturday in an older part of town, whose streets were filled with large, exquisitely appointed homes. Friends picked us up at 6:30 in the morning. We spent the night in the truck, in Wal-Mart's parking lot. We find, for festivals, it easier to sleep in the truck and be able to get up early and be where we want to be. I am not a morning person. Our friends took us to have breakfast in the historic Guenther House, which is a converted old flourmill. The King William's parade is more avant-garde than the bigger parades. School bands, the local belly dancing class, clowns and neighborhood business floats went down the main street. Along the parade route were booths serving such fare as gorditas, flautas, carnita (a spicy beef) tacos and the very popular turkey legs. The crafts were the best we'd seen during all the events.

The Flambeau Parade was later that night, but we were too hot and tired. All this partying was finally wearing us out. Not wanting the evening to end, our friends drove us to River Walk where we found an outside table and enjoyed the shops and people along the promenade. The riverboats, trees, restaurants and people were all lit up with the holiday spirit.

The last event of Fiesta is called *Charreada* and takes place in the Mission area of old San Antonio. It is the forerunner of the western rodeo and its purpose is to preserve the dazzling horsemanship that has long been a part of the Mexican culture. Some participants are descendents of Poncho Villa's soldiers and work the ranches along the border of Mexico. Charreada originated in Spain in the 16th Century by the Conquistadors and was brought to Texas in the 1700's by the Franciscan missionaries. They taught the American Indians how to ride, rope and brand the cattle. Now these events are the national sport of Mexico. Originally, rich landowners put on Charreadas as a form of entertainment. Their lavish haciendas were the backdrops for the ten events that make up the competition. The Fiesta Charreada, starts with much pageantry, welcoming the King of Fiesta and his court. A Mariachi Band played the national anthems of America and Mexico with style and enthusiasm. Then the games began. Roping, horse handling, bull riding, and bull tailing were just a few of the events. Our favorite was *Escaramuza.* Eight young girls, in traditional costumes, rode sidesaddle through intricate patterns. Their fast pace, looked like they were going to collide. It left the audience gasping.

A special note about Fiesta: There was so much more to be seen like the Battle of the Bands, The Oyster Fest, the Mariachi Competition and the Texas Calvary River Parade, that I know we will definitely be planning a trip back. The key to enjoyment is to pace yourself and not try to do everything.

Chapter Seven

Still in Texas

Guadeloupe River State Park is named for the gentle river that runs through it. We had heard it was great for canoeing, tubing and swimming, but the water was a little too cold for us. The land is flat with lots of low-lying cedar, ash and persimmon trees. Wildflowers such as Winecups, Texas Bluebonnets, and Indian Paintbrush were in bloom along with the cacti that had yellow and purple flowers. The landscape was bursting with color.

Our trip was extended because of truck troubles. A loss of power and a pinging sound gave us concern. A few mechanics we checked with said we needed to replace the engine, but our friends recommended their mechanic to us. They replaced the muffler and did a diagnostic check of the engine which showed a sensor that needed to be replaced. That seemed to do the trick.

While waiting for the truck to be repaired, we took a hike with the ranger who shared with us some history of Texas. We learned that in the early 1700's, cattlemen ranched sheep and goats here for mohair and wool. Around the late 1800's, the Spaniards introduced herding longhorns. As the cattle roamed the vast plains, barbed wire was used to fence the cattle in. This swiftly changed the cowboy's character from ranching and herding to mending fences. Traditional jobs such as branding cattle still took place, but the long, tedious cattle drives became a thing of the past.

Back at the campground we were paid a visit from armadillos. They are docile, prehistoric creatures whose main diet consists of roots. Since they are low to the ground, they can be heard swishing in the undergrowth. Several times we were able to shine flashlights on them but were careful not to touch them because they are one of the few animals that carry leprosy.

You never know what a trip to the bathroom will reveal, especially in the evening when the nocturnal insects come out. One night, I noticed a couple looking at the wall of the bathroom. When asked what they were looking at, they said they were counting "sticks". Sticks are insects that look like twigs with very thin legs that curl at the end to grasp branches. They had counted 54 sticks and one scorpion. Not believing there was an actual scorpion, they shined their light and there it was. It was very scary!

The town of Gurene (pronounced Green) was on our "Must Do" list. It is said to have the oldest dance hall in Texas and is where John Travolta filmed his famous dance scene in one of my favorite movies "Michael". Located in the center of town were five buildings dating back to the 1840's. Back then, the dancehall was where everyone gathered. Most buildings were well preserved and reminiscent of an old western town. Bringing Gurene into the twentieth century, the general store had been converted into an antique shop, and another store into an ice cream parlor. The buildings brought to life how the town must have felt when the old dancehall drew the community together. Liking antiques, it was fun seeing the difference between east coast and Texas antiques. Shelves were filled with old cowboy boots, saddles and hats, along with the usual knickknacks and glass items. Lots of ropes, horseshoes, horse riding paraphernalia, and several items featuring the star of Texas rested on the floor. Dale Evans and Roy Rogers would have felt very comfortable shopping here.

After touring the town, it was time to visit the dance hall. Spared the ravages of fire, the long wooden building is still in use today. The first thing we noticed when we walked in was the small bar area. Cases of beer were neatly stacked in the corner and above the beer were various neon signs advertising beer makers. Around the dance floor were pictures of famous artists who performed there. It is said that Lyle Lovette and George Strait got their start there and that Willie Nelson and Garth Brooks are frequent performers. In talking with the owner, he said that a lot of country performers like playing the dance hall because of its authenticity. A chalkboard behind the bar advertised that Dennis Quad would be playing with his band that night, but it was sold out. He was in Austin filming *The Alamo* because the original Alamo is located in the concrete jungle of San Antonio.

Our used camper was showing signs of wear and tear. The rust in the refrigerator was bothering me as was the mold on the canvas. We decided to look at new campers and found the improvements astonishing. The new campers had a three way, rust free refrigerator that could be operated by propane, battery and electric. They had a 6-gallon propane heated hot water tank, more storage, and a crank placement that made it easier to operate. The outside shower was a bonus. Veronica at Crestview Campers in Salem, Texas made us an offer we couldn't refuse, so we traded in our old camper for a brand new one. Most important was the bumper-to-bumper warranty promised at signing.

After 13 days of camping at Guadeloupe, it was time to head on to our next destination in our brand new camper. Our friends highly recommended seeing Big Bend National Park (NP).

On the way to Big Bend, we heard another "must see" was John Wayne's *Alamo* movie set. On a dirt-lined street stood an authentic stagecoach, parked in front of the Wells Fargo office. Next to it was an old adobe church that begged for sinners to repent. Some of the movies filmed here were *Bandelero* with Raquel Welch, *The Last Command* with Ernest Borgnine and *Two Rode Together* with Jimmy Stewart and Richard Widmark. The museum was very well done with larger than life posters from those movies along with lots of memorabilia. With our eyes closed, we could hear the spurs of John

Wayne's boots as he walked around town making sure everything was all right.

You know you are in the Texas desert when the trees turn to shrubs and the ground goes from dirt to sand. Ornate iron entrances displayed the mark of the ranches. Flying B's; jumping J's, and swerving S's were some of the decorations. As we traveled along Rt. 90, barbed wire fences went on for miles. At the border town of Del Rio, we realized we were lost. A wrong turn almost wound us up in Mexico. Sensing a high level of anxiety at the border, we were happy to get directions that set us right. Roadblocks were set up at frequent intervals as the border patrols looked for illegal immigrants. We were asked to pull over a few times, but once they realized we were no threat, they smiled and quickly waved us on.

Big Bend was a couple days ride from San Antonio and being retired, we could take our time getting there. On the map was Seminole Canyon State Park, located west of the boarder town of Del Rio, Texas. That was to be our next stop. Arriving late, our neighbors, a group of bikers camped across the road, were helpful in acclimating us to the Chihuahua desert with some of their homegrown cocktails. Growing up in South Philly, I never gave the desert much thought. Now I was in it. A sunset walk showed the desert in bloom. Hummingbirds hovered over the red and yellow flowers of the cactus and roadrunners crossed the road with lighting speed. There was nothing on the horizon except God's country and the setting sun. That night, the stars welcomed us and a cool wind blew. A large canyon with overhangs left the imagination to wonder as to what or who lived there.

The days were hot and the nights were cool and we were able to sleep with the windows open. The camper has lots of windows and it was a wondrous feeling waking in the morning and hearing the birds serenading the desert plants and seeing the sunrise turning the world golden. All this from bed.

A hike with the park ranger led us to pictographs under the bluffs in the canyon. "Fate Bell Shelter" is believed to be the second oldest inhabited cave, with pictographs over 4,000 years old. *Chauvet* in Lascaux, France is said to have the oldest. It is here we learned the difference between *archaic* and *historic*. Archaic refers to the cave dweller and historic refers to the early American Indians. The archaic man's beliefs revolved around Shamanism. A "Shaman" is a leader who has the power to go between the world of the living and the universe beyond. They believed that all creatures, human and animal, shared a cosmic soul. The Shaman would digest potent plants and listen to the drumbeat to go into a trance-like state. The paintings on the walls were a result of the trance, which were drawn by apprentices so as to share the Shaman's vision with the tribe. These pictographs are hard to interpret because no other evidence has been discovered as a key to their language. As we know, it is hard to interpret a dream state. The paintings showed the Shaman floating in air and you could tell if he was descending or rising because of the way his hair was flowing.

The ranger described the first cave as the "bachelor pad" because there was no evidence of plants such as Sotoel bulbs, which were used for food or Lechugillia that was used for mats. This room was probably where the Shaman held his ceremonies. In the cave next to it, you could see where mats covered the floor (for sleeping) and where cooking fires burned. Several rocks were smooth, indicating that animals were slaughtered and prepared here for the evening's meal. Lots of pictographs lined the cave.

A large rock with ocean fossils was pointed out to us. At one time a river flowed near the mouth of these caves whereas prior to that, the ocean covered the whole area. A dam was built that covered some of the caves and most of the drawings are now gone. We are fortunate to have a few to remind us of this ancient past.

The archaics disappeared from the landscape probably because of the climatic changes and loss of water. It is thought they settled in Mexico. When the historic American Indians arrived, they did not settle in these canyons because they felt this was a sacred place.

Several campers recommended the Langtry Visitor's Center, and for good reason. The Visitor's Center did a wonderful job depicting its famous resident, Judge Roy Bean. At one time, the area around the Pecos River was a tent city for the building of the Southern Pacific and Central Pacific Railroad. This area had gotten so tough that the railroad executives needed law and order, so in 1882, Judge Roy Bean was appointed Justice of the Peace. The railroad tracks came together with much fanfare on January 12, 1883 with a silver stake marking the railroads completion. It took over a year and more than 1,800 tons of steel to build a bridge crossing the Pecos River. At the time, it was said to be the eighth wonder of the world. An ethnic melting pot went into the building of the railroad. Chinese crews worked eastward from El Paso, while German, Irish, Italian, Danish, Greeks and Mexicans worked westward from San Antonio. San Francisco would be linked to New Orleans and the Wild West was wilder than ever.

Roy Bean became the first Judge to bring order to the tent cities and was known as the "law west of the Pecos". There was little protection against Indian attacks since Fort Stockton, and the Texas Rangers, were 100 miles away. That meant that Judge Bean could deal with law and order his way and sentences were decreed from his bar and pool hall known as the *Jersey Lillie*. The actual bar has been preserved just as he left it. A sepia tone picture showed him holding trial on the front porch as the town gathered around. Always looking to make a profit, he made lots of money selling liquor from his saloon, especially on trial days. Sometimes part of the fine was to buy everyone a drink, including his pet bear. Judge Beam was madly in love with the English actress Lillie Langtry and named the town after her. He even built an opera house in her honor, hoping she would visit. Although he never met her, he wrote to her often. Lillie Langtry did eventually visit America and the town named after her, but the poor Judge had died several months before.

The Visitor's Center was located in what would have been the middle of town. On one corner stood the stagecoach depot and on the opposite corner was the "Jersey Lillie" bar. Several holographs lined the wall in the Visitor's Center depict the events of this period. One holograph showed Judge Beam administering justice as two men took their bar fight into the streets. The fine was $10 and when they protested, the fine went up. Another holograph showed the building of the bridge over the Pecos. A recording at the Silver Spike Ceremony hinted that the Judge stole the silver spike and replaced it with a metal spike. Here, history comes alive. It is one of the great joys of traveling and discovering our country's past.

Finally we reached Big Bend National Park. It was a lo tedious drive getting there, as the scenery remained the sam mountains in the distance and desert in foreground. Heat and more heat were forecast and the prospects of camping there was dauntingly hot. The distant mountains were more inviting, so we did a big loop of the National Park and then headed for the hills. As we exited the Park, the landscape reminded us of the moon. In fact, we later discovered that this is the area where NASA tested their lunar modules before landing them on the moon.

Another long drive, 350 miles to be exact, brought us to Fort Davis, which proved to be the right move. It was early May before we found cooler temperatures. Our site was nestled amongst trees and the dry riverbed was a testament to the drought.

A short ride from Fort Davis sits the McDonald Observatory. It is located on one of the highest hills in Texas and on certain evenings "star parties" are given. We were there on the right night. Before sunset, a line of trucks and cars drove around and up the hill. The "party" started at 7 p.m. with an excellent video showing the advancement of the telescope. The observatories main focus is to study objects in the heavens and understand the ever-changing compositions of stars. Through these observations, they hope to learn more about the solar system and observe the planets. Outside the amphitheatre, a scientist pointed out, with a special flashlight, the constellations and planets. Several telescopes were set up to view Jupiter (with its two equatorial bands and three moons), Saturn, and a star cluster in the Big Dipper that cannot be seen by the naked eye. Some of these stars were 30,000 light years away. The evening ended with happy campers descending the mountain.

Not far from Fort Davis is the artesian well of Balmorhea with its major attraction, a huge swimming pool with fresh flowing water. On our way there, we went through Wild Rose Pass and stopped to read the historical marker. It said, "In early days, the Indian trail through these mountains followed the gorge below. To avoid the floods, travelers such as the Buffalo Soldiers, supply trains, immigrants, and the mail chose the higher pass which quickly earned the name for its wealth of wild roses." It was not hard to imagine the gallop of horseback riders and the rumble of wagon wheels taking settlers to a new land. Once they arrived at the springs, they found a pool where the water temperature stays between 72 and 75 degrees and the water so clear that fish could be seen swimming 50 feet down. Like the early settlers before us, it didn't take us long to put on our bathing suits and go swimming.

Nearby is the Solomon's Dive Shop. Scuba gear could be rented for people to dive and observe the fish. The owner, a Cherokee lady, chatted with us about the land. She lived here for many years and remembers when this area was all farmland. She said that the land was changing due to over grazing and that sand dunes were forming where grass used to be. The drought here is now in its tenth year. She said that last year she saw one dust storm and now it seemed to be happening every week.

Driving back to our campsite, we noticed that the tops of the mountains were very unusual as they looked like pudgy fingers reaching up to the sky. Volcanic action pushed the sandstone up to form the "fingers". They felt alive, like a nursery story where the mountains resemble huge human figures that walk and talk.

Taking advantage of the cool weather, we stayed at Fort Davis State Park for about a week. There was a lot to see and do. One such place was Fort Davis, named in 1854 after the Secretary of War, Jefferson Davis. The Fort had gone through many changes since its inception. In the early days, it was an important post that protected the settlers and provided escorts for the wagon trains, stagecoaches, emigrant parties and railroad workers. It was located on the Great Comanche War Trail, so when trouble was brewing, it was quickly known. The government stipulated that two units be "colored men" and they became known as the Buffalo Soldiers. The Cheyenne Indians gave them that name because their curly hair resembled that of the Buffalo. The "Buffalo Soldiers" were a very courageous all black regiment who fought gallantly with no loss of life. It must have been very hard for them, as they served under white officers and took a lot of unfair ridicule. However, they were always loyal and professional. At that time, enlisted men got paid $13 a month. The Comanche and Apache continued their raids until the 1880's.

Of all the forts that protected the settlers in this vast land, Fort Davis was the largest. It had over 100 buildings and housed 400 men and their horses. Life was hard as the area was desolate, but without the protection from these forts, the West could not be tamed. We enjoyed exploring the infirmary, the officer's quarters and several other buildings restored to preserve its history.

Fort Davis State Park was a very peaceful place. Unbeknownst to us, it was famous for its birds and wildlife. Many bird watchers come from around the globe to see the rare Montezuma Quails as they come down from the mountain to drink from a nearby stream. Next to me was a fellow from Germany who waited patiently with his very expensive camera and long-range lens. Once the quail was spotted, a flurry of birdwatchers got their cameras ready to take pictures.

We had now been camping for two months and the heat returned when we came down from the mountains. When we reached El Paso, it was so hot that we decided to get a hotel room using our Marriott Frequent User Points, which we get, by using a Marriott credit card. The border town of El Paso sits in a heavily populated, flat area in the shadow of the Franklin Mountains. Thru El Paso runs the ancient road known as the *Camino Real.* This ancient route brought trade to the new Americas and is the oldest road in America. That night, a dust storm obliterated the view of the city and we were glad to be indoors. It was wonderful having a hotel room with clean sheets, a big bathroom, WiFi (Internet access) and cable TV.

It was the Saturday before Mother's Day, and with passports and money safely tucked in a pouch under our shirts, we ventured into Juarez, Mexico. A short walk over the Rio Grande River bridge led us to a street lined with drugstores and dentists. Having studied the map, we quickly found the local market and church, which was past the tourist area. Everything was in Spanish. We wandered through the crowded streets of the market and had coffee in a bakery where we were the only Americans. It was early morning and the heat and wind hadn't set in yet.

Outside the Cathedral of Our Lady of Guadeloupe Church, was a square filled with vendors selling artificial flowers (made in China). Since it was almost Mother's Day, there were a lot of people paying their respects to the Virgin Mary, inside the church. One young girl crawled, on her knees, down the aisle to place flowers at the Virgin's feet. It was very touching. We purchased a bouquet of flowers and walked down the aisle to pay respects to my husband's mother. The petals were embossed with "I love you". Charles bought me a bouquet for Mother's Day, which is now a treasured item from our travels.

It's funny that many Mexicans cross to the United States to buy linens, clothing and food while many Americans cross the border for drugs and doctors.

Our last stop in Texas was to visit the Tigua Indian Reservation and gift shop. We were fortunate to arrive as the young people, in costume, were performing ritual dances that were passed down from their elders. In the corner of the courtyard, huge mud ovens baked delicious breads over hot coals. The gift shop had lots of items made by the kids, along with the fresh baked bread. Further down the road was the ancient Ysleat Mission. A wedding was in progress and we watched outside as the bride's family and friends fussed over her. The groom hadn't arrived yet. It was a scene that could have taken place many years ago when the Spanish migrated northward on the *Camino Real*

We bade adios to Texas and the next day headed into New Mexico.

Chapter Eight

Cowboys, Indians and Ancients

As soon as we crossed over into New Mexico, the architecture and feeling changed. We went from western towns and ranches to adobes and haciendas. The contrast was almost immediate.

Our next campsite was carefully chosen because of its proximity to places we wanted to visit. The town of Truth or Consequences had hot tubs, along with an interesting name; White Sands National Monument had sand dunes; and, Cloudcroft was known for its mile-high golf course. High on our list of things to see was the cave dwellings at the Gila (pronounced HE'-la) National Monument.

There were three campgrounds on the Caballo Reservoir. One was very barren and another was right below the dam. We found the perfect spot at the third location called Caballo State Park. It sat high on a bluff overlooking the reservoir. Across the reservoir rose jagged mountains that were desolate and oddly beautiful. The play of light at sunset was fascinating as the mountains turned gold, red and then burnt sienna. A short hike led to benches, which were provided to take in all this beauty. This was a good place to stop for a while and make it our home. That meant putting out the welcome sign along with a reflective metal frog that marked the entrance to our site. Inside, I hung mobiles and stained glass ornaments and on the table was the flowers purchased in Juarez, Mexico the day before Mother's Day. By staying in one place for a while, a sense of community prevails. Neighbors chat with neighbors and good information is shared about what to see, where to eat and favorite campgrounds to visit.

Surprisingly, we were still in the Chihuahua Desert, which covers parts of Texas, Utah, Arizona, New Mexico and California along with nine Mexican states, a fact that totally amazed this city girl. Water is scarce and they say the drought here has been going on for five years, so we were lucky to find a spot overlooking water.

On the way to Caballo Reservoir, the road lead through desolate mountains and passes. Dotting the landscape were a few small ranches with rusted cars in the fields and a horse or two out back. The terrain left us to fantasize about the American Indians who once lived here, with their teepees and corralled horses. It was easy to imagine cowboys running from the law crisscrossing the land. Later, we found out that we were on *Geronimo's Trail.* This trail leads to the hot springs town of Truth or Consequences. To the locals, it is fondly known as T n C. It is said that Geronimo, along with many other cowboys and Indians peacefully bathed in the town's hot springs.

Our campsite neighbors were a young couple with a six-year-old daughter. They traveled in a mini-van and planned to spend the night in a small tent. The father had enjoyed camping out as a kid and wanted to share this experience with his family. He had a special dinner planned and brought lots of toys for their daughter. We were invited to share their campfire. It was a beautiful night, clear with many stars shining above. Chatting, they told us they were both struggling academics. She was originally from Shanghai and was doing environmental research of the area. He was from Kansas and was studying computer science. Finding wood for the campfire was difficult, as the desert yielded little tree growth. Part of the hunt was to find sticks for roasting marshmallows, which we enjoyed searching for with flashlights. We supplied the chocolate and graham crackers and they had the marshmallows. So began the initiation ceremony to camping – the making of s'mores. The sunset magically lit up the mountains that gleamed on the waters below. Behind us, a mother quail lead her babies out for their evening meal.

After the little girl went to sleep, our conversation turned to travels, current events and religion. I asked the wife if she believed in God, curious of the customs she grew up with in China. Jasmine told me that religion was forbidden in China for a long time, but that her grandparents believed in God. She said she was an atheist, but believed in a divine spirit and that there must be an eternal force that created the beauty of our world. It was a profound realization. Thinking back to the petroglyphs we saw in Seminole Canyon, we talked about Shamanism and how the ancient people (now extinct) also believed in a divine spirit that guides, protects and heals. The evening ended as we watched the Big Dipper move eastward in the night's sky. That night, the temperatures plummeted to the low 40's and when we awoke, our new friends were gone. Snuggling under the electric blanket along with the camper's heater, we waited for the day to warm up.

The next day, all energies left my body and I was unable to get out of bed. For whatever reason – too much excitement, too hot, too cold, dehydration – it was time-out for me. Dealing with sickness is not one of my strong suits and I prefer to deal with it by sleeping. After sleeping all day and all night, life retuned to my body and I felt much better. Charles puttered around the campsite while keeping a close eye on me and making sure I was drinking plenty of water.

Feeling much better, the next day we planned a loop route that would take us west to Silver City and then north to the cave dwellings at Gila Cliff National Monument.

The town of Silver City lies at the base of the Gila Wilderness Area and the gateway to Gila National Forest. It is also part of the *Billy the Kid Scenic Trail.* Silver City was once a prosperous mining town whose copper mine was owned by William Randolph Hearst's parents. Great devastation came to this town in the form of a flood. On July 21, 1895, a wall of water, 12 feet high and 300 feet across, came crashing down the mountain. It carved a 35 foot ditch that was

Main Street. Subsequent floods dropped Main Street another 25 feet. It is now called "The Big Ditch Park".

It is said that young Billy the Kid was raised here. He was originally born in New York City, but moved with his mother, brother and stepfather to Silver City to strike it rich. Billy was a high-strung youth whose father wasn't around much. His mother suffered from tuberculosis, adding to Billy's struggle. At age 15, he was jailed for stealing from a Chinese launderer and escaped through the chimney of the jailhouse. Two years later, at age 17, he killed his first man who was bullying him in a bar. He escaped from that jail too. A description of Billy was that he was thin and wiry with jet-black hair and eyes that were as dark as a moonless night. An important rancher and prominent citizen befriended him. His name was John Tunstall and he treated Billy like a son. In 1877, John Tunstall challenged the local monopoly for a lucrative U.S. Government contract to move cattle through Texas. Tunstall was murdered and that started the Lincoln County Wars. The war lasted four bloody years. Gunslingers and vigilantes came from miles around to join in the fight. Billy was taken prisoner and later escaped. This is where Billy got his reputation for being swift and cunning. He used fellow Mexican prisoners as decoys and they shot their way out to waiting horses. Billy was the only one who got away. There is no evidence as to how many men Billy killed, but his numerous escapes from jail were legendary. Sheriff Pat Garrett killed Billy, then age 21, near Fort Sumner, but more about that in Year Two, when we visit Billy's grave. One can feel Billy's spirit riding through these hills and hiding in its small towns in and around Lincoln County. He was often a welcomed figure because he spoke fluent Spanish and was very charismatic.

From Silver City, the road took us to Emory Pass with its elevation of about 8,500 feet with surrounding peaks over 10,000 feet. At an overlook, we could see the switchbacks that we just traversed and were eye level with a soaring hawk. Going down the mountain, I clung to my seat with my foot on the imaginary brake. Charles did very well on the descent.

A two-lane road took us through the Gila Mountains to the cliff dwellings of the Mogollón (MUGGY'-on) people. The cliff dwellings were perched 180 feet overhead with a rocky switchback footpath leading upward. We hiked up from the stream that was once the Gila River, a source for their water and food. There was an awesome presence of mystery and self-sufficiency of these people. They are said to have occupied this area as early as 600 A.D. We were allowed to explore some of the 42 rooms that made up the settlement. The first room was a "Kiva" (religious room). This was where the men smoked "reed cigarettes", performed ceremonies for good crops and fair weather, and stored items used in religious ceremonies. There was also a Kiva for women. The dwellings were made from mud and sand that they carried up from the riverbed. The people farmed the land, fished the river and planted their crops. Here, they prepared meals, raised families, made clothing, pottery, tools and weaved baskets. Up and down the cliffs they scampered as they practiced a simple lifestyle. The Mogollón lived here as late as the 13th Century. By then, their population had grown and the land was not able to sustain their growth. So, they came down from the mountain to be assimilated with other tribes in nearby Mexico. Teddy Roosevelt made this the first "Wilderness Area" in the United States on June 3, 1924.

It was 8:00 p.m. when we arrived back at our campsite after a very long day of driving over 350 miles in mountains, deserts, and forests. It was fun meeting the cowboys, Indians and Ancients along the way.

The next day's forecast called for high winds to gust over 50 miles per hour and sustained winds of 30 to 40 miles per hour. A dust storm was brewing, which is not unusual for mid-May. Bravely, but with some apprehension, we were looking forward to it, to observe how the camper would react in high winds. Also, the down time gave me time to reflect on yesterday's adventure. The wind started to howl and the camper filled with tiny dust particles. We took everything off the shelves, lowered the table and opened all the windows reasoning that the wind would go through the camper and we would be okay. Charles moved the truck at an angle to the camper, which deflected the prevailing winds. Sitting comfortably on the floor, we both hunkered down with a book until the winds stopped. With a little clean up, the camper survived very well.

In large, bold print, *Truth or Consequences* really stands out on the map. With a name like that, how could we not explore it? The town of Truth or Consequences was originally named "Hot Springs". Some may remember the TV show, *Truth or Consequences* hosted by Ralph Edwards. On the show, there was a contest for a city to rename itself Truth or Consequences and in turn, through the TV show, the town would gain national exposure. The people of "Hot Springs" mailed in their form describing their unique mineral baths, which bubbled up from aquifers beneath the town's surface. Mr. Edwards liked the idea and they won. It was a funky little town that has several bathhouses and cottages. For $5, Charles and I took off our clothes and stepped down into a large, private tub to relax in the hot springs.

In the town of Truth or Consequences is the *Geronimo Springs Museum*. The exhibits were amazing. The first thing you see when entering the museum is a life size statue of Geronimo, a famous Indian chief, with his picture in the background. Another picture showed the last of the Indians being moved (by freight car) to Pensacola, Florida. Another picture was a blow-up of an Indian woman said to be Victorio's sister. Victorio was a brave Indian who did not want to live on a reservation. He led numerous raiding parties and held up many stagecoaches. It took the Buffalo Soldiers two years to hunt him down.

In another room was a display of pottery and jewelry from the Mogollón (Gila Cliff Dwellers) period. Designs of animals and fish appeared on their beige pottery. The intricately carved jewelry had scenes from their every day life. The animals they saw, the plants they knew, were all carved on shells which were then filed down to be worn or sewn on their clothes.

The history of the Wild West came together in a room that featured paintings by Keith Humphries. Large pictures showed the Spanish Conquistadors, the Mexicans on the *Camino Real*, the Indians, the Cowboys and Poncho Villa. The artist grew up on a nearby ranch and had a passion for the stories of the old West. Before starting a picture, he was able to interview the elders of the area and visualize what he wanted to portray. His works presented a microcosm of that time. A few examples of his subjects were a mule train going through a pass, an Apache raid on a homestead, two of Billy the Kid's escapes, the stagecoach dropping passengers off at Fort Sumner, and the Buffalo

Soldier's standoff against Victorio, the last warring Indian to capture.

The last room at the Geronimo Springs Museum had a TV from the 50's. There we sat watching a prank from the original Truth or Consequences TV show. It was the one where a wrecking ball smashes a man's car. The husband and the car owner were in on the hoax and enjoyed watching the wife's horror as the plot unfolded. It was very funny. In years past, Ralph Edwards would lead a parade through T n C. The ploy kept the town alive because even if someone didn't know of the TV show, the name stood out on a map.

When staying in an area long enough, its treasures unfold. Alamogordo, New Mexico, was such a treasure. The day started with a trip to the "Space Museum". Memorabilia from Sputnik and Ham, the chimpanzee the Russians sent into space, can be seen there. The year was 1961 and the race for space had begun. Two challenging interactive programs were part of the display. One exhibit simulated the arm on the robotic repairman challenging us to make a repair to the Hubble Space Telescope. The other exhibit had us landing a shuttle. It was difficult, but after several tries we were able to land it without much problem. Working the arm of the spacecraft proved more challenging.

Not far from Alamogordo is White Sands National Monument. This is a very diverse area. It is here that Special Forces are trained and where the shuttle lands when weather is bad at Cape Canaveral, Florida. Close by is the White Sands Missile Range where they close the highway every day while testing missiles. It's a little scary to me. In the distant mountains was Trinity Site, where the world's first atom bomb was exploded on July 16th, 1945.

But that was not the reason we wanted to visit White Sands. As the name implies, mountains of powdery gypsum form incredibly high sand dunes. An eight mile interpretative trail goes through this stark, white landscape. Visitors are free to climb to the top of the dunes and slide down. We took off our shoes and tested the sand. Expecting it to be hot, because we were in the desert, it surprised us to find the sand cool. Brisk winds move the dunes about ten feet a year covering all vegetation. Roads here are ploughed like snow and the stark whiteness even looks like snow. This phenomenon is all part of the Chihuahua Desert. The temperature was a balmy100 degrees.

The afternoon was fast approaching, so we headed to a mountainside town called "Cloudcroft". A railroad baron built the Cloudcroft Lodge in 1899 as a railroad rest town. The name is derived from old English and means "a clearing covered in the clouds". Resting 9,000 feet above sea level, it is supposed to have the best golf course in New Mexico. We checked out the Lodge's packages and found a romantic two-day package for $200. It included Chateaubriand for dinner, a bottle of champagne and breakfast for two. The setting was lovely and we thought about it, but decided to save this luxury for another time. However, it was nice walking around the Lodge and pretending we were guests.

Back down the mountain we discovered "Three Rivers Petroglyphs Site". A short hike from the parking lot brought us to a rock bed filled with petroglyphs. With the fading light of the day, it was a photographer's delight. The area was thought to be a passage used by many traveling tribes, but the terrain was too rough for a settlement. "Three Rivers" is also the home of the Teapot Dome Scandal of 1912, involving possible corruption in the Department of the Interior.

After driving another 350 miles, we arrived back at our campsite just in time to watch the full moon rise over the mountains. From our special bench overlooking the Caballo Reservoir, we pondered about how much history we knew and forgot. It feels like we are time traveling through a history book.

Chapter Nine

It Was 95 Miles to Carrizozo

It was late in May when we headed northeast. The highway seemed to go on forever. Our destination was "Valley of Fire". Charles kept saying, "It's around the next bend", but it wasn't. Suddenly, an extinct volcano rose in the distance and the landscape on the horizon turned black with lava fields covering a large area. We figured we were close to Valley of Fire Bureau of Land Management (BLM). Since BLMs are on government land, our Golden Card lets us stay for half-price. Many campgrounds have hosts who are there to help you. Sometimes the local police check in with them to ensure the safety of the campers. At Valley of Fire, we were warmly greeted by Jack and Mona with an invitation to stop by later for a cold beer. They had been campground hosts at the Valley of Fire for about three years. As soon as I saw Jack, I knew there was a connection. From the sparkle in his eye, I could tell he had an interesting life. They offered their phone line so we could retrieve e-mails, but we couldn't get a connection, so we spent the evening on their patio and listened as

Jack told us stories of his family and a first hand account of what the Wild West was really like. He said his great-great-grandfather ran a mule train through these mountains and his great-grandfather was evicted from the state for killing a man. The only reason he didn't hang was because his uncle was the judge. Jack said that "outlaws" who wanted to stop their evil ways and settle down to raise a family started the town of Carrizozo (pronounced CARA' zoo zoo).

Jack had us laughing all night. One story he told was about the time he and a buddy joined the Air Force. Being from the southwest, neither of them had seen the ocean. When they were in California, they brought a jug of wine and a raft and went to the beach. Unaware of the tides, they got drunk and fell asleep on the raft. He said they had to be rescued by the Coast Guard because the tide had swept them away. Another time, Mona (an accomplished horsewoman) took Jack on a moon lit ride to the top of the mountain. Jack had both saddlebags filled with beer. When the horses got spooked, Jack's horse couldn't run because of all the beer in the saddlebags. That was a good thing because Jack would probably have fallen off the horse and gotten hurt. They both arrived safely at the summit.

Upon Jack's advice, the next morning we stopped in Carrizozo for a milkshake at the local (and only) drugstore. At one time, this was the center of town. The soda fountain counter had the familiar green Formica countertop with the chrome trim popular in the 50's. What would an ice cream parlor be without stools that let customers swing around? It was fun going back in time and sharing a malted shake with my sweetie.

Speaking of going back in time, do you remember when Smoky the Bear became the mascot for the National Forest Service Fire Prevention Campaign? That happened back in 1950 when the fire fighters rescued a small cub from a forest fire nearby. We heard "Smokey the Bear's" final resting place was in a town called Capitan, which wasn't that far away. Resting peacefully, under a tree and by a man-made stream, were the last remains of the original Smokey the Bear. Across the street from Smokey's grave was an interesting museum paying tribute to the fire fighters of then and now. It had lots of memorabilia and equipment on display along with a video showing the progression of how forest fires are fought.

From Capitan, we drove to Lincoln County to live another chapter in the story of Billy the Kid. The jail there was one of the places that Billy the Kid escaped from. The landscape getting there was miles and miles of flat land surrounded by rocky outcrops. As we drove, we imagined the posses chasing Billy while Indians hid in the rock crevices. Images of old western TV shows with the Lone Ranger and Roy Rogers were brought to mind. Billy was brought to Lincoln to be hanged for murders committed in the Lincoln County Wars. He escaped, but not before killing the sheriff and his deputy.

At night, we walked around the Valley of Fire campground and were amazed at its beauty. The sunsets were awesome and the landscape of black lava hills was surreal. A concrete walk way made it easy to hike down into the lava flow to see a variety of plants growing because of the lava's nutrients.

The TV news station warned that a cold front was going to pass through. Around 8 p.m., high winds began to blow. Sure enough, it blew a steady 35 miles per hour and gusted up to 50. We thought that the camper was going to rip apart and Charles was even considering taking it down and spending the rest of the night in the truck. Unlike him, I had faith in the camper's construction and how it handled heavy winds before and slept pretty well. The camper held firm but Charles vigil made for a sleepless night. The next day, I stayed in and worked on my pictures (editing in Photoshop) so Charles could take a nap. That afternoon, Jack and Mona invited us to experience green chili cheeseburgers with them at the local saloon.

It was a great old bar with a few pool tables and lots of animal heads hanging on the wall. Jack proudly told us that all of the animals had been killed in the nearby mountains. He also told us of the time his friend Bud Crenshaw's son, Kenny, was shot in the bar. It is said that someone was always taking a shot at Kenny because of his antics and that when he died, he fell out of his coffin, leaving his father to say that "Kenny was always messing things up". Mona and Jack both remember neighbors who would bring their horses into the bar just to amuse the tourists.

The hamburgers were great and the stories amusing. When we left the bar, Jack and Mona gave us a tour in their four-wheel drive pick-up. We were very happy to have locals show us around. Carrizozo was a railroad town and is still a crossroads of two major highways, Rt. 54 and Rt. 380.

In the middle of town was a white building that had a sign over a door that read "Ice House". Jack explained that these were lockers where folks would store their meats before modern refrigeration. Across the street was the old telephone company where Jack's mother was employed. Those were the days of the old punchboard consoles. If there was an emergency, the operator always knew how to reach someone. Even if there wasn't an emergency, the operator always knew what was going on.

From there, Jack and Mona drove us into the hills, which we could see from our campsite. The bar in the old town of White Oaks had a sign that read "No Scum Allowed in Saloon". Unfortunately, the bar was closed on Tuesdays. It was one of Jack's favorite drinking holes. Rumor has it that Billy the Kid used to visit the brothels of White Oaks and was known to have frequented this bar.

We then drove further into the hills and the paved road became dirt which Jack's four-wheel drive truck was very accustomed to. In the back hills, Jack knew just about everyone, whether they lived in a shack or mansion. Every place had a story. He then took us to an old graveyard to pay our respects to Mary, the Mountain woman. She lived there during the depression trying to eke out a livelihood panning for gold. Next to Mary's grave was a one-room schoolhouse. A lot of people lived in these mountains during the Depression trying to survive by panning for gold.

Charles asked about gold mining and Mona assured him that there was still plenty of gold in those hills. She leapt out of the truck and grabbed a shovel from the back bed and proceeded to search for a fork in a dried riverbed. She said that is where gold can be found. She seemed to know where to go and scooped up a pile for Charles to sift later.

I asked Jack about his lineage and to tell me more about his great-great-grandfather. He said that in addition to being a mule train driver, he was a preacher. It was easy to be a preacher in those days, and if you were someone in trouble with the law, the law was more lenient on the person if they knew the scriptures. His grandfather was a rancher, and before the Great Depression, he owned a general store and a few bars near Carrizozo. He said his father was a mining engineer.

We came to a stop sign in the middle of nowhere and Jack said it was because there were a lot of drunks driving out there and the reason there were no cars today was because the bars were closed.

Before leaving Valley of Fires, Jack gave us one last tour around the campground. It had two levels. The upper level was for the bigger rigs and had hookups, while the lower level was for tenters and had no hookups. He pointed out a local mesquite plant and talked about the spirits that inhabited the caves in the tenter's area. Then he showed us where he hid to scare the high school kids who were getting rowdy, usually from drinking too much beer. We can just see Jack coming out of the dark, with the lights of his golf cart flashing and him whooping and hollering. Hee Hee Hee. That's Jack laugh.

So with warm thoughts of Jack and Mona, we leave with images of the good old west.

Chapter Ten

Enchanted in the Land of Enchantment

The map showed Salinas Pueblo as an historic sight on the way north towards Colorado. Having plenty of time, we stopped at the information center. A brochure explained that the Mogollón occupied the Salinas pueblo as early as the 10th Century. These were the same peoples who lived on the Gila Plateau. In ancient times, the Mogollón inhabited the plateaus, while the Anasazi lived in the valley. A map showed that the Salinas Pueblo sat high on a bluff. From the remaining foundation, we saw carefully crafted stone houses that looked like apartments. They reminded us of urban civilization. The Kiva was the first room we explored, followed by a visit to their homes, a storeroom, and two churches. The first church's foundation was still intact, along with the baptismal. More interesting, though, was the second church. It was much larger and had many rooms. This church was built by the Indians for the second priest to preside over the community, but was never finished. The Indians revolted in the "Pueblo Rebellion of 1680" which put an end to their required manual labor as well as to being forced to worship another religion. At one time, the Salinas Pueblo was an important trading village of 10,000 residents because it was located at a crossroad. Cartographers were plotting the land to better understand this community and to preserve this site for the future.

It was the end of May and very hot. We were in desperate need of cool weather and searching the map, we found that Monzano State Park was in the San Juan Mountains. Higher elevation meant cooler weather. It was dry camping (no electricity or water) but the campground was set amidst tall trees and cool breezes. Since we were only staying one night, we didn't bother putting up the table or getting out the dishes. Instead, for dinner, we built a fire and found sticks to roast hot dogs and marshmallows for dessert. It was very quiet at night and the stars entertained us with their brilliance and density.

Our next stop was to visit friends, Paul and Patricia, in Albuquerque for a few days. Their house sits on a hill, overlooking the Rio Grande River and Sandia Mountain range. Anxious to experience the southwest, they directed us to Old Town Albuquerque. The first vendor we saw was selling ristras. These are dried red chili peppers threaded together for hanging. It is believed to bring good luck to those who display them from doorways that welcomed friends and guests. We enjoyed walking through the old town with its shops, museums, crafts, and restaurants and believed we found the southwestern flavor.

There are a lot of ghost towns around Albuquerque that are being brought back to life by young and old artisans. Northeast of Albuquerque is the town of Cerrillos (pronounced Sir-E'-os). It is located on the railroad tracks that once brought coal and turquoise down from the mountains. On this particular day, Cerrillos was being inducted into the National Historic Register. The town's folk were very excited for the recognition and celebrated with a festival. Locals displayed their crafts and the fire hall served local cuisine of tamales and enchiladas. A parade of one fire truck, a mariachi band of young performers, a large papier-mache puppet and a few children in costume went down the dirt road that was Main Street.

An amazing sight was kids riding their horses through the town while visiting friends. They were as comfortable on their horses as city kids are on their bikes. It was very hot, but no one seemed to mind. Exploring the neighborhood, we saw many doors and windows painted turquoise. The turquoise color is believed to keep the evil spirits away and bring prosperity and good luck to those who live there. The Indians related turquoise to capturing the spirit of water and sky. It was said that Thomas Edison spent some time in Cerrillos trying to find an electrical component to extract gold from the nearby fields.

Santa Fe is a must for anyone wanting to capture the essence of the southwest. After a leisurely breakfast of banana nut pancakes topped with whipped cream that Patricia made, we were off. In the center of Santa Fe is "Our Lady of Light Chapel", also known as the *Loretto Chapel*, were a famous miracle happened. The story is that in 1878, the wooden steps to the choir's altar caught fire and the nuns had no money or resources to replace the steps. So they prayed for help. Along came a man named Joseph who built the steps with no nails. Supposedly, the wood that the steps were made from was not from the area and no one saw them delivered. Today, it is considered an engineering marvel.

In the center of Santa Fe is the Palace of the Governors, built in 1610. Through the years, the Palace functioned as the seat of the Spanish, Mexican, and American governments. Today, the plaza houses the State History Museum where we saw an exhibit on the history of the Jews in the southwest. Many photographs showed miners, farmers and bankers along with some of their possessions, including Jewish artifacts. It was very interesting to see my heritage portrayed with a southwest feel. The portico outside the Palace is a gathering place where local American Indians make and sell their art, jewelry and crafts.

Considered a major art center throughout the world, its streets are lined with galleries, containing top-notch sculptures and other art. The jewelry stores made my heart race. Not far from the shops of Old Santa Fe is Canyon Road where studios of potters, glassmakers, painters and sculptors live and work. One gallery had wonderful prints of the Wild West and another sculpture garden, while another featured modern art. All the houses were adobe style and very close together. It was fun getting lost in the neighborhood and peeking into gardens and driveways to see the fountains and statuary.

Memorial Day's weather was perfect for a picnic. Paul barbecued for a few of their friends and Patricia baked a special apple pie for the occasion. Under their strong urging, that evening we visited the Jemez (pronounced HE'-Mez) tribe for their pow-wow. As we drove closer to the site, there was a sudden transformation of the land. High cliffs turned red and the mountains started to take on definition. The pow-wow was located in the middle of a red cliff canyon. It is a very reverent ceremony in which dances are done to honor the elders and their spirits.

Two rows of tables circled the arena. The outside circle was where women sold their crafts such as turquoise necklaces, hand-painted pottery and beaded bands. At intervals in the inner circle, sections of young tribal men sat around a big drum. In the center of the circle were the Indians dancing in full costume. When we arrived, the dancers from a particular tribe were being judged on their style. One section of drummers beat out the tune and chanted a song while their group danced in a circle. The songs were in their native tongue, and every once in a while, a man would screech or pound the drum extra hard. The rest would follow. Their costumes were stunning. Most wore leather with feathers, fringe, shells, headdresses, and bells on their feet and arms. Some carried ceremonial objects like special feathered batons. Hanging in the back of their headdresses were golden eagle feathers and their moccasins were beaded with intricate designs. We couldn't believe we were there. Since this was their religious ceremony, no pictures were allowed and one must refrain from asking questions and from touching their ceremonial garments. I only have my mind's eye to remember the vivid colors and beautiful faces of that moment.

Adolescent boys were the next group that performed, followed by their elders and then the women. The pow-wow ended when everyone from the local tribes were asked to join in the circle. Young kids mimicked their fathers and young women twirled beautiful shawls around their bodies, all the while, tapping to the beat of the drum. There are 19 pueblos in New Mexico and each has its own celebration and dance. The Visitor's Center has schedules of these ceremonies and can tell you where demonstrations are given so you can take pictures.

It was time to leave our friends and venture further northward. About 80 miles south of the Colorado border is the U.S. Army Corp of Engineers of Abiquiu (pronounced A-BA'-queue) campground. It sits on a bluff overlooking the Abiquiu reservoir and for us seniors, the cost was $7 a night including electric and water. The first order of business in a new place is to find the local library to retrieve e-mail and the post office to pick up and send mail. The library was located across from a large adobe church. A sign told us that this church was established in 1888. A mental note was made to come back for Sunday mass.

We had reservations to take a tour bus to see Georgia O'Keefe's house, which is located in the small pueblo of Abiquiu. The tour cost $15 per person, which we thought was a little expensive, but we are admirers of her canvases and the cost went to the preservation of her home. Sadly, no pictures were allowed, although I did try to sneak a picture of her garden and got caught.

Georgia O'Keefe's work has always stood out in my mind, especially her colors of flowers on large canvases and stark skeletons of cattle skulls on a bright sky blue background. She lived in a time when her art was being recognized both here and abroad. Her husband, Alfred Stieglitz (1864 – 1946), was a famous photographer who institutionalized photography as an art form. His studio in New York was open to the public and featured Georgia's work along side other artists of the day. America was coming out of the Depression and art was on the rise. Alfred and Georgia lived in New York City for a while, but Georgia got tired of the New York life style and settled in the remote region we were now camping in. She was a very independent woman, especially during a time when female independence was recognized only by a few.

Georgia's house was built in the mid 1700's. Occupation of this land dates back to a time when the cliff dwellers from Mesa Verde came down from the mountain to farm the land (in approximately 1500 A.D.). The land lay fallow till about the 1700's when the Spanish gave land grants to the Christianized Indians. In 1945, O'Keefe bought an adobe dwelling from the Archdiocese of Santa Fe and took three years to make it livable. Many of her famous works were done in this house's studio. It was astounding to walk through her gardens and gaze at the mountains that inspired her.

On the tour we met a lady from New York City who was very excited about a trip she had taken the day before. She was driven up into the mountains by friends in search of the "Church of the Desert Monastery" and was eager to return. She asked if anyone else would like to join her as she had rented a four-wheel drive car and was ready to go. Excited about the adventure, we raised our hands and hopped into her vehicle. Soon, she pulled off the main road and traveled up the mountain onto a dirt road. At first, this afforded us the most spectacular scenery one can image. The huge cliffs had multi colored stripes starting at the top with yellow, and then a layer of beige followed with red at the bottom. Through this wonderland ran the Rio Chama River. A driver approaching us warned us not to go any further as the road was slippery because it had just rained. After a few feet in that direction, his words rang true. The road was getting dangerously slippery, even for a four-wheel drive.

After we safely came down from the mountain, she took us to "Ghost Ranch", which was another of Georgia O'Keefe's homes. It is now a conference center and in a display case was a picture of her rendition of a mountain. The mountain looked very familiar and was indeed the same mountain that we could see from our campsite. A note beside the picture quoted Georgia as saying, "It belongs to me, God told me that if I painted it enough, I could have it".

Our New York friend said she was craving Mexican food and invited us to join her at a restaurant that she was particularly fond of. We drove into the nearby town of Espanola. In the middle of town, was the "El Paragua" (meaning umbrella) Restaurant, which was aptly named because part of the restaurant was built around a tree. Each room was small and cozy and the food very tasty. We ordered their specialty of Tostada y Chile Relleno and Enchiladas de Carne. It was fun spending the day with her and having a special adventure.

The next morning, we awoke to an amazing scene. Now that we were getting acclimated to our surroundings, we found ourselves in the middle of a Georgia O'Keefe triangle. At one apex was the

Abiquiu Pueblo, Georgia's first home. At another apex, situated in the high, colorful bluffs was the Ghost Ranch, Georgia's other home. To complete the triangle was Georgia's Mountain. A note at an exhibit in Ghost Ranch said that when she died, her ashes were scattered on top of the mountain. At the bottom of this grand landscape was the Abiquiu Reservoir. A short hike behind our campsite and we could see it all and each morning felt the many moods as weather brightened or dampened the scene. We went in search of Georgia O'Keefe and we definitely found her.

I must confess that Charles and I are campfire moochers. It seems we have trouble getting a fire started and once started, we find that maintaining it is labor intensive. Instead, we prefer to seek out others who enjoy building and maintaining fires. That is how we met our camping neighbors, two couples in their late 70's. For two nights, we watched as they built nice fires and on the third night went over and introduced ourselves. They invited us to join them and over the next few nights, enjoyed their company, their stories and their campfire. They advised us to follow the river up to Taos, and take the mountain road back. Heeding their advice, we followed the Rio Grande as it ran through high bluffs. On the way, we stopped at the Santa Clara Pueblo. In the middle of town were adobe buildings, dirt streets and weathered-faced people. Two churches were located directly across from each other. Services in both were underway and the music flowed out into the streets. We visited their cooperative and cultural center and admired and bought some of their artwork.

At the Taos Visitor's Center, we were surprised to find that it cost $10 per person to see it. Also, it cost $5 to take pictures and pictures of the people were forbidden. So, disappointed, we drove straight through to the Rio Grande Gorge Bridge where we had lunch and then headed home. The recommended mountain road back went through the Carson National Forest, which had a wide expanse of hills and valleys. The new green color of spring foliage swept the landscape even though it was early June.

That evening, at our neighbor's campfire, we recounted our day. It was also fun listening to them recall various places they had visited and stories of their adventures. I asked if they would impart some of their knowledge, and they were happy to oblige. They told us how they too started in a pop-up and then moved up to a fifth-wheel. They loved camping and a few years ago did a trip to the West coast. Another night, we joined them and the discussion turned to walking sticks. I had been collecting Sotol, which makes good walking sticks, but that was the extent of my stick knowledge. Lonzo went into his trailer and brought out a wide variety of sticks that he had collected. He shared his techniques with me and told me what to look for. Now I have a new hobby.

It is amazing how fast people become friends. Sharing a campfire for a couple of nights and the warmth spreads into the heart. One morning we got a knock on our door and it was Lonzo stopping in to say goodbye. They were heading north that afternoon. He gave us his journal of their camping places to read, which I quickly entered into our computer's data bank for future use and returned it to him with a sad goodbye.

We couldn't leave Abiquiu without experiencing a service in its old church. Most of the service was in Spanish and was conducted by a traveling priest. It was a solemn, Catholic service with about 30 in attendance. At one point, everyone joined hands and sang. We were included as part of the congregation. The inside of the church was sparse, with wooden pews and a few saints' pictures on the walls while the glow of the people's faces gave it a rich, warm feeling.

When we returned to the campsite from church, our new friends were gone and our hearts felt empty. We were glad to be heading north the next day.

Chapter Eleven

A Million Dollar Mile

The air seemed so much cleaner once we crossed into Colorado in early June. High snowcapped mountains appeared on the horizon, which was a stark contrast to the barren, flat desert of New Mexico and Texas. Cows and horses grazed in the lush green meadows. Pagosa Springs was located halfway between Abiquiu, New Mexico and Durango, Colorado. A lot of towns have the word "springs" in their name, but Pagosa Springs actually has hot springs. The Tourist Information Center, located in the middle of town, directed us to a hot tub complex a few steps from their door. There were many different hot tubs to choose from, ranging from 98 to 106 degrees. Names like "Paradise", "Red Lobster", and "The Plunge" appeared on signs in front of each hot tub. For a minimal cost, you could spend the day soaking. The San Juan River tumbles on the fringe of the complex and in a few tubs you could have your body in the hot water and your feet in the cold river.

We found a private campground located on the banks of the San Juan River. Generally, we like to stay in state and national parks because of the ambience and cheap rates, but when that isn't possible, private campgrounds will do. That night, sleep was accompanied by the sounds of the rushing water as it flowed past our window. The cool waters and cool air came from the melting snow on the nearby San Juan Mountains. Texas and New Mexico were so very dry and hot, that the coolness was exhilarating. As we walked around the campground, we saw a campsite that had lots of walking sticks lying on a table. We waited until the owner was there and then approached him with questions about his "sticks". He invited us to join him on a walk along the river. The area was dense with all kinds of trees, especially willow, which he said made very good walking sticks. As we walked, he took out his knife and cut a few willows down for me. They grew thick along the banks of the river. He then showed us how to peel and dry them. My collection of sticks was growing and fit very well under the shelf, in the cap of the truck.

Once we left the campground, it didn't take long to get lost. We were headed for McPhee Reservoir, a BLM campground, to be close to the *Durango-Silverton Narrow Gauge Railroad.* We didn't realize that there were two campgrounds with the same name. One was in Delores and the other was in the town of Cortez. At a crossroad, we had to make a decision, so we went left and wound up driving what seemed like a thousand miles up and down hills. When arriving at the Delores campground, the hosts were very happy to see us as there was no one else around. They probably hadn't seen anyone for a long time as they confirmed that this was a remote part of the reservoir. They said we probably wanted to be closer to Cortez and the town of Durango, our ultimate destination. It was getting late in the day, so we decided to spend the night.

The sites sit high on a bluff over looking the reservoir. This was barren country with no trees. Under the reservoir's water lies the lumber town of McPhee. At one time, this was the largest producing lumber mill in Colorado. Because of the Great Depression and several large fires, the site was closed in 1948. Most the town's machinery and houses were dismantled and moved to other cities. The reservoir was noticeably down and we wondered how long it would be before the streets of town were visible again. At the Heritage Center in Delores were pictures of what the town looked like before the dam was built including a picture and floor plan of a Sears & Roebuck house that lay at the bottom of the reservoir. Also, several exhibits showed the importance of the railroad and lumber operation.

A visit from our hosts added more drama to the area. They told us that at the base of the reservoir was an unexcavated Anasazi site. It took us a while to find it, but when we did, we had the site all to ourselves. It was fun exploring the walls and pretending that we were archaeologists. The day ended with a magnificent starry night. So I guess we weren't lost at all, just on a brief, adventuresome detour.

The next day, we found the campground that we were originally looking for. It was located in a tree-covered valley and close to the main road. This was to be our base camp for about a week. Trips were planned for the famous train ride out of Durango; a visit to the Mesa Verde National Park's cliff dwellings, and a ride over the Red Mountain Pass at Ouray.

On the way into the town of Cortez was the Anasazi Heritage Center, which was an interesting museum with computer models showing the Anasazi dwellings along with microscopes, which helped to see the details of design in their work. The Anasazi were an amazing culture. The funny thing about learning about these people is that I don't remember being taught about them in school. They existed in the southwest as early as 1 A.D. A short movie explained that the great Sage Plain covers most of Utah, Arizona, New Mexico and Colorado. Over a thousand Pueblo Indians (now referred to as the Ancients) lived here. There were early indications that these people were hunters and gatherers. As they traded with other villages, they became more sophisticated in their tools and resources. Turquoise from Flagstaff, Arizona, seashells from the Pacific Ocean and Gulf of Mexico, copper bells from Central Mexico were discovered along with foods that were introduced to them by the Spanish explorers. By the mid-13th Century, the area was abandoned. Speculation was the same fate as the other Ancients with lack of water to support the crops that fed an ever-growing population.

Our journey took us on an exploration of 12 houses and one Kiva located behind the Heritage Center. Being on top of a mountain was crucial as it provided a view of six directions. I knew north, east, south, west, but was introduced to zenith (above) and nader (below). In the middle of the Kiva was a special circle that provided an entrance for the spirits to enter.

In their earlier development, the Ancients lived in "pit" houses. As the name describes, these were houses dug into the ground and covered over with wooden beams. Most of the Ancient's time was spent outdoors doing chores such as weaving cloth, making tools, cooking and preparing for the winter. This was a prelude for what we would find at Mesa Verde.

Back at our campsite we hiked to a lookout. There we could see 360 degrees, much the same as the Ancient's dwellings. A candle lit dinner and a glass of wine completed another perfect day.

The *Durango and Silverton Narrow Gauge Railroad* was built to traverse the steep San Juan Mountains between Denver and New Mexico. To accommodate the steep grades, the rails ran about a foot and half narrower than the standard rail. In 1881, the connection to Durango from Denver was complete. This made Durango an important hub in getting supplies to the mines. Gold and silver ore poured down from the mountains, and towns prospered. Passengers also rode the train along with the mail. The very rich had their own private cars attached to the main line, with all the comforts of home. As gold and silver prices dropped, the mines closed. One by one, most towns fell into despair, however a few towns did survive. Thanks to rail enthusiasts and Hollywood, the *Durango & Silverton Narrow Gauge Railroad* survived. "Around the World in 80 Days", and "Butch Cassidy and the Sundance Kid" were just a few films that featured the steam engines and old cars of this now historic railway.

Excitedly, tickets were purchased from a lady dressed in period costume behind the original iron barred ticket counter. We had been told by fellow campers to sit in the open car and wear dark clothes because the soot from the engines would get us dirty. The day was cool (68 degrees) and sunny. Upon seeing the massive iron steam engine getting ready to chug up the mountain, brought tears to my eyes because of its historical significance. At 9 a.m., the train pulled out and traveled through the rich meadowlands of the Animas River

Valley. Skirting snow-capped mountains, the train followed the Animas River. Up we climbed as aspen filled the mountainside and waterfalls cascaded down to the meadows. Our neighbors to the right of us had two boys who loved trains. Their mother bought them the track guidebook and they read out loud what was coming. A game ensued as we readied our cameras to catch the train as it rounded a steep bend with a sheer drop into the Animas River or when it traversed precarious bridges over high gorges. At some places, the mountain's wall was so close, a person could touch the foliage and catch a leaf.

Our arrival in Silverton was greeted with, surprisingly, snow. The sky darkened and snow began to fall, followed by hail. We were prepared for the change of climate, but not for a snowstorm. Gladly, it only lasted a few minutes and was followed by a sunny, cool day. Silverton was amazing. In the summer time, the population can be as high as 1,000 and in the winter, drops to a few diehards with snow as a constant companion. It was fun seeing this old, cold western town that hadn't really changed much. A poster in the local saloon said there was going to be an old timers parade on the following Saturday. Wow, that sounded like a party.

Another recommendation from several campers was to ride the bus back. The return trip was entertaining as the driver told us stories of all the interesting sites on the way. A few miles into the descent, he asked us to look back and notice a tiny ribbon of a trail along the mountainside. That was the old stagecoach and Pony Express route up to Silverton. Further down the road, he told us we were not far from where Butch Cassidy and the Sundance Kid jumped off the mountain to escape the law, into the river below. Butch Cassidy and Sundance were known as the Robin Hood of the West because they never killed anyone and shared their bounty with the needy. It was late when we arrived back at our campsite and that night I dreamt of Butch Cassidy riding in the wilds of Colorado.

Mesa Verde National Park is known for the well-preserved cliffs housing the early settlement of the ancient pueblo people. It was here that the nomadic people began associating in groups, and building small villages. These were the first known hunter-gatherers who became farmers. Dominated by switchbacks, the ride up to the

Visitor's Center wound around the mountain and took over an hour to reach the top. After a while, a person wonders how they found this place.

In 1888, two Quaker cowboys were herding cattle and discovered the cliff dwellings of Mesa Verde. It was so amazing to them that they called it "Cliff Palace". It sits under a rock cliff, 7,000 feet above sea level. On the Park Service tour, we were told that we would be climbing three, ten-foot ladders to enter and exit the dwellings. Cliff Palace is the largest cliff dwelling in North America. Because Spanish archeologists were sending artifacts back to Spain, President Teddy Roosevelt passed the Antiquities Act to keep the artifacts in this country and made this area a national park

Our guide explained that "The Cliff Palace" was a storage area for the people who farmed the land on the mesa as well as the meadows below. Looking at the cliff dwellings, they resembled apartments. Five years ago, archaeologists began to reveal the true story of Mesa Verde. They originally thought a large population occupied this site. Now they see it was occupied by a small band of "caretakers" responsible for overseeing the commerce of several tribes. The cliffs were ideally located, slanting to the south for sun. We climbed down many steps to reach the dwellings. In the time of the Ancients, rainfall on the mesa averaged 18 inches a year. That made the soil good for crops of corn, squash and later, beans. By 900 A.D., the Ancients had mastered their building technique and started building more rectangular, sturdier rooms. Mortar was made from clay, sand and ash. Entry into these stacked dwellings is through a small, square opening accessed by climbing ladders or footholds. There had to be a lot of cooperation among the families to co-exist in this tight space. One can only imagine the leg muscles on these people as the scurried up and down the rock wall carrying baskets of goods. At one time, 30,000 people lived on the mesa and its surrounding area. Today, the population of Montezuma County (Mesa Verde) is about 18,000.

Wondering how the cliff dwellers got their water, our guide told us that in the back of the rock was a pool of water called "seep springs". The water was only a foot deep, but it had a constant flow. We were invited to climb carefully through some of the dwellings and the park rangers were very helpful in answering questions and providing a hand so that no one got hurt exploring the dwellings.

No one knows the particulars about the demise of the Ancients, but it is known that they were faced with a 27-year drought. The Ancients used trees for cooking, building and tools. Slowly, their supply was depleted. Archaeologists tell us that the trees in this area were slow growers and no evidence of older trees have been found. Even today, Montezuma County is experiencing a five-year drought. It made us wonder about the effects of global warming.

The National Park's museum at Mesa Verde displayed a lot of their pottery, utensils, clothing, and had a detailed history panorama that showed that around 1450 A.D. the Utes and Navajos moved into the area. This was about 100 years before the Spanish arrived. It was all very overwhelming and we decided to save the other dwellings for another time. Another way to explore this fascinating land is to take a tour by the local Ute Indians. In their four-wheel drive vehicles, they can take you to places not often seen as many more cliff dwellings were spread out over two mesas. The Utes are still here, preserving the land.

Coming down from the mesa, a wild turkey wandered onto the road. It was fun stopping traffic and making sure it found its way back into the bush.

Saturday morning dawned with temps at 58 and sunny. We heard that back home in Maryland, it had been raining forever! With an early start, we pointed the truck towards Silverton's Ice Cream Social. We could have taken the same road that paralleled the Durango train, but the map showed us another road that locals called "The Million Dollar Mile". Up and across steep mountains, the road connected mining towns to the railroad. The railroad was the lifeblood of the miners who worked in shafts way below the ground. Many people think it was called the "Million Dollar Road" because of the cost, but another theory is that the "fools gold" used as building material was the real thing! The scenery was breathtaking.

Ouray sits in a valley surrounded by vacant mines. All terrain vehicle (ATV) rides are a specialty of this area as well as a large, public spring-fed swimming pool. The ride from Ouray to Silverton was the scariest road I had ever been on. For three miles, the road wound around the mountain gaining in elevation. At some places, the road can't be seen ahead as it passes over ledges and climbs 11,018 feet to Red Mountain Pass. There were no guard rails and the gorges were steep. I was so scared that I would have climbed into Charles' lap if he had not been driving. At one time, this road was used for mail, mule teams and miners until the rails were complete. After much screaming, laughing (my nervous reaction) and crying, we safely arrived in Silverton. In such a rugged terrain, it is mind boggling how such a road could be built and how the miners survived.

The parade and celebration, "Step Back in Time" was just getting started. About fifty of the town's folk dressed in period costumes paraded down Main Street. Men were on horseback, dressed with leather chaps and carrying pistols and shotguns. Wild Bill Hitchcock, Annie Oakley and Bat Masterson were part of the parade. It was a small gathering, but the scenery of the old town and the huge mountain backdrop made it seem like a "step back in time". The band played in the gazebo and the Lady's Club served ice cream. If someone wasn't in costume, a Keystone cop would harass them and give out a $1 ticket. The ticket was then exchanged at the local saloon for a garter that was put on your arm so that you too would be in costume.

The ride home was much less exciting. Being on the other side, we hugged the mountain and didn't have to look down into the steep gorges. Now that I could open my eyes, I could see many of the deserted mineshafts as they came into view.

In the late afternoon sun, we approach Telluride Ski Resort and found the ski lifts still operating. Camping neighbors said they were free and well worth the trip. We couldn't resist a ride. Several levels of trams took us up the mountain; high in the aspen forest while the fairytale town of Telluride was shrinking below.

The next few days were down days. That meant I slept in, wrote and downloaded photos while Charles piddled. Then it was time to leave Colorado and enter Utah.

So far, the camper and truck proved to be the ideal combination for whatever we wanted to do. Feeling comfortable with our new life style, we set three goals for ourselves. 1) A "must see", must be obeyed; 2) try not to drive more than 250 miles a day, and 3) stay in shorts. Images of the movie "Follow the Sun" came to mind. Not a bad credo for popping up across America.

Chapter Twelve

Utah's Treasures

Southern Utah was to be a big surprise. Originally, we were heading to Arizona, but camping friends in Abiquiu said that we didn't want to go there, because it being mid-June meant it would be hot. They asked us to bring our map over so they could show us a route that encompassed five national parks. It looked like a snake crawling from Zion to Bryce Canyon, then up through Capital Reef, down to the Natural Bridges and up to the Arches. It was to be an adventure that we hadn't planned on, but one that begged to be done.

Our plan was to head first to the Arches, the northern most National Park we wanted to visit. Most of the private campgrounds along the way were unacceptable because they were flat, dusty and had no trees. The fee of $20 was also high for what we would get. To us, the ambience of a site was more appealing than a swimming pool out on the dusty plain. After searching the map, we found a site at Devil's Canyon State Park. The price was right at $2.50 a night and was situated in the Manti-La Sal National Forest. It was that cheap because it had no utilities. Dry camping wasn't our favorite way to camp, but it did get us back to basics. We still had the comforts of home with refrigeration, powered by the propane, and lights and pressure for the 10-gallon water tank from the battery. Our only restriction was to be conservative with our usage.

Devils Canyon got its name from the emigrants traveling west who couldn't cross the Canyon. They had come a long way and still had a long way to go. Imagine their disappointment when they found out they had to go around the canyon because it was too steep to go through. Devils Canyon is located in the bottom of a "V". On one side is Capital Reef National Park and the other side is the Arches National Park. For the early emigrants, this land was very foreboding. For the modern traveler, it is awesome country.

"The Needles" was on the way to the Arches. From an overlook we saw the vastness of the sagebrush plain where the Ancient's farmed. With binoculars, the ATV trails looked enticing as they shared the valley floor with the Ancients that once lived there. A sign gave the history of the valley floor and surprised us by mentioning that the Ancients occupied this area in the same time as when the Roman Empire occupied Europe and the Middle East. After the Ancients left, Spanish Explorers used this road looking for a route to the missions of California. This period was followed by the "Ute" Indians and then by ranchers. At one time, over 10,000 cattle grazed in this valley. The rocks we climbed glistened with various minerals and the snow-covered mountains in the distance, made it feel like a fairyland.

A flash of the Golden Age card enabled us to visit national parks for free. With our ambitious plan to visit five national parks, this card saved us a lot of money.

Arches got its name from the 2,000 plus catalogued arches in the park. Created over 100 million years ago by violent forces pushing and pulling at the earth's crust, what was left was an inviting playground. "Delicate Arch" (the state's symbol) came highly recommended. The brochure we received at the entrance classified the hike as moderate and 1.5 miles, one-way. Charles was brilliant when he thought to bring a golf umbrella to provide shade. By the time we reached the Arch, it seemed more like five miles of difficult hiking. The rock cliffs went on and on and the elevation went up and up. Piles of stone marked the path. We finally made it to the top, after a lot of stops to catch our breath and drink water as the elevation climbed from 6,000 to 8,500 feet. We should have been forewarned as the faces of the folks on their way down were red from the heat and they looked exhausted. Once at the top, we were not impressed and have to say that we wouldn't do it again, especially when we found out that we could see the formation from the road. The hike left us almost too tired to see any of the other Arches. We then went to inspect the National Park's campground, which was very nice, and a "must do" for a future visit. Days could be spent here, hiking and exploring arches and canyons. For now, a quick dunk of our heads under a waterspout awoke our adventuresome spirit to forge ahead on a few easier climbs including side canyons that revealed awesome stone formations. The scenery of high, red rocks carved into many shapes played with our imagination. As we left, the formation near the exit, called the "Three Sisters", seemed to wave goodbye.

Driving toward Capital Reef, the map showed a campground located at the headwaters of Lake Powell. The route there led us through varying shades of red rock mountains rimmed by white canyons. One could see how the Ancients would have farmed this land and stored their crops in the canyon crevices. Each turn was amazing.

John Wesley Powell discovered Lake Powell in 1869 while looking for a northwest passage. We were able to dry camp on the banks of the lake for free in a desolate place called Hite. This stop was a total surprise, as we didn't plan on stopping here, but who could resist exploring the headwaters of Lake Powell as it ran into the Colorado River? Across the lake, houseboats docked in canyons, just like their advertisements boasted. As we explored the area, it was shocking to see the lake down by about 50 feet. Huge cinder blocks, that once stabilized a dock, lay exposed in the dry mud that once was Lake Powell. It was here that I had a big scare. Charles was rushing around setting up and I begged him to slow down. It was hot and there was no shade. He paused next to the camper and the next thing I knew, he passed out. Fortunately, I was there to catch him. It didn't last long and I helped him into the camper to lay down with cold compresses on his head. That day we learned to take it easy in the heat and drink plenty of water. He has been fine ever since.

The red rocks accompanied us all the way to Capital Reef National Park. The different colors in the rock marked different eras. With the passage of time, the beauty of the sculptured rock could have been in a Smithsonian exhibit. In fact, early pioneers called it "Capital' because the rock color reminded them of the United States Capital and "Reef" came from the difficulty sailors had crossing them. Every turn was breathtaking. The land changed from mountains to sage plain and then back to mountains. The colors of the mountains changed too, from red to white to gray. Seeing it for the first time left us in awe.

At Capitol Reef, the amazing scenery went on. This time, the cliffs were sprinkled with petroglyphs. A unique geological stratum called a "Waterpocket Fold" makes Capital Reef special because of unique rock formations high on the plateau. The Fremont River runs through the park and brings much needed irrigation to the surrounding grasslands. The Mormons tried to cultivate this land and in the middle of the park are the fruits of their efforts, the town of "Fruita". A one-room schoolhouse survives along with a few homes that showed their resiliency for survival. The park service maintains several of the orchards that grow a variety of fruit.

We found a wonderful, private campground outside the town of Torrey. It had a pool and utilities for less than $16 a night. A cookout was planned for that evening and on the menu, for a nominal fee, were steaks and the fixings. At dinner we met a young couple from Switzerland who had three months to explore the United States. Bruno and Danielle had rented a four-wheel, all terrain vehicle for the day and explored some of the backlands of the park. That night we roasted marshmallows around their campfire and shared stories. We stayed an extra day to enjoy their company and lounged at the pool. Bruno's hobby was photography and it was wonderful seeing pictures of their trip as well as discussing various web sites he used to share his photos with friends. Having a laptop makes sharing pictures easy. We parted ways with a promise to stay in touch. Camping is so much more than camping. It is a great way to make new friends from all walks of life.

The amazing scenery continued as we skirted the Grand Staircase Escalante National Monument Park to arrive in Bryce Canyon. We had heard from a lot of campers that Red Canyon National Forest was the place to camp and for us, it was. The alternative was to camp in the national park, which was located next to a large gift shop and hotel that was a bit too touristy for us. At the Red Canyon campsite we met Deb and Dan and their four-year-old grandson. He seemed very shy, but when I got out my bubbles, he warmed up to us. It is a special moment when we connect with someone at a campground. It makes it feel more like home, where there are friends and camaraderie.

Bryce Canyon National Park was about 15 minutes down the road. Famous for a specific kind of rock formation called "Hoodoo", we managed to see this spectacle as the sun set. The whole area is called an "amphitheater" because of the thousands of colorful, hoodoos and a landscape that stretches for miles. The rock formation looked like fingers jutting up from the canyon's floor. In Indian lure, it is believed that these stones were once people who betrayed the gods. The next day we took several hikes through these formations and it was amazing. We couldn't believe how far we had come. The funny thing was that we found ourselves in places we had not planned to be in. Conversations with other campers had opened eyes to the amazing country that is America!

Chapter Thirteen

Hot Vegas and Cold Ghosts

It was a long, hot drive to Las Vegas. The trucks outside thermometer read 117 degrees, which in my imagination, felt like the truck and I were going to burn up. I have never been in temperatures that hot. Surprisingly, it all held together and the air conditioning didn't miss a beat. It seemed too hot to spend time in the camper, so we stopped at "Circus, Circus", where we heard they had the cheapest rooms in Las Vegas. A security guard showed us a nice shady spot to park the truck and camper and pointed the way to our room.

It was too hot to enjoy the day. It was even too hot to go to the pool. The only logical time to venture out was at night. That is when Las Vegas sparkles. With comfortable shoes on, we stopped at the front desk for the lay of the land and discount coupons for food. We took our maps, coupons and list of events; set our internal warning antenna on high, and ventured into the street. The air conditioned trolley seemed like a sure bet to get familiar with the town. From the windows of the trolley we saw Caesar's Palace, the Monte Carlo, the Luxor and the ending of the Pirate Show at the Mirage. As we passed the Bellagio, someone said that the infamous couple of J-Lo and Ben had just spent the night there.

Entering the Tropicana was a slot machine with a "free pull". Everyone wins a deck of cards and some win 2-for-1 tickets to the *Folies Bergere.* We got the deck of cards. At the redemption center, we were told we could "earn" free tickets to the *Folies* by playing two hours of slots. Not being gamblers, we figured the slowest machine was Poker with deuces wild. The wild card made the game easier to win. We sat at machines that were next to each other and analyzed each other's hands. It was fun and became even more fun when we started using the coupon for free drinks. Las Vegas was everything we had imagined. In the middle of the casino was a floorshow complete with gorgeous, high kicking, showgirls, duet singers and a trapeze act. The trolley was our designated driver, so we could let loose. Isn't that what Las Vegas is all about?

Back out on the street, the veil of night was cooling the air. The finale of the evening was the fountains at the Bellagio. They were beautifully choreographed and set to a soundtrack that could be heard from various points around the hotel. All of the Bellagio, that we could see, was beautiful. The gaming rooms were elegantly designed with deep red velvet upholstery, where blackjack started at $100 a hand. The lobby was most impressive with exotic flower sculptures and an Italian tile floor that belonged in a museum. Even the bathrooms were luxurious with marble tile and brass fixtures including an overhead light in case you wanted to read Hoyle's Rules of Games while doing your business.

The next day, we ducked in and out of the air-conditioned casinos as we made our way to a free dinner and the longest running show in Las Vegas, the *Folies Bergere.* Beautiful showgirls strutted around magnificent scenery with high, feathered headdresses. Their choreographed dancing and the dinner was the epitome of Vegas. All in all, it was a very entertaining night for a couple on a budget, as you can't beat "free".

Speaking of free, the Freemont Experience was our next stop. Once the center of the Vegas strip, it went into decline as a new wave of casinos were being built. Now it is having a resurgence. A "must do" was seeing the light show above the enclosed strip. Coordinated lights flashed images of Elvis, Tom Jones, Louis Prima, and Sammy Davis, Jr. along a 1,400 foot vaulted ceiling. The show ended with Frank Sinatra singing *Luck be a Lady Tonight.* Driving home, we saw a sign on the drive-thru wedding chapel that read $135 to get married.

A major decision was whether or not to cross Death Valley. With Vegas being so hot, it was hard to imagine how hot Death Valley would be. We really didn't want to go through it as we had missed the "cool" season, so we decided to skirt it by taking Highway 95 north through Nevada. A program on our computer called "Streets", showed that the distance was shorter and elevation higher. That meant it would be cooler. Departure was set at 5 a.m. to avoid the heat of the day. The road started out desolate and bleak and put me right to sleep. I felt the truck turn onto a new road and I awoke and needed to go to the bathroom. What a surprise to find us outside "The Cottontail Brothel". Charles didn't realize where we were, but I knew. PBS did a special report on "The Cottontail Brothel" about a year ago, because it is one of a few brothels still open in the United States. I couldn't bring myself to go in and with some embarrassment (although no one was around), I let loose on the side of the road. Sometimes a girl has to do what a girl has to do and being comfortable was a major objective. However, I do regret not going in, at least for a T-shirt.

For many miles, the landscape was barren. There weren't even any fences. Around a bend, a few cactuses appeared. Then more and more. Around another bend, and they began to disappear. A few more miles and there was an oasis with one home, in the middle of nowhere. Temperatures were a comfortable 65 to 72 degrees because we had climbed to 7,400 feet in elevation. In the distance appeared snow-capped mountains, which contrasted to the starkness we were seeing. Another bend revealed a few fir trees, and then slowly, a forest of trees began to fill the landscape. The land was becoming more fertile and then we saw a sign that read "Welcome to California". Hallelujah!

The California roads were newly paved as compared to the older asphalt roads of Nevada. It was strange to see the change from the deserts of Nevada to the greening of California all by crossing the state line. We did about 350 miles that day, about 150 more miles than I would have liked. Our destination was Mono Lake, which is a main water source for northern California. It was late afternoon when we found a private campground and settled in for the night. The next morning we explored Mono Lake.

Back in the 1940's, southern California redirected much of the water from Mono Lake to irrigate its fields and fill its swimming pools. So much water was drained, that the lake's most famous features, the white towers of a calcium carbonate, became exposed. They are called Tufa (Too-FAH'). Today, conservation measures have curtailed the water flow and Mono Lake is on the rise. No fish live in the lake, as the water is very alkaline, but trillions of alkali flies and brine shrimp provide an excellent source of food for over 90 species of migrating birds.

Forty miles north from Mono Lake, and at an elevation of 8,000 feet is the ghost town of Bodie, once a large town with a big mine in the middle. The dirt road entrance was three miles long traversing the hills of the Sierra Mountains. There was nothing to see for miles around but the barren land. The National Park Service preserves about 170 buildings here. Fortunately, the devastation of time was kind to these buildings because they were made from cedar wood. Gold was discovered in its mountains in 1859 and the Mother Load in 1877. The town quickly grew to over 10,000 men. At one time, over 30 mines operated in Bodie and produced $35 million in gold and silver. With 65 saloons, it is said that Bodie had the roughest, toughest, meanest men in the West. Its population was made up of Indian fighters, ruffians, bounty hunters and entrepreneurs. Alcohol and gambling were the town's only activities accompanied by a lot of prostitution. It was a lawless place with no decent woman or religion, and where life was hard and the weather inhospitable. The pay for a day's work was $4 and there was always the chance you may lose your life either to the mine or by the gun. Peering into the windows of homes and businesses, we saw the beds, the kitchen and furniture just as it was left. Yards were littered with rusting mining equipment and a few old cars. When the gold vein dried up in 1888, so did the town. All around town were wild irises that seemed to be the souls of the people who died in Bodie. Bodie became a State Historic Park in 1962, and the guards tell of ghosts they hear in the night after everyone had gone home.

Before the sun set, we found ourselves exploring the 15 mile June Lake loop that winds through a glacier canyon. Several campgrounds were located on a few of the four lakes and it seemed to be a fisherman heaven. In the office of one of the campgrounds, we studied the map and I was surprised to see the Ansel Adams Wilderness. The owner told us that Ansel Adams' daughter ran a restaurant down the road, and recommended the photographic exhibit there. Another kid joined in the conversation about where to eat, and he recommended the "Mobil". I though he was getting smart, recommending a gas station. But he was not. It turned out that the "Mobil" was the place to be. The first sign of a good restaurant is limited parking. As we walked towards the convenience store in the Mobile station, a drum circle was playing in the parking lot and there was a wait for a table. Inside, a sign over the food case said we're eating at "Tioga Toomey's Nellie Deli". The atmosphere was jovial and the mango margaritas and lobster taquitos were excellent. We shared our table with a couple from Great Britain and had jolly-good fun!

Not far from the "Mobil" was Tioga Pass, peaking at 9,945 feet. It is the gateway to Yosemite, our next destination. The climb gave us some concern, but we took our time and stopped to admire the beauty of Tuolumne Meadows where lakes, waterfalls and pastures graced the surroundings. As we got more into the park, massive redwood trees outlined majestic towers of rock and the blue sky stretched across the horizon. The vastness was breathtaking. Campsite availability was almost non-existent, as the summer tourist season had begun. A wilderness campground had just opened for the season and sites were available. We started down the recommended road when a sign appeared and read, "Not recommended for trailers or motor homes". The only problem was, there was no place to turn around. We were committed and it was very scary. Once again, Charles did an outstanding job navigating the ruts of a two and half mile winding road and kept us from falling down the side of the mountain. I was too scared to look.

Our campsite was deep in the valley floor. Next to our campsite was a metal box with a heavy-duty latch. For precautionary measures, it was recommended to empty all the food into this box so as not to tempt the bears. Not only was this dry camping, it was wilderness camping. There we were with backpackers feeling grateful to be in the pop-up being up off the ground and having the three burner stove to cook our meals. That afternoon, we hiked to where a steam flowed through a forest of virgin redwoods and huge boulders. Tiny purple flowers carpeted the ground around our camper. One of the most impressive sights was the range of flower colors. From deep yellows, to baby blues, to deep pinks and light pinks, to soft white; Mother Nature's palette was in full bloom.

Our first day was sunny and warm, but the next day brought clouds and a cold wind. We had a foreboding feeling that we might be caught there. Visions of cold rain and a slippery, rocky road back to the top scared us. An early afternoon departure was planned with hopes of having the road all to ourselves. We didn't want to have to pull over because there was no place go or to have the road fall away due to erosion. After several hours of white knuckle driving, we reached the top.

Because of the change in weather, Charles had gotten a cold in Yosemite and was sick when we arrived at the 49er's Ranch in Columbia. Columbia is said to be one of the oldest occupied gold rush towns in Northern California, but as we were finding out, everyone claimed to be the oldest. During the gold rush days, wagon trains and other travelers used the 49er's Ranch to rest and rejuvenate. It was a comfortable place for Charles to get well. Lots of rest and vitamin C helped him get back his health. The radio station said we were in "Mother Load" country. Chinese Camp, Angels Camp, and Sonora were a few of the old ghost towns nearby that thrived during the gold rush.

We had been traveling for four months. Other than heading west, there was no focus on a destination. Our country's incredible diversity and beauty went beyond our imagination. Being newly retired was like being a new baby. Seeing everything for the first time and having time to savor it was an exhilarating feeling.

It was June 25 when we got to the last campsite of our westward journey. Half Moon Bay State Park is located right on the Pacific Ocean and is 50 miles south of San Francisco. The white tiled bathrooms were "Unisex" and were a testament to cleanliness. They were big enough to fully enjoy a shower with your mate.

I was starting to feel that whatever Charles had, was getting to me. However, nothing could diminish the joy of seeing the Pacific Ocean. There we stood with tears in our eyes and disbelief in our minds. We had done it.

A lady from the "49er's Ranch" campground said her parents would be camping at Half Moon Bay that weekend and to look for an older "Minnie Winnie" (a Winnebago camper). Their names were Val and Van, which was easy to remember. Imagine our surprise to be camped right next to them. It was an even bigger surprise to them, when we called out their names. Fond regards from their daughter were given and a glass of wine shared to celebrate the coincidence and our arrival on the west coast.

Chapter Fourteen

The Beat Goes On

Before venturing to San Francisco for a reunion with friends, it was suggested that we drive down the coast to Año Nuevo State Park. Here is where seals can be seen up close and personal. Being late June, it was the season when male bulls congregate to challenge each other for dominancy. This spectacle went on in the water and on land with a viewing area arranged so that you could get close to them, which you didn't want to do, because they stink!

On our arrival in San Francisco, our friends, Bill and Julia, had our room ready. After settling in, we shared a ride with Julia to one of our favorite cities – San Francisco. A cable car ride took us to the place where we had our wedding reception – Pier 39. The seals were still there clapping their approval of our eleven-year marriage and our good fortune to be able to see America.

It was great being with old friends. Julia's son came over with his wife and three boys for dinner. I remember when he was nine and Julia and I were single parents.

For the next few days, I stayed in bed feeling awful. It is amazing how rest, plenty of liquids and vitamin C actually work! We were proud to "self medicate" and believe that it makes the immune system stronger. It took us both about two weeks to shake the bug.

On Saturday, Julia and Bill took us for a picnic in the hills surrounding Point Reyes. Sandwiches, wine, fruit, cheese and the scenery made for a wonderful picnic. We hadn't seen them since our wedding, yet, it seemed like only yesterday, but for a few gray hairs. Coming home, Julia drove like Mario Andretti navigating the twists and turns and a detour that took us around Mt. Tamaplia. At one turn, we were able to see the famous fog rolling in to cover the city.

Our tentative plans for July 4 were to visit friends in Salem, Oregon. However, Julia and Bill had another idea. They insisted that we join them for their 20th annual July 4 party at their cabin in Truckee, California and "no" was not an option.

It was a pleasant five hour drive from San Francisco to Truckee. Rt. 80 took us across the state to the beautiful mountains of the Sierras. As we approached "Emigrant Gap" I was reminded of the winter camp that the Donner Party made there as they waited out winter on their trek to the West coast. Today, ski lifts dot the mountainside.

Their cabin sat two blocks from Donner Lake and at the base of a rock wall. It was rustic and charming and tall pines lent shade from above. Our pop-up fit nicely between Julia and her neighbor's cabin. This was to be our home for the next week. Slowly, friends arrived, then neighbors joined in and the next thing we knew, a party was going on and lasted for five days. The neighbor's ages ran from 10 to 80 so it was a good mix of people. The day before July 4, was the day when the whole neighborhood decorated their houses and joined in for a potluck dinner. July 4th started with a huge breakfast for the twelve people staying in the house plus us. The pop-up was working out just great. It fit in with the surroundings and no one seemed to mind. Having the extra bed space was what made it possible for us to join in the celebration. The drinking of California wines started around 11 a.m. Then came the games. Bocce ball, beanbag toss and baseball where played throughout the day with great gusto. I was surprised at my competitiveness playing bocce ball. One of the house guests was an exchange student from Barcelona, Spain, and she was my partner. We kicked butt and took second place.

July 5th was Donner Lake's annual sandcastle contest. A brainstorming session took place at the kitchen table the night before and the kids decided to build a sunken ship with an attacking octopus. The rules specified that only two adults could supervise. Julia and Jeannette got up early and found the necessary supplies to create this masterpiece. Happily, they won first place and more California wine was consumed to celebrate. On Sunday, everyone left and a strange quiet filled the cabin. Julia and Bill were staying on for a few more days, so we decided to help ease the transition. Charles was able to play golf with a few of the neighbors and the rest of us tried to clean up and recover from partying.

It was sad to leave, but we had to be moving on. Bill suggested that we travel north, through Lassen National Forest. He said we would find some good campgrounds there and that the scenery was awesome. Our original plan was to travel up the coast, but since Donner Lake was in the northeast part of the state, Lassen National Forest was a good choice. McArthur-Burney Falls Memorial State Park was a nice place to spend the night. Within the campground was a lovely waterfall and huge lake. This was all within an easy walk from our campsite and the dock on the lake, provided a nice spot to sit and watch the sunset and moonrise. A ranger chatted with us about his adventures in Yellowstone, which we listened to with envy.

Mt. Lassen National Park was close to the state park and along the roadside, snow was piled twelve feet high, even though it was mid-July. The brochure said this park was famous for its sulphur springs, however the most famous one was unattainable because of snow. At a few other stops, it was an easy hike over boardwalks, to see the bubbly springs. Hot water pushing up through the earth's crust makes one wonder what is happening here.

At the Visitor's Center, a chart showed 14 volcanoes in the Pacific Northwest. Seven of these have erupted in the last 1,000 years. Mt. St. Helens is the most active, having erupted three times and doing some belching in 2004. One day we toured a "volcanic tube" that was created by the force of a lava flow and lay 30 feet underground. What made this cave interesting was to see the terrain above it as well as below. It was then that we realized the miles and miles of land, that we had seen traveling here, were on top of these tubes.

Packed up and moving on, our path led us through Klamath Falls to Crater Lake in Oregon and again we experienced incredible scenery and geological history. Our campsite was nestled under large trees and although we did not have any amenities such as water and electricity, being surrounded by the lush greens of towering pines and a babbling creek nearby and it just didn't get any better.

Crater Lake was made by an implosion. Mt. Mazama was once the tallest volcano in the United States and stood 12,000 feet high. When it imploded, it dumped up to eight inches of ash, enough to cover what is now the state of Oregon. Maybe that is why Oregon's soil is so fertile. Snow and rain filled the caldera (inside the dormant volcano) to create the deepest lake in the United States. At an evening program, the ranger passed around a big chunk of pumice rock that made up the walls of the volcano. It was light and felt like Styrofoam.

The Crater Lake Lodge was charming. It had a superb restaurant that overlooked the lake. Decorated with pillars and planks of local Ponderosa pines, it had a very homey touch. Two huge fireplaces greeted guests (residents and non-residents) with a warm welcome. The menu was very appealing and inexpensive. We decided to have breakfast and lunch there instead of just dinner, so we could extend our enjoyment of the room and its view.

On a day trip, we explored various parts of the rim and found a lovely flower garden interspersed with a waterfall. At another overlook was Vidalia Falls that gushed from the crevices above. Kids nearby clamored up its rock face for the perfect picture.

The drive to Salem, Oregon took us through the North Umpqua River Trail. The elevation dropped from 5,000 feet to 400 feet while the Umpqua River meandered along the highway (Rt. 138). It traversed hills covered with large conifers and valleys where the river ran. There were lots of places to raft, tube, fish, camp and enjoy. Wildflowers let us know that we were still in spring, even though it was July. A-h-h-h!

The one thing that is immediately noticeable when entering Oregon is their love of coffee. Small shacks were everywhere advertising drive-thru "Espresso". Even the Visitor's Center had free coffee.

Arriving in Salem, we were reunited with friends who moved there from Frederick, Maryland. It was fun being with them. Their son, Michael was eight years old and a pleasure to be with. One day we all took a hike to the top of Multnomah Falls as Michael played hide-n-seek amongst the rocks. Another day we visited Cooley's Iris Farm where incredible strains of irises are grown for transport around the world. A special trip with Michael was to the Gilbert House, where we all got to act like kids. The Gilbert House commemorates A.C. Gilbert, the inventor of the Erector Set. Evenings were filled with wonderful dinners and much reminiscing.

Again, it was hard to pull ourselves away and continue north. Our next visit was to friends that we met during the July 4th party. They live in Tacoma, Washington, and their house sits in the shadow of Mt. Rainer. They insisted we stop by and said we could park the camper in their driveway. Besides, Julia and Bill would be there to celebrate Jeannette and Julia's birthdays and having the camper was like having an extra bedroom. Jeanette, a huge Mariner's baseball fan, purchased tickets for all of us. I couldn't let a birthday pass without some recognition, so Julia and I went to the hospitality office to try and get a birthday wish with their names on the billboard, but we were too late. This had to be done four weeks prior to the game. As compensation, they gave us a Mariner's hat, shirt and banner. When we got back to the stands, friends and fans sang a loud rousing "Happy Birthday" and Jeannette loved the Mariner's gifts.

We had to go to Annapolis, Maryland on business for two weeks. Jeannette and Doug said it was no problem leaving our camper in their driveway. One of the biggest surprises of the trip thus far was the reuniting with old friends and meeting new ones. We were amazed at how welcome we were made to feel. Being with Charles 24/7, I didn't realize how important it was to talk to "girlfriends". It is just a fact that women need their friends. Charles is a wonderful companion, but girlfriends share feelings on a different level.

Chapter Fifteen

Old World Forest and Ancient Cultures

Our flight home couldn't have been better. Leaving SeaTac Airport, the pilot tipped the plane's wing for a great view of Mt. Rainer and luckily I was sitting on the right side. On the way back, we were able to see the majestic mountains that make up the Cascade Range. The peaks of Mt. Jefferson, Mt. Hood, Mt. Adams, and Mt. St. Helen were dwarfed by Mt. Rainer.

Friends told us that a short ride from their home in Tacoma was Port Defiance, and there we would get our first taste of the Pacific Northwest. Located on the banks of the Puget Sound waterway, the Pacific Northwest spread before us. Large mountains reached down to kiss the cold waters as blue azure skies shinned above. Port Defiance is a five-mile motor loop with many attractions. The rose and dahlia gardens had an incredible display of flowers. Laid out in a geometric pattern, the colors and textures were anchored by a lovely gazebo. An area called *Never, Never Land* was a great place to play. There was the old ladies shoe, and Jack's beanstalk. Another section included a boathouse were canoes could be rented. Not far from the boathouse was the Washington State Ferry that left Port Defiance and sailed to Vashon Island, the gateway to the San Juan Islands. As we continued around the loop, Mt Rainer showed herself. Snow capped and clear, she smiled at the fishermen going out the Hood Canal in search of a fish dinner. At another stop, a pier reached out into Puget Sound where locals were catching Red Rock crab.

Departing Tacoma and back on the road, we found Illahee State Park on the Kitsap Peninsula. This park rests on the tip of Bainbridge Island, which is near the Puget Sound and the Hood Canal. On the map, in red italic letters read, "Scenic Beach State Park" located on the Hood Canal. It was a short ride to the beach which had huge trees strewn along the shoreline as a reminder of the power of the surf. Also on this beach were phenomenal oyster shells. I collected a few with thoughts of making them into a soap holder or using them as condiment dishes. That night, our site was under the canopy of old growth forest. Sitting outside, we watched as the sun set. The light coming through the moss-draped trees was golden. It highlighted the texture of boughs that reached to the sky.

The ranger at Illahee State Park recommended Dungeness Spit State Park for the next night. The drive crossed the Hood Canal and ran north on US 101. Not wanting to get lost, we asked directions from a survey worker. He said, "Go to Kitchen Dick Road and make a left on Lotsgazel Rd. That road goes to Olympic National Park". The first state park we came to was Sequim State Park (pronounced Skwim). We found a nice site with hookups and parked the camper. Having a home base allowed us to explore other campgrounds. Since it was early, we headed out to find Dungeness Spit State Park. I was really enjoying saying *Dungeness Spit*. It had a nice ring to it along with the image of a Dungeness crab spitting before it went into the pot to be cooked. There were numerous open sites there, so we left our lantern on a table to mark our possession and drove back to Sequim and picked up the camper. We were glad we did because Sequim was booked for the weekend and that would have left us homeless. Sequim was located on Sequim Bay, but our new location was on the *Straits of Juan De Fuca* (another fun phrase to say).

Time was moving quickly. It was late August when we arrived at Dungeness Spit and it was the perfect place to stop. Not far from our campsite was a trailhead that lead to the spit; a five-mile stretch of land (the spit) that reached out into the Straits. A lighthouse at the tip could only be reached by hiking there during low tide. Massive storm tossed trees covered parts of the spit, making the walk difficult. We didn't stay on the spit too long for fear of the incoming tide. At night, a short walk took us to an overlook of the Straits. It was a great platform to watch sunsets and the night sky. A low-pressure system was crossing the area bringing high winds and white-capped waves crashing to shore. Neither weather nor tide allowed us to hike on the spit to the lighthouse.

Port Angeles is where you board one of three ferries that crisscross the Straits and Sounds of the San Juans. Information booths with real live people were non-existent, but lots of brochures were easily accessible. The library at Port Angeles was very modern and had large windows that overlooked the Straits. It was a joy to download e-mails and write stories as I began to fantasize being published.

A flyer on the library bulletin board said there was going to be a wooden boat festival in Port Townsend, so we drove over there to investigate. Port Townsend is a lovely Victorian town with quaint shops and restaurants that reminded us of St. Michaels and Oxford on the eastern shore of Maryland. The road back to the campsite took us through "Pick It Yourself" fields of fresh flowers. Sequim is noted for their lavender fields.

Our next venture from our home base at Dungeness Spit was Hurricane Ridge and the Olympic mountain range. Mt. Olympus sits at 7,965 feet looking as regal as the god it is named after. Much of the top was snow capped and it towered over the other mountains in the range. With peaks averaging 6,500 feet, the mountain range covered the whole horizon. The scene was so immense that there are six glacier fields in the mountains folds, many of which spawned rivers of the Olympic National Park such as the Hoh, Elwha and Queets. All of these rivers are laden with salmon in spring and fall. Thanks to conservation efforts, all these rivers run through the ancient, undisturbed, old growth forest. That is what makes the Olympic National Park so special. We hiked the ridge loop trail and met Mount Angeles. Mountains jutted up around us and some of the trees were bent over and bore witness to the name of Hurricane Ridge. As we were leaving, a lady kindly suggested that we stop by Neah Bay that weekend because the Makah Tribe was holding their annual pow-wow. She said an Indian in the Visitor's Center could give us more information. The Makah Indians are known for their skills as whale hunters and are the only tribe that still hunt whale from their canoes. Sitting at a table, stringing beads, sat a man of middle age with a dark complexion wrinkled from the sun. He gave us a list of events and suggested the Sunday canoe races and craft fair as the festival's highlight.

The most northwestern point of land on the continuous continental United States is Cape Flattery. Close by is Neah Bay, home of the Makah Indians. We got up early, made a quick stop at the drive-thru Espresso bar, and arrived at the celebration by 10 a.m. It was exciting being on the most northern continental coastline in North America. The Straits of Juan De Fuca is a major waterway connecting the Pacific Ocean with port towns like Seattle, Tacoma and Olympia. It also separates Canada from the United States. Freighters, tug boats, ferries and fisherman all share these waters.

At Neah Bay, tents lined the main street and families were gathering to support their kids in the canoe races. It was a very strenuous row out to an island and then 3.5 miles to finish. This portion of water channeled around an island where the current was brisk on both sides. The first race was men and women. The second race was men and they had to go around the island, twice! Their canoes were wooden, painted black with a red, white and black eagle design on the bow. Their distinctive art form of these three primary colors fascinated me. The Makah Indians have been inhabiting the beach and forest of this coast for over 1,000 years. At one time, there were five tribes. Today, only one exists. Most of the tribes were wiped out when the Spanish arrived and brought disease with them. Neah Bay is a poor village, but their sense of pride shines in their culture. After the races was a salmon bake on the beach. A large hut housed a fire pit where salmon was being smoked on hickory sticks. Corn and flatbread shared the menu. One of the cooks offered us a sample of the delicious smoked salmon.

The Makah Cultural and Research Center explained that the Ozette tribe disappeared because in the 17th Century, a mudslide buried the whole village. Archeologists were able to discover over 55,000 artifacts from the tribe's daily life. It was mind-expanding being part of their culture for the day.

When we left the next morning to find a laundromat and grocery, our neighbors (with a boat) told us not to eat dinner as they were going to bring home that night's meal. We wished them luck. When we returned, they had two very large pots cooking Dungeness crabs. A bottle of wine and garlic butter made for a complete dinner. No offense to the Maryland crabs, but these crabs were huge. The claws yielded copious amounts of sweet crabmeat.

As we traveled, the scenery went from old growth forest, to deforestation and to reclamation. Some bald hillsides showed the ignorance of an early age. About six miles from Neah Bay is Cape Flattery. There we watched the waves of the in coming tide crash on Tatoosh Island where a lighthouse warned sailors of the dangerous coast.

Looking forward to exploring more of the coast, we moved our campsite to Ozette, a national park site with primitive camping only. This site was extra special because we had learned of the tribes' demise at the cultural center. With propane, we could heat the camper, have fuel to cook on the three-burner stove and keep the refrigerator running. The only thing I missed was our electric blanket. To compensate, we changed to flannel sheets and wore our hooded sweat clothes to bed. The daytime temperatures were averaging 60 – 75 degrees and at night, a low of high 40's. There were two trails that led to the coast with promises of seeing sea stacks and tide pools, but they both had to be done at low tide. The timing just wasn't working for us.

With Labor Day fast approaching, we were anxious to find a comfortable campsite to call home through the holiday weekend and beyond. An early arrival at Sol Duc Hot Springs National Park awarded us with a perfect site. It seemed folks packed up and left around 9 a.m. and it was helpful to be there to get the spot just as they were leaving. As a group of young boys were getting ready to leave, they guaranteed that we were getting the best spot in the park.

"Sol Duc" is a Quileute Indian phrase meaning, "people living at the place of the clear sparkling water." A major feature of Sol Duc is the hot springs. With our Golden Age Pass, the $12 fee cost us $6.00 and the hot springs gave seniors a special rate. The park was located right in the middle of an ancient rain forest. The trees reached up to the sky with a dignity of surviving hundreds of years. Being among these giants felt like we were in a prayer and was very humbling. The towering giants protected us against the rain. Behind our site ran the Sol Duc River. We checked in and met our camp host whose license plate read "Bluehwy". The Blue Highways, A Journey Into America was a book written by an American Indian named William Least Heat Moon and portrayed his reflections as he traveled cross-country. It had special meaning as this book was a going away gift to us and I read portions to Charles as we traveled some of the same routes.

As we entered Sol Duc, a feeling of peace and awe overcame us. After settling in, a hike to the hot springs and a dip were the order of the day. This was another "dry" camping site and to compensate for the length of time we were going to be there, Charles purchased an electrical cord that attached to the battery of the truck to extend the camper's battery life. We used candles for light to conserve energy and found that candles added extra heat that kept the camper warm but we were careful to make sure they were extinguished when we left the camper and before we went to bed.

We awoke to a heavily overcast day and decided to do our wash and make phone calls, as our cell phone didn't work in the forest. Forty miles down the road was the town of Forks and it had all the amenities. In the afternoon, the sun came out, so we drove to Rialto Beach. Rialto Beach is part of the Olympic Coast National Marine Sanctuary, where, surprisingly, backpacking is allowed on its beaches. Even more surprisingly were the "huts" people had built from the driftwood to sleep in. At first, we thought it was something that the kids built, but as we ventured further onto the beach, we saw families walking with backpacks on.

In the distance, large rock formation called sea stacks rose from the ocean and looked like fabled castles. Through the binoculars, we could see the spit becoming exposed by the outgoing tide and people walking on the spit toward the sea stack. We decided to do the same. Entering between two large boulders, it seemed that we crossed through a portal. The beach receded behind us and a jetty was in front. The jetty led straight to the sea stacks. How exciting it was to be standing on land that was just covered by the ocean. The stones on the sand were rounded and warm and there was a lot of driftwood scattered about. After lingering a few hours, we could feel the danger of the changing tide, and climbed to higher ground. As we left, we stopped at an overlook that was once the home of the Quileute Indians. This area was a perfect place for a settlement. Food was provided by the sea and forest and there were lots of resources for tools and implements.

The day ended with our feet tingling from the rock climbing, our bodies sun bathed and our hearts happy to return to the old growth forest and our new home at Sol Duc.

Determined to see as much as we could, the next day we hiked in the old growth world of the Hoh Rain Forest. It was like being in another time when the world was fresh and the air clean. Giant trees stood like soldiers protecting their species; moss draped limbs resembling lace curtains. Through parts of the forest flowed the Hoh River whose headwaters came from Mt. Olympus. They say the salmon are starting to move upstream to spawn. All they needed was a little rainfall and the "staircases" would be filled with salmon. Here, the trees are living legends. and rate as the biggest in the world. A plaque near a Douglas fir said it "rose above the forest floor to a height of 298 feet and a circumference 37 feet".

A sign in the forest read "And with all your strength, with all your mind, with all your heart, preserve it for your children, and love it…", said Chief Seattle.

Chapter Sixteen

Ida Who? Ida Wow!

It was mid September when we started heading east. Yellowstone was still our destination and we hoped to get there before winter moved in. Traveling on the Oregon side of the Columbia River Gorge, we could look across the river and see Washington State. The Columbia River Gorge has high canyon walls and the expanse of the Columbia River skirts its shores. Lewis and Clark navigated this part of the river on their way to the Pacific Ocean. Today, many dams control its waters as well as provide power and irrigation to towns like Portland and Salem.

A friend said the salmon ladders and the sturgeon pond at Bonneville Dam were worth a stop. The Bonneville Dam has a viewing station on the lower floor where they keep count of the salmon. Peering through three large windows, we watched the salmon and trout climbing up the ladder. There was an auditorium-like room with bleachers to watch the migration. Off to the right was another room that channeled a few fish, one at a time. A synchronized camera took pictures as they reached the center of a measurement line. The purpose was to monitor the health of these fish. In a nearby pool swam sturgeons that were over ten feet long. The biggest one was called "Bubba".

We camped at LaGrange Campground, which was part of the Corp of Army Engineers and was on the John Day River. The $8 fee (Golden Pass rates) came with hookups. Our site was a short walk from the confluence of the John Day River and the Columbia River. Strong winds were forecast for the evening. As a precaution, we didn't fully set up the camper and just pulled out the beds and had everything put away before we went to sleep. The weatherman was right and that night strong winds blew. The camper was hit hard and broke one of the Shepherd's poles that held up the canvas over the bed. It didn't take us long to get the camper down and sleep in the truck. The stars were magnificent and the truck was warm and comfortable. The next morning we called Fleetwood's 800 number and was told we could get it repaired in Boise, Idaho. We bought our camper new and have been very pleased with Fleetwood's commitment to their "bumper to bumper" warranty as well as their coast-to-coast network of dealers.

We spent the next night in a hotel where we watched Hurricane Isabelle spin off shore and head for the Chesapeake. We too, were facing a weather situation. Two cold weather systems were building in the northwest making our quest for Yellowstone questionable. A friend, who grew up in Idaho, recommended seeing the Sawtooth Mountains. The next day we picked up the camper, which was ingeniously repaired, and headed toward central Idaho. It would be a nice side trip while we waited to see what the weather was going to do.

Our plan was to camp at Crater's on the Moon National Monument, but with the afternoon waning, it was too far. Upon entering Idaho, we noticed lots of signs for "Sportsman's Access". These all seemed to lead off the road to special places for camping, fishing, and hunting. One road led us to "free" camping on the Big Wood River. Over a culvert, we saw a camper in a wooded area and knew that was our spot. Within 15 minutes, the camper was set up and we hiked to the river. A hawk flew over our heads to its nest in the trees and a mink played on the distant shore's rock ledge.

Back at our campsite, we heard kids on dirt bikes playing ESPN extreme sports LIVE. It was entertaining watching them as they as rushed around curves, flying off of hills and jumping the ruts. As evening approached, they left and even though we were not far from the road, it was very quiet.

The next morning, we saw a utility truck checking a hydrant. Being from Maryland, we were a little like rock stars and found that people were astonished when we told them where we were from. The fact was we are pretty astonished too! Chitchatting about the area, they strongly recommended that we "must see" the town of Stanley. So, off we went.

The Galena Summit (elv. 8,701) gave us a bird's eye view of the valley below. Large cliffs with jagged edges reached to the sky and looked like a lumber's saw. The day was clear and we could almost make out the headwaters of the Salmon River. A roadside marker showed a map of the river's course as it flowed through the states of Washington, Oregon, Northern Colorado and Idaho. We pictured the Salmon River as a ribbon connecting all the states we have just visited.

On the way to Galena Summit we passed through Sun Valley. It seemed that all of a sudden, the houses started getting bigger and the airport had many private jets. We wondered what industry would support these luxuries. Chatting with a local at the Galena Summit, he told us that Sun Valley was the playground of the rich and famous. Jamie Lee Curtis, Arnold Schwatznager, and Tom Cruise supposedly have homes there. The man also agreed with the utility workers that we must see Stanley. In addition, he recommended exploring the once prosperous gold mining ghost town of Bonanza and home of the *gold gusher.* He said that not far from the gold gusher was a town called Challis. There we could find a campground with a spring fed pool and hook-ups. That sounded like a plan as we kept our eye to weather still trying to make it to Yellowstone.

During the depression, gold fever was at its peak. "The Yankee Fork Gold Dredge" was invented to extract gold from the valley floor. This huge three-story machine looked like it was out of a science fiction movie. It had large drill bites and several shoots that extended from the main body. In the process of extracting gold, it would eat up a whole valley. Discarded rocks made huge hills along the river. Gladly, the gold gusher didn't get very far and was put to rest at the same spot where the gold was first discovered. Over three million dollars in gold was extracted, with a major portion of the profits going to the mining company.

Close by was Bonanza City that was laid out in 1877 to accommodate the gold fever. At one time it housed over 600 residences and supplied the surrounding mines. Today, only a few buildings remain. We hiked to a cemetery located a few miles outside of town. There, a plaque listed the names of the departed and what they died from. Many of its occupants died from disease, accidents at the mine and shooting each other or one's self.

We passed through Stanley and didn't see what was so special. Maybe that was because it was a winter resort or we were more interested in the hot tubs that awaited us at Challis. Challis Hot Springs Campground sat on the banks of the Salmon River and had spacious sites with full hookup. The pool was huge and clean. On a nearby mountain, we could see where the springs had worked their way down the mountain by following the streaks of white sulphur. Soaking in the hot spring pool was wonderful. Fire fighters are flown here for a much needed break from fighting the wild fires in the north. Taking advantage of the 10 p.m. closing, we floated on our backs while watching the stars overhead.

A few days later, I woke up with a pain in my neck (and no, it wasn't Charles). It had been over a week and wasn't getting any better. Even the hot springs didn't seem to help. The campground's office recommended a Chiropractor in Challis. The office also let us use their computer to check e-mails and weather. A cold front was on the move over Idaho and promised winds in excess of 50 miles per hour. Locals said the night's freeze would bring snow to the mountains. All things considered, we decided to spend the night at the Challis Lounge and Motor Lodge. That way we didn't have to worry about weather and it was a short walk to keep an early appointment at the Chiropractor's office. An evening stroll through town showed buildings dating from the early 1900s.

The morning arrived with black clouds on the horizon. The Chiropractor came in extra early to help me out. After the session, we drove south, heading through a canyon that looked like the abyss. I had my foot pressed down on the imaginary gas pedal in an attempt to out run the storm. As I looked back in the rear view mirror, the clouds were getting more ominous and were closing in. To our surprise, many of the trees on the hillsides were bright reds, oranges and yellows. It seemed fall had come overnight.

We passed ranches where cowboys really herded cows from horses. At one point, we were in a snow shower. How did we ever get ourselves into this predicament? It was time to "get out of Dodge". Faster, we pushed south. It was beginning to look unlikely that we would make Yellowstone.

About two hundred miles south was the town of Lava Springs and more hot tubs. Rt. 15 went through the Blackfoot and Shoshone Indian Reservations and the Caribou National Forest. We were very lucky to get to the campground without serious weather problems. A fellow camper was not that lucky because he experienced fifty mile per hour winds on the road through the Blackfoot mountains. We must have just missed it. Another camper had just returned from Yellowstone and said it was cold and snowy. That made us glad that we changed our course. The cold weather system was expected to last for the next two days.

The Cottonwood Campground earned its name because it sits in a canyon surrounded by Cottonwood trees. The silver leaves shimmered as the wind blew, but we never got the sustained winds that were predicted. Some sites at the campground were near two beautiful waterfalls that flowed into a trout-laden stream. Three blocks away were the hot springs that were hot and a delight to be in. The bubbling water came from an ancient volcano and was naturally filtered so there was no sulphur smell. Idaho supposedly has the most hot springs in the United States, according to a tourist brochure. The soaking really seemed to help my neck.

It was cold and drizzling when we broke camp. It would have been nice to stay for a few days, but the lows for the coming night were forecasted to be in the 20's. We needed to head further south and warmer weather.

Outside of Ogden, Utah, we found ourselves in between two weather systems. To the left of the road, gray clouds engulfed the area. To the right of the road were blue skies. Gladly, our path headed towards the blue skies. The local radio station continued to forecast a low in the 20s and winds were expected to reach 50 mph. Thanks to our Marriott Rewards credit card, we had enough points to get a nice room in Provo. The weather channel's weekend forecast was for sunny skies to the south, so we changed our plans and headed to Zion National Park and then the Grand Canyon. Yellowstone would have to wait for another time.

Chapter Seventeen

Amazing Places and Fun Times

On our way to Zion, the temperature finally started to rise. Zion National Park possesses a grandness of space and time that is very spiritual. Named by the Mormons, it stands for a "place of refuge". Several campers told us of its spirituality, but I couldn't image what they meant. Then we saw it and felt it. Massive vertical cliffs dating from 260 million years ago rose 3,000 feet above us. During the course of Zion's history, the oceans covered and receded from this land twice, leaving behind sand that formed today's plateau. To make this land even more mystifying, on top of the mesa are Ponderosa pines.

Entering Zion from the east, you are greeted by a rock face with an unusual checkerboard pattern. At first glance, it looked man-made, but later we found out that this formation was caused when an ancient sand dune was lashed by cross winds, then frozen and thawed. Next, you drive through a narrow tunnel, which made some of the bigger rigs shudder, as it was 16 feet high and 22 feet wide, but with our pop-up, it was not a problem.

Vibrant colors lit up the rock face with the passing of the sun. Pinks and whites of the rock layers gleamed with a touch of red and gold as the sun faded. The feeling was as awe inspiring as the great cathedrals of Europe. Unlike the Grand Canyon and Bryce, were you look down into the canyons, in Zion you are in the canyon looking up. The National Park Service runs a shuttle through the canyon from April through October and goes to sites that are majestic. The shuttle also cuts down on traffic and pollution, preserving the austerity of Zion. One bus driver pointed to rock climbers ascending a sheer rock face. He told us that it takes the climbers at least two days to reach the summit and at night, they will be sleeping suspended in mid-air. Charles wondered how they took care of their personal hygiene from the suspended positions. Look out below!

Water seeped down many layers of rock that supported a tropical garden. Plants such as watercress, Golden Columbine and even orchids bloom in its lushness. Most of Zion is made up from sandstone that is capable of storing spring water for a very long time. Scientists were surprised to learn that the water in the rocks carbon dated back to over 2,000 years. Plants that shouldn't be thriving in the desert thrive here. Cactus co-exists with oak trees and Maidenhair fern can be seen along the road. The colored layers and heights of the canyon's walls equally baffle scientists and are a thrill to behold.

The Colorado Plateau continues to rise and change. The sandstone rock tells the story of the continent's evolution. Scientists predict that in another millennia, Zion will probably look like the rock formation we see today in the Grand Canyon.

At another stop along the bus route, we looked up 7,000 feet to see the Court of the Patriarchs. A Presbyterian Minister was exploring this area in 1960 and was so in awe of the peaks, he named them Abraham, Isaac and Jacob.

The Virgin River runs through Zion's canyon. It leads through a slot canyon called the Narrows. Today, the river is a gentle creek, but after a good rain, it is known to fill its banks rapidly. The river descends 71 feet. For every mile it travels, the water can rise eight feet in a minute. A popular hike is to walk up the middle of the river, where high canyon walls surround it, hence the name "slot canyon". We met a family with two kids and enjoyed their company walking up the river. The kids scouted ahead as their mom, wearing flip-flops, struggled to keep up. I think she was grateful for our company and support.

There were two types of campsites at Zion. The one that had hookups was full. Reservations are highly recommended. The other was dry camping, and a little more primitive but comfortable. Our campsite was very close to the bus and Visitor's Center. At dusk, we would ride the shuttle just to see the rocks light up at sunset. At night, the stars reigned supreme because Zion is located far away from everything. The Milky Way stretched across a horizon that seemed to go on forever.

On the west end, outside the park, is the town of Springdale. It has lots of hotels, shops and an Imax Theatre. Most impressive were the rock shops.

Zion was, as many campers said, "A very special and spiritual place". The Park Service has excellent, free programs describing the geology and history, which we highly recommend. Schedules can be found at the Visitor's Center.

It was the middle of September when we drove from Zion, to the North Rim of the Grand Canyon. The night before, temperatures dipped into the high 20s, so a lot of campers left. A woman at the Visitor's Center said we probably wouldn't have any trouble finding a camping spot in the park. Normally, these sites are booked months and even years in advance, so we were happy with our good fortune. At the Grand Canyon's North Rim Lodge, we sat on the veranda's rockers overlooking the canyon and sipped a glass of wine. Next to us was a couple that hiked from the top of the south rim to the top of the north rim. They trained for months to be able to accomplish this feat and as a reward, that night they had a room in the lodge. The next day will take them another twelve hours to return to the other side.

The bar at the lodge was named after Teddy Roosevelt's Rough Riders and on its walls were wonderful caricatures and cartons of his time. The bar looked like the kind of place that he and his men would have come for a cold beer. The lodge also served as a base for his many hunting forays. That night, a star party was planned on the veranda. A very knowledgeable astronomer set up telescopes so we could see many star clusters and even Jupiter and Mars.

Because of the unpredictable weather, a sense of urgency was taking hold. We headed further south to Albuquerque. En route, we spent a free camping night at the entrance to the Petrified Forest National Park. It was the perfect place to spend the night being very close to our next day's destination. The desert landscape of the Petrified Forest was littered with petrified rocks. Our morning hike made us feel like we were on another planet. In gray dirt mounds lay petrified trees in this 225 million year old forest. The logs had a marbled texture and their quartz gleamed in the morning sun. Located in the middle of this arid land was the Puerco Pueblo. In prehistoric times, this area was a vast flood plain. Through erosion and uplifting, silica crystals replaced the original trees and turned the wood into quartz. The Petrified Forest National Park joins the Painted Desert at its northern end. It was nice to have an early morning hike before the long drive to Albuquerque.

After about four hours on the road, I needed to stop. My butt hurt and I needed to stretch. Winslow, Arizona had a huge truck stop and a Visitor's Center within easy walking distance. The name sounded vaguely familiar and at the Visitor's Center it became clear. *"Well, I'm running down the road trying' to loosen my load, I've got seven women on my mind. Four that wanna own me, two that wanna stone me, one says she's a friend of mine. Take it easy, take it easy. Don't let the sounds of your own wheels drive you crazy"*. These words, by the Eagles, were printed on a bookmarker given out at the Visitor's Center. Charles got a big kick when I sang him the song as he was pumping gas. Now we both knew where we were.

Refreshed and back on the road, we were temped to stop at many places along the way, but they would have to wait for another time. The famous Albuquerque Balloon Fest was next on our "must do" list. In Albuquerque, we found several campgrounds already filled because Balloon Fest was fast approaching. To get our bearings, we chose to spend a few nights in an upscale RV park near Santa Fe. The size of some of the "rigs" totally amazed us. Some were fifth-wheels pulled by Freightliner trucks. A few coaches had garages in the back that housed Harleys and antique motorcars.

In Santa Fe I found a synagogue where I could spend Rosh Hashanah (the Jewish New Year). While I was in services, Charles scouted the area and found an Army Corp of Engineer's campground on the Cochiti Reservoir. The "Golden Age" price was $5.50 a night, with electricity, water and a great view.

This campground sat high on a mesa overlooking the reservoir. Our site was carved out on the side of the mesa, so we would be protected against high winds. We were the only pop-up there, and were surrounded by bigger RV's. Our neighbors had been there for a couple of months and we could see why. Cochiti is located halfway between Albuquerque and Santa Fe. It is also in the middle of several pueblos. It had all we needed, even a pet tarantula who we named "Mr. T". Our first night, it made its presence known and then we didn't see it after that. Not far was the Cochiti Golf course, ranked 15th in the state. This was Charles' first experience at a desert golf course and he loved it. Several signs warned of rattlesnakes, but he didn't see any.

I felt a strong desire to be home in Frederick, for Yom Kippur (the Day of Atonement) so Charles drove me to the Albuquerque Airport where I boarded a plane and headed home for a few days. One morning, Charles called to tell me that he was on the grounds of the Balloon Fest and was volunteering to be on a chase crew. He sounded very excited. He signed me up to volunteer for the coming weekend. My flight back to Albuquerque was uneventful and it was good to be reunited with my husband. The camper looked great and a bouquet of flowers was on the table to welcome me home. Charles already knew the lay of the land and made friends with the Canadian balloon crew called "Sundance". An exciting event was about to unfold.

We volunteered for the "Dawn Patrol", so we got up very early the following morning to drive the 50 miles to the Balloon Fest for a pre-sunrise flight. This is where several balloons ascended to check out the weather for the ascension of over 700 balloons to be launched later that morning. This particular day was "special shapes" and the conditions were right for launching. How funny to see *Smokey the Bear* next to *Frosty the Snowman* while a *happy face sun* floated down the canyon. Wherever we looked, balloons were getting ready to lift off. Balloon enthusiasts come from all over the world to participate in this event. Lots of folks had on vests that were covered with pins of their favorite balloons they collected over the years. It was fun watching them trade and tell stories of past festivals. The colors of the balloons, the camaraderie of the crews, and the food and crafts made for a memorable day. That night we found a spot alongside the road to watch the fireworks. That positioned us to be on the road before the crowd left the field.

We stayed at Cochiti for a few weeks, spending several days at the Balloon Fest and visiting Santa Fe and Albuquerque. An interesting day trip was to Bandelier National Monument. Bandelier is a maze of tall canyons and flat mesas where the "cliff dwellers" from the Anasazi's era made their home. The remnants of an ancient pueblo existed here between 1100 and 1300 A.D. This settlement had over 2,400 sites, but only 50 have been excavated. Wooden ladders enabled us to climb up into some of their dwellings. It was awesome to walk in the Ancient's path.

Not far from Bandelier National Monument and through the Jemez Mountains was a vast grazing area known as the Vales Candlier National Preserve. We heard that if you got there before sunset, there would be large herds of elk grazing in the pastures. And sure enough, that is what we saw. When I was waiting in line at Baltimore Washington International (BWI) Airport, I overheard a fisherman relate a story about fishing in the preserve. He said that in one day he caught over 75 fish. Was this a fish story or the truth?

After a delightful time with the Indians of New Mexico and the sights of the Balloon Fest, we headed south towards Roswell, New Mexico. The whole town was alien obsessed. We visited The International UFO Museum and Research Center, which lived up to its name. Their explanation of terrestrial life and what really happened in 1947 when aliens were supposed to have crashed in a nearby mountain was very intriguing. The government supposedly apprehended the ship and its contents while the media was kept at bay. In the museum, there was evidence of the rescue and there was even a display of an operating room where the patient was an alien. Every storefront had pictures of aliens in their windows, and blowup alien dolls even greeted us at the doorway. I picked up a glow-in-the-dark can opener, shaped like an alien, as a gift for a friend who drinks a lot of beer. When we saw an airplane from a nearby military base drop a few parachutes, we thought we were seeing flying saucers.

Not far from Roswell is Carlsbad Caverns. Brantley Lake State Park was close by and a good place to spend the night. The next day we spent below the earth's surface exploring enormous caves. Some were bigger than a football field. The Park Service did a fabulous job of backlighting the terrain. From an enchanted rock forest to a lunar moonscape, every turn had something for the imagination. On a tour of the "Great Room", the guide turned out the lights and we were enveloped by total darkness. It made us wonder how the early explorers found their way around down there. Our day ended in front of the cave, where at sunset, thousands of bats leave for their night's journey to feast on insects.

Back at the campground, we saw that our neighbors were from Virginia. After polite conversation, they told us they were new to camping. They had a big Class A, which housed their office as well as their home. To celebrate the fact that we were both from the Washington, D.C. area and both previously sailors, they brought out their fine crystal glasses for drinks. I was very surprised, as plastic cups where more the style of campers. They said they wanted a touch of class for their camping experience and couldn't part with them. Who were we to argue? We enjoyed camping with them so much that we extended our stay for an impromptu potluck dinner. Almost every day brought wonderful surprises.

Chapter Eighteen

Cajun Country Revisited

A nice pause in our traveling lifestyle was visiting friends. In Houston, Texas we reunited with Sharon and her husband. Sharon and I go as far back as kindergarten. Our reunion came about a few years ago through Classmates.com and we make it a point to visit when we are near Houston. She remembers so much of what I have forgotten about our early days in South Philly. While in Houston, we took advantage of the highly rated medical facilities there and had annual check-ups such as a mammogram and pap for me, and a PSA for Charles along with blood work.

Fausse Pointe State Park is the gateway to Cajun country and the bayous. It took seven hours to drive from Houston because we had gotten lost. The Visitor's Center was a good place to find our way, but it was closed. Our predicament at the closed Visitor's Center was that there was not enough room to turn around. As we pondered what to do, a man drove up and asked if he could help. He saw the trouble we were having and offered to show us a better way. We followed him through the countryside that led to the highway. Getting lost in southern Louisiana is a chance to meet the people and experience their hospitality they call "Lagniappe" (pronounced Lan-YIP'). It means giving "with a little extra". The Cajuns are wonderful, kind people with deep roots in the bayou.

It was hot and humid when we arrived at Lake Fausse Pointe. Our campsite was right on the bayou and there was a platform to tie up a boat or to throw out a fishing line. A ranger stopped by to chat and gave us a bottle of bug spray with Deet. Off in the distance, in the middle of the swamp, a blue heron was perched on a cypress tree. It was all part of the Atchafalaya (pronounced A-CHAF'-a-lie-ah) basin. Not long ago, Fausse Pointe was under water until a levee was built to hold back the estuaries of the Mississippi River. This is very fertile land that yields crops such as sugar cane, rice and mosquitoes.

New Iberia is a small town on Bayou Teche. At one time it was an active center for the commerce of cotton and sugar cane. In a local restaurant, we picked up a copy of *The Times*, which lists all the music in the area. The proprietor of the restaurant wanted to make sure that we knew where we were going and pointed out some well known names in Cajun and Zydeco music playing in the area. To repay his kindness, we had a glass of wine with him and a few other folks at the bar. There we met a couple that noticed Charles was wearing an Aircraft Owners Pilot Association (AOPA) hat. They were going to meet friends at a restaurant nearby called "Lagniappe Too". One of their friends was a pilot so they invited us to join them. It was Friday night, which is Shabbos and if there is a Temple in the area, we like to go to services. New Iberia's synagogue was built in 1903 and on this particular Friday, the service was lead by the president of the congregation. It was a nice, short service and I was given the honor of lighting the Shabbos candles. Returning to my seat, the glow of the candles warmed our hearts and we were thankful to be able to explore this wonderful land.

After services, we joined our new friends at "Lagniappe Too". As we entered the restaurant, seated at a table in the middle of the room were ten jovial people. We were immediately recognized and chairs were added and drink orders taken. Charles and Richard, the birthday boy and pilot, got along very well. After dessert of a pina colada rum cake, the table's conversation turned to the upcoming local election. Several other patrons in the restaurant jumped right in with their thoughts. They laughed at the negative press coverage and said that it was tame compared to some previous years. After dinner, we were invited back to Richard's house for more drinks. We were lucky to find our way home, as the state park was a lengthly drive along some very dark roads.

Saturday was just one of those "off" days. Zydeco breakfast at "Cafe Des Amis" in Breaux Bridge ended earlier than expected. Fortunately, we did catch about an hour of the band and ate a delicious crawfish gumbo. We then drove to Opelousas for the Yamilaya (Yams) Festival. Opelousas is the birthplace of Zydeco so we expected to hear some good music, but during the day, it looked like any other carnival. I am sure it heated up at night, but our timing was off. From there we went to a flea market that just had junk. Since we were on a roll of disappointments, the local daiquiri bar drive-thru was the next stop in trying to rejuvenate our spirits. Then we went to the Opelousas Music Fest, held in a stadium, and found that the music was too loud. Not to waste good music, we boogied in the parking lot. The ride home was interesting as we watched the sugar cane fields being harvested and large trucks bringing the cane to the processing plants. Even a bad day is a good day in the bayou, especially when a daiquiri bar is not too far.

Food is very important to the Cajuns. Gas stations called boucheriers carried local items such as file' powder, Cajun crawfish boil, and alligator patties. Homemade boudin and andelouea (pronounced an-DUE'-e) are local favorites. Boudin is a sausage made with rice and ground pork and andelouea is a sausage made with chunks of meat (not ground). Both are made with recipes passed down through the ages and flavored with local spices.

At the previous night's dinner, a couple recommended dinner at Pat's located on the levee. They said driving the levee road would not be a problem. In keeping with a bad day, the food at Pat's tasted like yesterday's leftovers. The stuffed crabs were dry and the gumbo, cold. To top off a trying day, going home, we got stuck in the mud on the levee. It had rained while we were eating and the dry road we had taken earlier turned to mud. Charles tried very hard to stay in the middle, but our wheels got stuck and we couldn't move. There was no sense of danger because on our side of the road, the ground was fairly level. The other side would have been a lot more dangerous because it dropped off to the bayou and that is where the alligators live. Thunderstorms were booming in the distance and slowly advancing toward us. The stars above became covered with clouds, but the rain never came. Before we got stuck, a 4-wheel, high ratio truck passed us with two boys in the front seat and three girls in the back. As they passed, we asked about the road condition. They said "not a problem". Luckily, they came back our way and found us stuck. The boys stripped down to their skivvies (showing great bodies in the truck's headlights), and got down in the mud with a rope and heavy-duty hook and connected us to them. Then gently, they pulled us on to firm ground. At times it felt like the running boards were deep in the mud. As the boys were cleaning up, I chatted with the girls. They said the boys loved helping people. We got their address and later sent a check with a note of appreciation.

Sunday was a down day, just in case the bad air was still around. Charles washed the truck, especially the mud off the sideboards, and I went for a walk around the campground. Close by was a shack that rented canoes and kayaks. In the office, on the counter, were two photographic books of life in the Atchafalaya basin. There were pictures of alligators, Cyprus swamps and families of the bayou. Their faces were rich in vitality and wisdom. Louise, the shop owner, said she was born and raised here and shared stories that went with the photographs. One story was of an old family who lived in the bayou all their life. Her husband passed away just before Hurricane Andrew came through. With repeated efforts and warnings from friends and authorities, the wife would not leave. After the storm, at age 85, she was found fixing the roof. Her companions were several dogs. When the relief boat came with supplies, she requested "Piranha" dog food but meant "Purina".

Outside, at the boat rental dock, Louise's husband had a pet alligator that lived in the swamp. He obliged my request to see it by calling for "Baby" (the alligator's name). After calling "Here Baby, Baby" he would click his tongue. After several tries, he determined that "Baby" was not in the area. He said it usually responds. I think I would have lost it if I saw the alligator's bulging eyes advancing towards me.

Louise and her husband were Cajuns from up the river and lived on a houseboat called a "Camp". She explained that camp is like going camping. It is a place to play, fish, swim and have fun. The camps of southern Louisiana are what fishing cabins are called. Many are located along the bayous with alligators, snakes, coons and herons as their neighbors. Camps usually are not inhabited year round, although some families stay.

In search of Zydeco, the campground office recommended the "Mystic River Bar". He said live music was performed on Sundays from 4 to 8 p.m. Locals described it as a "juke joint on the levee". If one can imagine, it was a large room with a bar in the back, tables in the middle, a wooden dance floor toward the front and then the band. Behind the band was a window that could have been a painting. The scene was of moss-laden trees fading into the twilight of sunset. Inside, the joint was jumping. Young, old, black and white gyrating on the dance floor. The accordion played the melody and washboard kept the beat. We danced up close to the band and filled our souls with this happy, lively music, which brought an end to our stay at Lake Fausse Pointe State Park.

Still in southern Louisiana, but due east, is Bayou Segnette State Park. It's about 100 miles from Fausse Pointe and is near the city of New Orleans. Getting there, we passed towns with names like Boutee and Bayou Bouche and the local restaurants advertised the best "Po Boys" and fresh "crackling" (fried pork rinds). Behind buildings and in the yards were stripped-down floats from last year's Mardi Gras. Soon they would be transformed into next year's masterpieces. All along the road, the bayous followed us. Bayou Segnette is where we stayed at the beginning of our trip and it was hard to believe that it was the end of October and we were on our 8th month of popping-up.

The local radio station, KBON, played both Zydeco and Cajun music while exclaiming that it is "Louisiana Proud". Southern Louisiana has its own brand of music called Zydeco and Cajun. Originated from the exiled Arcadians from Nova Scotia, it is the heart beat of the bayou. The difference between Cajun and Zydeco music is like the famous chef, Emeril Lagasse kicking his food up a notch by adding spices. Zydeco has the "heat" of red beans and rice while Cajun simmers in a more folksy style gumbo.

Once settled in, we took a day trip south to the *Barataria Preserve of Jean Lafitte National Historic Park*. It seems questions still abound today as to whether Jean Lafitte was a famous, fortune seeking privateer or feared pirate. We do know that he was most famous for helping Andrew Jackson defeat the British during the Battle of New Orleans in 1812. "Letters of Marque" enabled Lafitte and his men to roam the waters of the Caribbean and Gulf of Mexico looting and capturing foreign ships. Lafitte reinforced Jackson's troops with hearty men from the nearby bayou known as Barataria (pronounced Bear-a-TEAR'-e-a). As early as the 1700's, this was a fishing village made up of struggling Cajuns. Over a thousand men rose to the idea of quick cash through piracy. Reflecting their heritage with a sense of humor, the name Barataria means "dishonesty at sea". These men were a scandalous bunch of buccaneers and smugglers who knew the backwaters well and could disappear into the mist of the bayou, in a matter of seconds. In the early 1800's, much contraband flowed between the Barataria and New Orleans and some say treasure can still be found in its swamps. The history of Jean Lafitte could be seen at the Visitor's Center in a town called Jean Lafitte. A display of marionettes cleverly portrayed Lafitte's life. Scenes showed Lafitte signing contracts in his blacksmith shop in the French Quarter; another displayed ships laden with treasures. A third portrayed the capture of his brother for illicit importation of slaves. There were twelve fascinating windows to peer into.

The ranger at the park recommended the easy-to-walk Bayou Coquille (pronounced Koe-KE'-Ah) Trail. A boardwalk over the swamp ran along the waterway. This trail straddles both Bayou des Families and Bayou Barataria, which further down, connects with the mouth of the Mississippi River. It was said that Jean Lafitte's ships would traverse these swamps to get to the city of New Orleans. There he would conduct business and visit with the courtesans of the French Quarter.

As we approached the trail, a local fisherman seemed to appear out of nowhere and joined us. He was around five feet tall, dressed in jeans and had jet-black hair. His tan and casual stroll hinted that he was a waterman. In a soft spoken voice, he said he had a shrimp boat and fished about three days a week catching shrimp and catfish that he sold to local markets. When not fishing, he liked to walk this bayou for exercise. He said his family has lived on this land for over 100 years. I asked if he knew any stories of Jean Lafitte. With a twinkle in his eye, he said there was a good possibility that his ancestors fought with him during War of 1812.

It was nice to have his company, as he was an excellent guide. We ascended the handicap friendly boardwalk when his trained eyes spotted three alligators. One was small and resting near the shore while a larger gator sunned itself on the distance banks. Another alligator was deep in the reeds and hard to see. He helped me to stand on the railing to see it. It must have been 16 feet with big, bulging eyes that were looking straight at us. We would have made a tasty meal if one of us were to fall in. He said a few weeks ago, an alligator with thirteen babies trailing behind her crossed his path. Then he met a man walking on the trail looking for alligators, when a big one was right behind him.

Following the trail, we approached a platform overlooking the vast expanse of the prairie. He told us how the deer here developed webbing on their hoofs to adapt to the marshy land. Later that day, I inquired about the deer at the Visitor's Center and was told by the ranger that he thought it was Cajun folklore.

Approaching the end of the trail, our new friend pointed out the remains of a four foot high Indian midden. Middens are mounds of seashells discarded by the Houma Indians who use to live there. Since shellfish such as shrimp, crab and oysters was their main food source, the middens could be very high. Today, a huge oak tree grows out of the pile of shells that is rumored to be where pirates met. As we looked down a waterway, we were told about the huge flea markets Jean Lafitte would hold in this bayou. Goods from the Spanish galleons that he raided were displayed here for sale. Clothes, linens, spices, and trinkets would be sold at a fraction of the cost and tariff free. Word would spread of this event and people would come from

.r away as Atlanta with laden purses, ready to shop! This duty e shopping greatly upset the government in New Orleans.

As we walked back to our truck, we said good-bye to our mysterious friend. As quickly as he came into our lives, he disappeared into the bushes that surrounded the parking lot. Could this have been a visit from the ghost of Jean Lafitte's crew?

Back at the Visitor's Center we watched a video depicting the lives of those who lived and grew up in the bayou. They weren't educated, but they knew how to work the land. Like the Indians before them, the swamp provided for all their needs. Knowledge was passed down from generation to generation for over 300 years. There were no doctors, but they had a keen sense of how to use herbs. One of their main beliefs, which exist today, is the spirit of Lagniappe. "Be kind to your neighbor, give a little extra, and be happy." That belief is very much alive today and we were fortunate to be the recipient many times during our stay.

Bayou Segnette campground is located about 20 miles from the French Quarter, via a ferry or a half-hour drive making it is easy to get into the city. Halloween is our favorite holiday and we try to find special places to celebrate it. In the past, the Village in New York City was our playground. This year we decided to celebrate it in the Big Easy.

Around mid-morning, we took the Algiers Ferry into the French Quarter because we wanted to experience the transition of a quiet day into a scary night. During the day, we strolled up and down the streets admiring the architecture and character of the people. One lady was walking her three dogs, all in matching leopard outfits. A few bars were decorated for Halloween, but the streets were fairly quiet. We figured that a majority of revelers must have been home taking naps. As night approached, the party began. On a street corner, swaying to the music, we met a couple from my hometown of Philly. Slowly, more and more costumed revelers filled Bourbon Street. We watched a devil lean against a door while the Incredible Hulk stumbled by. Around 9 p.m. the parade started with the clanging of fire engines followed by carriages carrying folks in wonderful costumes, waving and throwing beads. The party was heating up. Around 11p.m., we had seen enough and boarded the ferry home. As we exited the terminal at the Algiers' dock, more folks in great costumes were boarding. We overheard a couple comment that the party was just beginning.

November 1 is Charles' birthday. As a special surprise, I made reservations for lunch at the New Orleans School of Cooking. Kevin, the master chief, prepared gumbo, jambalaya and pina colada bread pudding. A mirror above the kitchen counter showed us his techniques. All this was done with great humor and fascinating tidbits about the culinary history of New Orleans. The best part was at the end when we got to eat his culinary delights.

As so our Cajun experience of taste and sounds came to an end.

Chapter Nineteen

Homeless in Florida

It was late November and we couldn't go home quite yet as our renter in Maryland asked to continue renting through February. "Of course", we said. He was a good renter and that put money in our travel fund. What to do, what to do? We knew that "snowbirds" fly south to Florida for the winter, so why not visit Florida? We had the time and resources to do it. As a child, I had visited Florida many times, so it didn't seem as exciting as going out west. However, to be in a warm climate for a whole winter was very appealing. I told my friends, who were expecting us home by now, that "we were homeless in Florida".

A major concern was finding campground availability. Being in the sunshine state, in the winter, was competing with an influx of Northerners. We solved this problem by going to the local library to use the Internet. We logged on to "Reserve America", Florida's booking agent and found lots of campground availabilities.

Traveling across the state, many moons ago, Big Lagoon Campground was one of our favorites. We liked it because it was near Pensacola, Perdido Bay, and had towers overlooking the Grande Lagoon, the ICW and the Gulf. Being surrounded by different bodies of water, for us, was the ultimate spot. The pristine beaches, plentiful fishing and excellent seafood made us happy. Now we had the luxury of staying for a week. Buying fresh fish at "Joe Patti's", the local fish market, was a must. Picking up a few recipes at "Joe's" and buying the ingredients made for several special dinners.

Following I-10 across the panhandle brought us to St. Augustine. We had previously done a day trip to St. Augustine and loved it. Now we had the luxury to stay as long as we wanted. Actually, the state parks have a two-week limit, so we booked it. At Anastasia State Park, we got a great spot next to the bathrooms. These bathrooms were extra clean as they had a sign in/out sheet showing they were cleaned twice a day.

After setting up, we journeyed into St. Augustine to find the tourist information center and library. At the Visitor's Center, we picked up a brochure called "Nights of Lights". The holiday festivities started on November 22 and ran through January 31. We were lucky to be there when we were because, to our surprise and luck, Santa arrived on Saturday. Another surprise was the encampment of British soldiers at the fortification known as the "Castillo de San Marcos". The calendar of events listed a Christmas parade on Saturday. It was to wind its way along the waterfront. Listed for that evening's event was the reading of the "Christmas Proclamation" by the British governor. The British occupied St. Augustine from 1763 to 1784 and it was this time period that was being celebrated. Sounded like a plan.

Another flier in the Visitor's Center caught my eye. It read "Purevyns Songs of the Sea at the Taberna Del Gallo", Friday and Saturday nights. It said that this "was the oldest tavern in the oldest city on the east coast".

The last piece of information I needed to feel truly at home was the name of St. Augustine's oldest synagogue. "The Congregation Sons of Israel" would hold services on Friday night. Their brochure said, "This congregation was organized in the late 19th Century". A helpful volunteer said it was a small synagogue located near the "Old City" and he drew directions on a map.

On Thursday, we found a secluded beach and kicked back. Charles was comfortable under his umbrella and I was happy to have my feet in the Atlantic Ocean. Through the binoculars, Charles watched the dolphins play and I went for a long walk while being followed by a large blue heron.

Friday night was the start of a St. Augustine Christmas. Luminary night at the lighthouse was advertised for Friday at 6 p.m., but the brochure was wrong, so they let us in for free. Halfway up the 210 steps was a bucket that the light keeper once carried. It used to be full of lard oil to keep the light burning. A sign asked you to imagine how heavy it must have been. The view from the top was outstanding. It overlooked the secluded "Salt Run" cove that made this a very valuable harbor. Sailors call harbors like these "hurricane holes" and seek refuge there when the weather turns nasty. Even today, it remains a safe anchor for ships arriving from the Atlantic.

After the lighthouse, we went into town to celebrate Shabbos with the local community. Friday night services gives us the opportunity to say, "thank you" to God for all our good fortune. We parked in the *Lightner's Museum's* parking lot where a few musicians were unloading their instruments. They told us of a free concert there later that evening. As we left services, we heard music coming from the Lightner Museum and on a side street found a grand, marble staircase that lead to a balcony overlooking a small orchestra. They were playing *Joy to the World*. At one time, this building was a lavish hotel named the "Hotel Alcazar". Built by Henry M. Flagler in the late 1800's, his intent was to lure guests to the Florida sunshine.

Our visit to the "Taberna del Gallo" topped off an incredible evening as we were transported back in time to a pub scene from the 18th Century. Lots of folks from the reenactment were dressed in period costume portraying life during the British occupation. Soldiers, seamen, wives, officers, and trades folk were all drinking beer and singing sea shanties. Very few people were not in costume. All had a good time.

I don't think I will ever outgrow the thrill of seeing Santa Claus come to town. Saturday arrived sunny and cool. It was a perfect day for a parade. The parade route was lined with folks wearing Santa hats and earmuffs. A cold front was passing, so it was a little chilly and windy. This was the same cold front that produced two feet of snow in Boston just a few days before. Marching bands, antique cars with clowns, new cars with politicians, the girl and boy scouts, and the Air Force entertained the crowd. It was wonderful. Santa arrived in a sleigh, much to the crowd's delight.

We heard that the "Columbia" restaurant was a good place to eat and has been serving authentic Spanish cuisine since 1905. So we took a break from the British invasion to honor the Spanish, who discovered the city in 1565. We had to walk off the wonderful meal of black bean soup and paella de pollo, so we strolled to the military encampment outside the fort's wall. A military city had been recreated with white tents and cooking fires and everyone in period costume. One of the reinactors demonstrated how to put on a kilt. First he pleated the plaid (pronounced "played") tartan on the ground. He then laid down on it, tucked the waist into his belt and stood up. He then took off his knickers and socks while draping the tartan around him. It was amazing to watch.

In the distance, we heard the fife and drum corp. advancing towards the fort to perform colors, the lowering of the British flag. As evening approached, a crowd began gathering in the Plaza. With much pomp and circumstance, the town crier announced that the Governor was going to read the "Christmas Proclamation". The current mayor proudly played the part of the governor and with a "Hear Ye, Hear Ye", wished everyone a happy Christmas and healthy new year. Everyone lit a candle and followed men carrying large torches and proceeded down the street through the old quarter singing Christmas carols. Once we got to the gates of the city, a guard was posted and then the crowd marched back to the Governor's Palace to let him know that the city was secured. People carried candles because when the British occupied the city, they didn't want anyone wandering around because it might be spies or the enemy (Spanish or French or Indians). This portrayed a British custom of how Christmas was celebrated in the late 1700's.

One final stop that evening was to the "Taberna del Gallo" for some grog and a hearty welcome to the holiday season.

Two weeks went by very quickly. Traveling down the coast, we stopped at the NASA Visitor's Center and found it was too expensive for us. The part that upset me the most was that it was outsourced to a firm in Chicago. I expected a government facility to be managed by the government.

Located on the eastern seaboard, our next stop was Sebastian Inlet State Park also known as the Treasure Coast. It is called that because Spanish galleons, filled with gold and gems from Mexico and Peru, crossed the Gulf Stream here, on their way to deliver their treasure to Spain. Sometimes they were caught in treacherous hurricanes and sunk. Much treasure has been found on this coast and there are two museums that tell the history and show some of the riches. The State of Florida has the McCarty Treasure Museum and Mel Fischer has a museum, which exhibits artifacts and jewelry he found on the "Atocha".

Sebastian Inlet is a mecca for fishermen and a few fisherwomen. There were fishermen on the rocks, on boats at the inlet, on the catwalk under the highway bridge and on the distant shore. Not being into fishing, it was funny to see these men, mostly by themselves, casting, sitting and waiting. They did this for hours on end.

One day, we met friends for high tea at the famous "Breaker's Hotel" and for shopping in Palm Beach. It was only an hour's drive down the coast. On the way home, we noticed from the highway, the Christmas lights of Jupiter. It reminded me of Christmas in South Philly where lights are strung across the streets. Exiting the highway, we followed the glow of light to the holiday fantasy and shared in the merriment. Neighbors were handing out candy to the line of cars. Lights flickered to the beat of this holiday season wonderland.

Sixty miles inland is Orlando and Disneyworld. We took a ride there just to taste this mega world of entertainment and to see its campgrounds. After paying $7 for parking, we took a bus to the Fort Wilderness Resort and Campground. The sites were very nice and very expensive at $40 a night. We walk around and found the campers had their areas decorated in true Disney fashion. Lights were in trees, along the walkways and even outlined their rigs. Blow-up reindeers and talking Santas greeted us as we walked by. Of course,

Mickey and his friends were well represented. The holiday season was in full swing. So another two weeks quickly passed by.

Continuing south, down the coast, is Jonathan Dickinson State Park, our next stop before joining friends in Ft. Lauderdale for Christmas and New Years. We took a boat ride on the Loxahatchee River, to Trapper Nelson's home site. Trapper Nelson lived off the land and when the Tarzan movies became popular, he ran a small show from his home. Visitors would board a boat, much like we did, and once at his homestead, they would be entertained with an alligator show. The National Park Service preserved much of his home, dock and cages. You too can go back in time, with a visit to Trapper Nelson.

After the holidays, we crossed Alligator Alley to Koresham State Park heading to the Florida's west coast. To our surprise, we found a preserved 1894 settlement known as the Koresham Unity Society. This was a community where an alternative lifestyle was practiced, much like the Mormons and Shakers of that time. Koresham was ideally located for visits to Sanibel and Captiva Island where we spent the day shelling and exploring. Naples and Fort Myers was fun for admiring the stately homes, especially those belonging to Thomas Edison and Henry Ford.

Oscar Scherer State Park was another wonderful park about 80 miles north of Koresham. It was a short ride to the lovely city of Sarasota and the white, soft sands of Siesta Key.

It was mid-January and our plans were to be home by mid-February. Up the Florida coast, we spent several nights at three state parks: Myakka River, Rainbow Springs, and Manatee Springs. Each park was different. Myakka River flowed through the park; Rainbow Springs attracted divers to its springs and Manatee Springs had a boardwalk where manatees could be viewed. Florida has so much to offer for campers and tourist, alike.

The rest of the trip home was anti-climactic as sadness settled in. I don't think we were ready to go home, but we had to. Savannah and Charleston did take some of the edge off, but home we had to go. It was an amazing eleven-month journey and we couldn't wait to plan our next trip.

Year Two
On the Road Again

Introduction

Year two finds us on the road again. The experience we had the previous year was so unbelievable and so much fun, that it was like a dream. We felt we had to do it again, just to see if it was real and still as awesome. In our second year, we stayed out for six months and covered 13,000 miles. We continued to prefer the pop-up. In retrospect, it was practically maintenance free, we got very good gas mileage, it was easy to tow and the 360° view when the windows are open was a good cross between a tent and a trailer. The most important aspect of the pop-up, for us, was that it made a comfortable home.

After returning from our first trip, we found out that a neighbor had sold his condo for a very high price. We figured that if we were ever going to sell, now was the time to do it. We had been in Frederick, Maryland for eighteen years and as we all know, nothing stays the same. When we moved there, it was a small town. Now it had grown and all the problems of an expanded population went with it. The lovely downtown changed as the suburban malls grew. Roads became more crowded and that "small town" feeling was gone. Frederick had become a bedroom community of Washington, DC.

"Help U Sell" was our agent to test the market. Within three days of an open house, our condo sold. We doubled our money and were glad to have our health and spirits to start over again in a new place. Since we enjoyed the winter weather in Florida, we decided that was going to be our new home. With the help of the website, www.Realtor.com and a wonderful Florida real estate agent, we purchased a two-bedroom condo in the Tampa Bay area on the west coast. We moved in May 20, unpacked, and four days later took to the road.

Come join us as we do a reality check of last year's adventure. Will it be the same? Will it be better or worse? Only time will tell.

Chapter One

We're Off Again

With minds wide open to new places and new routes, we ventured on.

Fleetwood's "bumper-to-bumper" warranty had ended (although a few items were still covered) but we felt confident in their ability to service our needs in a timely and courteous manner. Now that the camper was in its second year, we hoped it to be trouble free. If there was a problem, a Fleetwood repair shop would not be too far and their 800 number service line had already far exceeded our expectations.

Our goal was to be in Albuquerque, New Mexico by mid-June so we could fly home to Frederick for a wedding. Hopefully, July 4th would find us partying in Truckee, California and then we'd continue on to visit friends in Salem, Oregon and Tacoma, Washington. "New territory" would be heading down the coast to San Simeon in California.

We left on Sunday, May 24, around 2 p.m. Heading north through the coastal towns of Port Richey, Hudson and Springhill, it seemed like the honky-tonk was never going to end. Finally, the tree-lined road stretched before us, welcoming us like an old friend. Highway 19/98 was an easy drive, especially when being escorted by an exotic bird called the "swallow-tail kite". This bird migrates to Florida in the summer and we were delighted with its company. Its four-foot wing span and V shaped split tail makes these birds stand out.

Manatee River State Park was our first night's destination. We had stayed there last January and really liked it. The Manatee River holds true to its name as manatees do swim there. A boardwalk follows the clear, azure blue water to a viewing area. Looking down in the water, huge fish, big turtles, exotic birds and yes, even manatees could be seen. That night, we had a special dinner of pasta, clams and champagne to celebrate the start of a new journey. The next morning, before we left, we took a dip in the cool springs. Two young girls showed us where the shallow end was and assured us of a sandy, not muddy, bottom. It was cold at first, but delightful once we got use to it. A group of divers from Atlanta were taking their certification test and told us of seeing bubbles from the headwaters of the underground spring. Once refreshed, we left heading north and then west across the Florida panhandle.

Many campers had told us that Port St. Joseph State Park (also known as Port St. Joe) was akin to Paradise. Fishing villages became more numerous as we got close to the Rt. 30 turnoff. If it weren't so late, we would have stayed to explore.

From the turnoff, it was a long 20-mile drive to the campground. There was nothing much to see but the green of the trees and fronds. If this was paradise, then we planned to stay for a few days. At the campsite, huge palm trees buffered each site making it feel very private. Off in the distance, the sound of the surf could be heard. It was the kind of place we liked to call home.

We were finished setting up about an hour before sunset. With beach chairs slung over our shoulders, we headed out to enjoy the uncrowded beach. Located on a peninsula that juts out into the Gulf of Mexico, its 33 miles of shoreline has white, soft sand and turquoise blue water reminding us of the Caribbean. As the sun set, we intently watched it drop into the horizon and eagerly awaited the "green flash". When the sun goes below the watery horizon, a green flash sometimes announces its descent. The colors of the spectrum, going from orange to red to green to blue of the coming night's sky become vivid. It happens so fast, that if you blink, you will miss it. We stayed on the beach until the stars came out and watched Mars drop into the western horizon. The big dipper rose high above our heads and the Milky Way splashed millions of stars across the sky. The cool breeze was relaxing as the day was hot and humid. In the distance, flares from Apalachicola Naval Air Station gave us a show.

Our neighbors across the road, also in a pop-up, had a Margaretville bumper sticker and they seemed very nice. After a pleasant greeting, we decided to do a beach day together. Donna and Buster were true beach goers. As they prepared for the beach, they had their cooler, towels, umbrella, fishing gear and a boom box on a carrier with big fat beach wheels. CD's of Jimmy Buffet and Zydeco music made for a perfect day at the beach. I believe there are people in this world we haven't yet met, but when we do meet, it feels familiar. That is the way we felt with Donna and Buster. Buster's real name is "Iris" and he said his name caused him lots of grief growing up, so the name "Buster" stuck. They were from a parish not far from Baton Rouge. Buster's dad grew up in Opelousas, (the birthplace of Zydeco), so their CD's were the real thing. At one point, Donna and I had to laugh as the boys, sitting under umbrellas, compared their skin problem. Of course, Donna and I were assuming the position, greased down and stretched out in the sun.

Buster is a fisherman and after a few folks on the beach started catching fish, he jumped into the water with his rod and reel. We watched him for a while. Soon he caught what he called a "lady fish". He fishes for the sport and let the "lady" go. Wanting to learn, I waded out and when he caught another one, he handed me the reel to bring it in. I did and once the fish took a look at me, it jumped right off the hook and back into the water. The hook barely missed my face as it swung back. Buster tried to teach me to throw out the leader, but I needed to coordinate my thumb on the reel to stop the line. On the first cast, I tangled the line so bad that the reel started spinning backwards. It was a mess! With the patience of a saint, it took Buster all day to untangle it and I'm not sure if he ever succeeded.

That night, they invited us over for some drinks and music. We danced to Zydeco, talked travel and had a great time. An invitation was extended to us to visit them anytime we were in Louisiana. Buster said he would take us fishing on the bayou and he would give me a "fool proof" reel. The campers were right in their description. This was Paradise.

Leaving Port St. Joe, we traveled along the panhandle to another one of our favorite spots, Big Lagoon State Park. This place is special because it was the campground where the reality of retirement first sunk in. I will always remember my poor husband sitting in the pavilion overlooking the Inter Coastal Waterway (ICW). His face showed signs of shock and disbelief. That was last March. This day, late in May, he was wide awake and ready to explore. Big Lagoon encompasses 678 acres. The marshes were alive with wild life and the beaches were beautiful. Across from the ICW is a barrier island, easily accessible by car. Our stay was short, but we did take time to visit the tower and watch the sunset. A hawk, not 100 yards from the tower, displayed his skill of hovering. With his neck extended, he looked for fish. Spotting one, he dove after it. After being briefly submerged, he flew off with his prize catch. As we left, a gray fox darted across the street reminding us of the pristine wetlands that surrounded us.

Bayou Segnette State Park was a long day's drive from Big Lagoon, but is was worth it as it was another one of our favorite campgrounds. To break the ride up, we stopped in Biloxi, Mississippi to visit the home and library of Jefferson Davis, President of the Confederacy during the Civil War. The gift shop had an extensive book collection on the War as well as current day politics. I, however, was more interested in the books on Southern cooking and purchased a book entitled Hot Beignets and Warm Boudoirs with thoughts of trying a few recipes while traveling.

The weather was hot and humid. Our first year found us here at the beginning of April. Now, it was the end of May and what a difference in the weather. It seemed it had been hot ever since we left Florida. To cope, we turned on the air conditioning in the camper and stayed in. It was somewhat painful to be so close to New Orleans and the French Quarter and it being too hot to play. However, our restless souls begged for an adventure. A visit to Blaine Kern's Mardi Gras World would help with our New Orleans' blues. So, with the air conditioning on in the truck, we drove over there. It was as fabulous as we remembered. Blain Kern is famous for making a majority of floats for the two month long Mardi Gras celebration and its parades. The gift shop still had a great library of books on the history of Mardi Gras. It was fun leafing through books showing pictures of floats from early days and the festivities that went with them. They also had an awesome collection of sun catchers, which I purchased for gifts.

Blain Kern's Mardi Gras World is located in the parish of Algiers. The ferry here takes passengers across the Mississippi and to the French Quarter. Algiers is a small community that rests on a curve in the Mississippi River. In a previous visit, we found out that Algiers was once home to many jazz musicians who played in "Storyville". Since they could not afford to live in the "Big Easy", they settled here. Storyville existed outside the French Quarter from the early 1900's until prohibition of the 1920's. It was famous throughout the world for its vibrant red light district and highly respected bordellos. Louis Armstrong, Jelly Roll Morton, King Oliver and Sidney Bechet were some of the many greats who played there.

As we left Blaine Kern's, a large picture of the famous voodoo queen, Marie Laveau, came into view. It was on the side of an old cedar-planked building. Above her picture was a sign that read "Seven Sisters of Algiers". Marie Laveau was known as the greatest voodoo priestess ever to have lived in New Orleans. "Come in and shop for a spell" was stenciled on a bench outside the door. My curiosity piqued and it was worth leaving the air-conditioned truck to explore. The seven sisters of Algiers that the sign referred to were the daughters of Marie Laveau. She didn't want them to follow in her footsteps, but the genes were too strong. A young, black girl with dreadlocks welcomed us to come in and see the museum. Voodoo was the religion of slaves who were brought here from Africa. Many items used in their ceremonies were carefully displayed. In a dark corner was a papier-mache doll called "Evil Eye Willie". A sign asked visitors to "Rub my left cheek, then drop quarters and dimes. A good spell I will be cast for you until the end of time."

Not to tempt fate, we rubbed his cheek and dropped our quarters into his hand and asked Evil Eye Willie for his well wishes, and cooler weather. Back out on the street, it continued to be oppressively hot. Our resolve was to keep going until our wish was granted.

Chapter Two

New Territory from Texas to New Mexico

From New Orleans, we drove west into the hill country of Texas. The last time we drove through Fredericksburg, Texas I picked up a local paper and found there was a campground called the "Lady Bird Johnson Municipal Campground". It said there was a swimming pool and a fishing stream. More importantly, there was the "Lady Byrd Johnson Golf Course". Knowing that Lady Bird was a great conservationist, it had to be worth playing. Fredericksburg is a quaint town founded by German immigrants. It had lots of shops, B&B's, German restaurants and bakeries.

A huge mistake we made before we left our last campground, was not securing the refrigerator door. When we opened the camper, the refrigerator door was ajar and would not come on. The thermostat read "0". At a payphone, I started to dial the 800 number to the Fleetwood repair center, when a camping repair truck happened to drive by. I flagged him down and he was happy to look at our refrigerator. He reset the system and left his cell number in case it didn't get cold. He said the thermostat should read 40 degrees. Fortunately, the reset worked and there was no damage. We learned a very valuable lesson that day. From then on, whenever we hit the road, we would take extra measures to secure the refrigerator door with a pillow jammed between the fridge door and the folded down sink.

The mornings were cool enough for Charles to play golf as I lingered at home, in air-conditioning, and savored a cup of coffee. The first day, I met him on the 17th hole and he said the course was lovely and difficult. After he played the 18th hole, he drove me around the course. It was very scenic with old trees and a delightful stream that meandered through the course. It made for a great photo shoot because it natural beauty was captivating. The last stop was the stone built clubhouse that sat high on a hill overlooking the stream and campground. Like most courses it offered a restaurant and big screen TV that was perfect to enjoy a cold beer while watching the golf channel.

The campground was adjacent to the "Gillespie County General Aviation Airport". We had seen some impressive jets flying in and out and decided to pay a visit. The "Hanger Diner" was a brand new restaurant with decor reminiscent of the 1940's. Billy Holiday and Duke Ellington played in the background. A motel next to the diner was built in a WWII military hanger. The Officers Club in the lobby, lived up to its name with a beautiful wood crafted fireplace, a grand piano for weekend happy hours, and an elegant pool table. A nice bar with comfortable leather chairs to lounge in completed the room. As we left the hanger/motel, a large billboard showed Rosie the Riveter proclaiming "I sleep like a baby at the Hangar Hotel". Next to the sign was a big, old round spot light from that era.

On the day of our departure from Fredericksburg, Texas, the weatherman predicted heavy rain and high winds. Our plans to spend the next night camping in San Angelo State Park had to be reconsidered because the weatherman was right and it started to rain hard. We continued driving to Big Springs and the rain followed us most of the way. The Chamber of Commerce in Big Springs said there was a state campground not far from the center of town. We drove up the road to a plateau and with a break in the weather, parked the camper. Concerned about the wind, we decided to take a hike and contemplate Plan B. On the way down the road, we stopped to see the prairie dog town, which was not far from the campsite. The ranger said the prairie dogs had disappeared for a couple of years and were just starting to come back so we had to say hello to the little fellows. We then went back to the truck and drove into town.

Plan B found us sitting in the parking lot of the VA Hospital, while we called a few motels. The Comfort Inn had affordable rates, wireless Internet, cable TV and a laundromat. So we drove back to the camper, hooked it to the truck and moved into the Comfort Inn. We had just bought a WiFi card to access the Internet from our computer and this was our first chance to use it. In one night, we were able to go on-line, get the laundry done and watch cable TV, being especially attuned to the Weather Channel. It was a very good stop. The weather continued to be hot and folks were saying that it was highly unusual for that part of Texas and that it felt more like July than early June.

Bottomless Lake State Park is located just outside of Roswell, New Mexico and was a cool spot for our next campground. The area leading up to Bottomless Lake was barren, dry, and flat. The road stretched for miles and miles with nothing much of interest. As we approached the lake, huge sinkholes filled with emerald green water started to appear. The largest pool was at Bottomless Lake. Not far from our site was swimming, paddleboats and lifeguards. The lake is fed by springs from an underground aquifer, which generated 10,000 gallons of water a day. It was very refreshing swimming in the ice cold water. It sure beat the heat of the last few days.

The town of Roswell proclaims it captured an alien space ship during the summer of 1947. On our last trip, we stopped in the museum, which we really enjoyed. This time, we were more interested in visiting Wal-Mart to stock the pantry. The town really plays up to the alien invasion. Green waving figures were painted on the Plexiglas bus stop enclosures. Even Wal-Mart had a mural of a flying saucer and the "Crash Site Café" had Internet access. But that wasn't all that Roswell was famous for. An informative man at the Tourist Information Bureau told us that during World War II, German Officers (not the SS) were detained there. They were treated fairly and after the war, they were released. To show their appreciation, they sent the town of Roswell a huge piece of the Berlin Wall. A note read "To the Citizens of Roswell. Thank you so much. Signed: German Prisoners of War". Twenty families returned to Roswell and settled there.

He also told us some of the history of Bottomless Lake. In the mid 1800's, it was a regular stopping spot, on the Chisum Trail, for cowboys herding cattle from Texas to Colorado. The trail was hot and dusty and when they reached the lake, they were happy for a refreshing swim. With the scarcity of water on the trail, this was like an oasis. Charles and I tried to imagine what it was like being on a cattle drive. Eating and sleeping outdoors in the heat; no water for miles around and the constant wind. No thank you. We were happy traveling with our pop-up and its conveniences. The town of Roswell was named for Roswell Smith who set up a trading post nearby. That is how the town got its name. We also found out that Billy the Kid's grave at Fort Sumner was not far.

Driving back to the campground, we stopped in a Mexican bakery. A burrito for lunch sounded appetizing. Upon inquiring as to the "heat" of the burrito, we were told they all were hot. She suggested another type of burrito, one filled with cow's tongue and cheek, which we respectfully declined and bought some sweet wheat rolls instead.

Our last night at Bottomless Lake, we lay in bed and watched the stars and moon. The big windows of the camper were open and a light breeze cooled us down. It was a lovely night.

After seeing so much about Billy the Kid on our previous trip, we felt we had to pay our respects. The road to Billy the Kid's grave was desolate. The land was flat and went on for miles. A dirt road intersected Rt. 20 and a street sign said it was "Tumbleweed Drive". Maybe there was life out there. The road was very bumpy and Charles fantasized that he was flying a plane that was experiencing heavy turbulence. I just held on.

It was early afternoon when we arrived at Fort Sumner. The town had wonderful murals showing what life was like in the old west. One mural showed cattle herding, another showed a blacksmith shop. Everywhere were signs for the "authentic site" of Billy the Kid's grave.

The Fort's history is a very dark one. Dealing with friction between the settlers in the plains and the Indians, in 1862, the Indians were rounded up and forced to live at the Fort. The Army thought they could teach them how to farm, but the water from the Pecos River was alkaline and it killed their crops. The Navajo and Mescalero Apaches were forced to walk 450 miles to Fort Sumner for colonization. Many of them died. Three years later, the Army admitted their plan didn't work and signed the Treaty of 1868 so that the Indians could return home. Today, there is a memorial to those who lost their lives. In 1968, the Navajo nation recreated the "Long Walk" in memory of those who died.

Not far from Fort Sumner is the cemetery where Billy the Kid is buried. The cemetery was sparse because so many graves were swept away by the Pecos River. During a particular rainy season, the land had been rearranged as the Pecos River changed its course. In the process, it wiped out most of the Fort. However, the "Kid's" grave, along with a few others, was preserved. His headstone read, "Billy the Kid. Born Nov. 28, 1860. Died July 14, 1881. The Boy Bandit King. He died as he had lived." A wrought iron fence surrounded his grave because there were several successful attempts to steal his headstone. Fortunately, each time it was recovered. On the "Kid's" grave, people have thrown coins, cigarettes and there was even a bullet casing.

Frank Perez, who worked in the museum, helped me understand the final days of the life of Billy the Kid. He said that in the cemetery was the grave of Lucien Bonaparte Maxwell. Maxwell owned, at one time, the largest tract of land held by any individual in the United States. He founded the First National Bank of Santa Fe and was one of the founders of the Texas Pacific Railroad. His daughter's name was Paulita Maxwell. She, too, is buried in the cemetery. It is said that Paulita was pregnant with Billy's child and that when Billy was visiting Paulita at the Maxwell house, her father called Sheriff Pat Garrett. The sheriff arrived and shot Billy dead. Most outlaws are buried outside of town but it is said that Billy was much respected in the community and the town mourned his death. His good standing permitted him to be buried in the local cemetery. I think Maxwell might be turning over in his grave to have Billy so close to him.

I asked Frank if the stories I had read about digging up "Billy's" body were true. He told me that there was a battle between the Sheriff of Lincoln County, the Mayor of Captain and the Sheriff of Fort Sumner who wanted the body interred. The rest of the town and most of the public couldn't care less. He thought it was more about politics and a possible book deal. He said that the movement was slowly falling apart and that the idea was so unpopular, that the Sheriff of Lincoln County was resigning.

I don't know why, but it was very exciting to see and hear the history of Billy the Kid. Frank said that last year, over 250,000 people visited the grave. As we drove from Fort Sumner, we could feel Billy's ghost riding the terrain between Lincoln City and Fort Sumner, a wanted man evading posses and narrowly escaping death.

Upon Frank's suggestion, we had lunch at "Sadies", a local Mexican restaurant. Charles feasted on a huge burrito that didn't have "heat" and I had a homemade enchilada. That night we camped near Santa Rosa and found it to be very far from anywhere. The next day we headed to Albuquerque and civilization.

Chapter Three

A Four Corners Storm

Leaving the camper and truck at the Albuquerque Airport, we flew home to Frederick for a June wedding. On our return flight, heavy storms over Atlanta put us five hours behind schedule. So, instead of arriving in New Mexico by 1 p.m., we arrived at 6 p.m. and found the camper and truck were fine. Due to the lateness of the hour, we spent the night in a motel.

The Weather Channel's seven-day forecast for the middle of June showed a slow low-pressure system moving across the country. We changed our route due to severe thunderstorms in Southern Colorado. Instead of heading north to Pagosa Springs, Colorado, we decided to head west towards the Four Corners. Leaving the congested city of Albuquerque, slowly, the hills became mountains and the vegetation sparse. Soon the scenery changed from flat desert to hills and canyons. Sagebrush was everywhere. Being from the east, we were used to sage being an herb grown in a garden, not blanketing the landscape.

Since we were so close to the Four Corners Monument, we decided to stop and see it. Fellow campers did not give it a good review and we soon found out why.

On Rt. 64, we crossed from New Mexico to Arizona and got all excited as the signs welcomed us to each state. We thought we were there. However, we did not see signs for Colorado and Utah. In the distance, the snow-capped mountains of Colorado gave us a false sense that we had arrived. A quick check of the map showed where the road dipped before reaching the Four Corners, so it was still a few miles away.

Finally, after a very dusty ride, we reached the tollbooth for the monument. "Three dollars per person", the Indian ticket taker said. Six bucks was more than we wanted to spend, but what the heck. It was a historic marker and besides, I had to go the bathroom. For that price, I pictured a nice Visitor's Center and clean bathrooms. Wrong! As we approached, there was a semi-circle of deserted booths around it. A few Indians were showing their wares. A sign for RV parking led us to the back of the shacks. A few yards from the parking spot was a row of Porta Johns. Surely there must be a Visitor's Center somewhere. Nope! The Visitor's Center had mediocre exhibits and no bathrooms. It was back to the Porta Potty – YUK!

At the actual spot of the four states joining was a disc with the crossbars. To get a better look, there was a platform that read "Only two people on platform. May collapse". For the price of $6, it was all pretty dismal. The park was open until 8 p.m., but around 4 p.m., the natives started closing shop. A quick look at the horizon showed a dust storm about to envelop the region. To the left, was a big orange cloud. We quickly ran to the truck and high-tailed it out of there. The dust storm was so bad that we couldn't see mountains that were visible only a few moments before. Tumbleweeds flew across the highway and made driving difficult. It was like playing dodge ball or should I say dodge weed. Some struck and clung to on-coming cars. We prayed that the desolate road would veer away from the storm. The Four Corners is the starting point of each state's mileage. All miles start at zero. Our destination was Cortez, Colorado, 36 miles away. Very slowly, the mileage markers increased as we counted our way to safety. We estimated the winds to be sustained at around 30 miles per hour with gusts of 40 or higher. Dust was everywhere.

We didn't want to camp that night as the thought of high winds flapping the tenting was not appealing, so we searched for a room in Cortez. Most rooms were in the $115 range, and without breakfast. The Sundance RV Park was about five blocks past the center of town. It sat low in a valley, which meant the wind would be over us. That night, we could hear the wind high in the trees, but felt nothing. The bathrooms were immaculate and they even had cable TV. Feeling very tired from the weather and having driven 300 miles, we decided to spend a couple of days there.

On our last night in Cortez, the local Indians performed ancient dances in full costume at their community center. The storyteller told wonderful tales of the dance originations and the spiritual significance. He told a funny story about an Indian and the Pope. "One day, the Pope came to visit the local tribe. Everyone was very excited and turned out to see him. This one particular Indian had to get close to the Pope, for a blessing. After the blessing, the Indian immediately took down his Teepee and ran away. When the elder of the tribe asked why he embarrassed them, the Indian said he did not. He explained that the Pope motioned up and down and then from right to left (signing the cross). To him it meant the Pope was saying, "Take down the tepee and get out of here!" The evening ended with a friendship dance. Everyone was invited to join hands and dance in a circle to the drummer's beat. The crowd was then invited to talk to the young people who were performing and take their pictures and ask question about their costumes. One dancer had on an ornate breastplate made from elongated seashells. She proudly said that her mother had made it for her. This was a very special moment, because during a pow-wow, picture taking is not permitted. It is considered an intrusion to their privacy and very rude. When visiting, it is very important to respect the culture of the people.

Chapter Four

The Red Rocks of Capital Reef

Four weeks after starting the trip, we finally found cool weather in Capital Reef. It was mid-June and the nights were a comfortable 60 degrees with the days in the 80's. No air conditioning or heat was needed.

Leaving Cortez, Colorado, we headed north to Utah, on Rt. 95 towards Capitol Reef National Park. The scenic route took us through "White Canyon" where deep crevices in white rock stretched for miles. Beyond "White Canyon" was "Dark Canyon" that stretched beyond the horizon. The map showed a vast, undeveloped landscape. The color of the rock ranged from peach on the top to maroon at the bottom. The artist's palate was astounding. Folds, like pleats in a skirt, reached down to the earth. Perched high atop the mesas were rocks the size that Atlas would lift. They hung precariously on the edge and it seemed that at any minute, one of them might come crashing down. Evidence of fallen rocks was everywhere, some large boulders split right in half from the force and speed of landing.

. overlook on top of a mesa, we saw where the Colorado wed into Lake Powell. They must have been draining the r irrigation, as there was none left in this part of the lake. It was a very sad sight. Through binoculars, we looked down into the valley and saw there was no water where the marina was last year. The landscape went from white to gray, void of vegetation. A strata of gray mounds leading up to the mesas looked like a moonscape. Big, dark rain clouds appeared on the horizon and our internal warning radar was turned on as we ventured forward.

The entrance to Capitol Reef was shrouded in rain. Rocks glistened as if snow had just fallen. As we neared 1,000 Lakes Campground, the rain stopped. This is the same place we camped last year.

The next day started off with plans to explore Capitol Reef National Park, but the truck had other ideas. Halfway between the campground and Capital Reef, the oil gauge read "no pressure". We had been having trouble with the truck since Albuquerque where a mechanic installed an oil sensor. The oil gauge showed the pressure dropping. Before panicking, we decided to let the truck cool as we hiked into the foothills. Following a wash deep in the folds of the mountain was exciting. It felt like we were honored guests in this pristine environment. Many varieties of flowers surprised us as well as one rather large, pudgy lizard. The rocks on the ground were brown with blue streaks. We thought we found turquoise, until it crumbled in our hand. Rose and yellow quartz were strewn across the surface. After several hours of hiking, we returned to the truck and it started with no problem so we headed back to the campground.

The last time we visited 1,000 Lakes Campground we were having a hitch problem because it was installed incorrectly and was pulling the back-end of the truck down. The owner's husband had a garage nearby and helped us fix the hitch. The same mechanic as last year looked at the truck and said it was a loose wire. He tightened it and that seemed to solve the oil gauge problem.

The scenery in Capitol Reef is breath taking. Always in search of a good campground, we found the national park's campground nestled among trees and near the orchards of the town of "Fruita". For a small donation, you are invited to pick the fruit.

A twenty-mile scenic drive took us along the "folds" of the mesa. At the end of the road was a two-mile hike that led deep into the canyon. All the delays with the truck were not in vain, as the hike started out in the hot, late afternoon sun, but soon turned cooler as the sun started to set. An umbrella would have helped shield us from the sun, but we didn't think of it. We did have plenty of water, hats, and comfortable shoes. A big lesson learned that day was that when hiking in a hot climate, it is best to go late in the afternoon or early in the morning.

Capitol Reef offers the visitor a lot of diversity. Mountains, canyons, and the Fremont River all are part of the landscape. Inhabited as early as 700 A.D., petroglyphs are still found on its walls. The "Waterpocket Fold" is a 100-mile wrinkle in the earth's crust and this effect can be seen from many lookouts.

Route 50 is known as the Loneliest Road in the country. Life Magazine gave it that name in 1986 because they felt the road yielded nothing of interest. The towns along that route capitalized on the name and a Survival Guidebook is available at the visitor's centers. For a certificate, all you need to do is get a card stamped saying that you have visited all the wonderful places along this "lonely road".

That road led us west to Great Basin National Park. Inducted into the park system on October 27, 1986, the Great Basin National Park is almost on the middle axis of the north-south state line. Parts of the great basin reach into Idaho, Wyoming, Oregon and California and encompass most of Nevada.

The fenced road up to the park surprised us with funny artwork. Doc Sherman, a local artisan, started putting white gloves on the posts of the fence and called it, "The Permanent Wave Society". Doc passed away last January, 2003 but like-minded artists of the "Post Art Impressionism", carry out his wit and humor. Besides the white gloves that waved, humor is still displayed. A stuffed animal of Snoopy sat on top of the fence and had a thigh trimmer for a bow tie. A golf club posed to tee off on an artificial green was glued to a block of wood attached to the fence. The "post" art went on for several miles giving us much amusement, gratis of Doc Sherman.

At the Visitor's Center, we were surprised to read in the *Park News* that "The region is bound by the Wasatch Mountains to the east, the Sierra Nevada to the west, and Snake River plain to the north."

Folks from the previous night's campsite said that "we must" camp at Baker Campground in the Great Basin National Park and not to miss *Lehman Caves*. Usually, campsites at national parks are unparalleled in beauty and our site was no exception. At least ten varieties of wild flowers surrounded us and right outside our window was a waterfall. Wild Columbine, Yellow Balsam Root, Monkshood, and Shooting Stars are just to name a few. Wild roses were everywhere and their scent was delightful. From our campsite, we could see Mt. Wheeler rising 13,063 high above us. The weather was warm and dry and all the windows of the pop-up were open to enjoy this beauty.

Fate intervened when we decided to take the 60-minute instead of the 90-minute tour of Lehman Caves. At the Visitor's Center, we met our guide, Kiah Conrad. This was his third year as a guide and besides being knowledgeable about the cave's history, he had a great sense of humor and as we found out, a musical ear. He later told us that he majored in music at Southern University at Utah. Our group was small and very interested in what Kiah had to say. Being the last tour of the day, he had the time to tell us many stories about the discovery of the cave and the people who visited it.

Originally, the Shoshone Tribe inhabited the area. In 1885, a miner named Absalom Lehman discovered the cave. Locals say that "A pack rat ran away with his lunch and he followed it into a hole in the earth. He fell in and it took a search party three days to find him". Amazed at what he saw, he started charging folks to go into the cave. He gave them a candle and said they were allowed to pick one stalactite or stalagmite to take home as a souvenir. To enter the cave, they had to climb down a rope ladder, which many ladies did in their Victorian dresses. Like most caves, it must have been very cool when they entered and provided relief from the summer's heat. Evidence of their picking was everywhere.

The tour started out as most cave tours do. We walked down a well lit stairway, and at one point, were directed to gather in a small group. Kiah gave a flashlight to a kid in the group and told him not to lose it. The lights were turned off and we found ourselves in complete darkness. It was a wonder how Absalom Lehman ever found his way around. The flashlight holder did a good job, so we wouldn't be kept in the dark.

As we walked through the cave, Kiah pointed out such features of his imagination as the Statue of Liberty, and a formation that looked like the Star Ship Enterprise. Deep inside the cave was a basin of water called the King's and Queen's Baths. The water level used to be 50 feet higher than it is today, so now it is only the King's and Queen's footbath. During the late 1800's through prohibition, these caves were filled with lots of activity. Nearby an arch was where folks married and in the next room was a formation resembling a wedding cake. Another room's rock formation was in the shape of an eagle near the ceiling. We were told that the Boy Scouts use to have campouts there. Walking down a stairway, Kiah stopped at what looked like a mouth organ and gently tapped the stalagmites to create musical notes. He discovered that he could do this because of his musical training.

The best part of the tour was when he led us into a room he called the "Party Room". This was the most popular room during prohibition. He shone his light onto the ceiling where a variety of signatures appeared. One signature was dated 1888. Another inscription read "Skating Rink". It got that name because the area used to flood and was often quite muddy, but that didn't stop the partying. In fact, this room was used for the initiation ceremony for the Knights of Pythious and we were promised to see pictures back at the Visitor's Center.

As the tour came to an end, we found ourselves in a long, dark hallway with evenly spaced lights. It was very surreal. In single file, the steep incline lead to the red exit light at the end of the tunnel. As we walked, Kiah started singing, in a delightful voice, "Amazing Grace". The somber notes left us speechless and gave us chills. Kiah had given the cave a voice and the whole experience was very spiritual. Just before exiting the cave, he asked that we stand in front of the wall and closed our eyes. Kiah then knocked on the stone and the sound reverberated throughout. He said it was the heartbeat of the cave and a living monument to Mother Earth.

After the tour, we joined Kiah in the Visitor's Center where he shared, as promised, the photos of the Knights. Lined up against the wall of the cave, they posed for pictures in their ceremonial garb. We were also shown photos of the movie set of the 1965 horror film called "Wizard of Mars". The last picture he showed us was of a "toll taker" at the front entrance of the cave. He was sporting a big, toothless grin and a sign above his head said the cost was five cents.

Chapter Five

Riding with the Pony Express

The same campers who recommended Lehman's Cave also recommended that we visit the Hotel Nevada in the town of Ely. Ely sits at the crossroad of Rt. 50, which runs east and west, and Rt. 93 that runs south and north. At this intersection sits the historic Hotel Nevada, where many movie stars stayed on their trek from Hollywood to New York City in the days before modern transportation. Finished in 1929, it was the tallest building in the state of Nevada and the only one that was fully fireproof. Inside was a nice cafeteria and lots of slot machines. One of the hotel's main attractions was their $4.99 prime rib dinner and their .99-cent breakfast. The billboard outside read "Rooms for $25 a night" which raised our curiosity. So after a brunch of prime rib and eggs, we asked to see a few rooms, which the receptionist nicely obliged. There were six stories and only the top floor was non-smoking. Of the six rooms upstairs, only one was $25, so it was advised to reserve ahead. A plaque at the top of the staircase said guests included Ingrid Bergman, Gary Cooper and

Jimmy Stewart. Brass beds, claw foot tubs and lots of lace made the rooms look cozy. However, one room (The Suite) didn't like me. I gashed my arm on the bar and somehow a big bruise mark appeared on my shin. Who believes in ghosts????

We crossed Nevada following the route of the "Pony Express". It wasn't difficult to imagine the harsh conditions the riders endured. On April 3, 1860, the first rider left St. Joseph, Missouri, to start mail delivery to Sacramento. The thirteen ranges across Nevada made the ride very difficult. To add to their misery, there were frequent Indian attacks as the Indians were not very happy with the invasion of their territory. At its peak, the "Pony Express" had about 190 stations with about 500 horses that stretched across its route. The "Pony", as it was called, lasted for 18 months before the railroad phased it out. Today, there isn't much left of the trail, but at Cold Springs was a partially restored building and an artist's diorama of the lives of these men. An unknown fact was that for a short time, even Billy the Kid was a carrier. They advertised for orphaned boy with a lot of spunk, which was a good description of the "Kid".

Late in the afternoon, we came to Austin, Nevada. The map showed it was in the middle of our route and a brochure said there was camping there, with water and electricity. We had covered 220 miles and it was time to stop. As we dropped down from a range, a junkyard with rusted vehicles came into view. Around the bend, we saw the campground. Besides our pop-up, there were two Class A's (they looked like a bus) camped there. After we settled in, a nice guy came over and introduced himself as Victor and invited us over for drinks. His wife was sitting under a tree overlooking the highway. Big trucks were either climbing up a steep hill, or coming down a steep hill. Reading our minds, Victor said he thought it would get quieter in the evening. We hoped so.

Carol and Victor lived in Yerington, Nevada but were giving "RV full-timing" a try. So there we sat, chatting, overlooking the highway and did I mention – the campground was in the backyard of a Baptist Church? We were glad it wasn't Sunday and that no classes were in session.

Stopping at the library in the town of Fallon, we collected e-mails and surveyed the area for that night's camping. Talking to librarians was very helpful. It looked like several state parks were within easy reach and we decided to camp at Fort Churchill. As soon as we got out of the truck to set up, mosquitoes attacked. Quickly, the camper "popped-up" and inside we went. The carbon monoxide detector in the camper went off as we covered ourselves in Deet. We tried to go for a hike, but that didn't work. The mosquitoes were relentless. That night we hunkered down to a cool and enjoyable evening in the camper. With the windows open, we sneered at the mosquitoes that couldn't get in through the fine, mesh screen. The next morning, we were out of there.

An interesting brochure we picked up said that Virginia City was, at one time, the richest city in the United States. Gold was discovered there in 1859 and Bill and George Hearst, (father of William Hearst) started their fortune there. I thought Charles was going to have a fit as the truck and camper struggled to climb the 20 percent grade leading up to Virginia City.

Old time western saloons lined the boardwalk along with novelty shops and attractions. It was possible to pan for gold or see a real western shoot out. We decided to take the *Virginia & Truckee Steam Train* to see the original mine where it all got started. The town fascinated us. One saloon was called the "Silver Queen". Inside was a large portrait of a lady whose dress contained 3,261 silver dollars. Many of them probably were coined from silver found in the nearby mines. The lady's belt had 28 "twenty dollar gold pieces". The sight of her must have bolstered the imagination of gamblers seeking Lady Luck. We asked if we could see a room and the madam said "yes". Then she added that the walls were thin and she could hear every word that we might utter. The stairs that lead up to the rooms were bleak and old and the wallpaper was stained from years of traffic. We could almost hear the laughter from the prostitutes, gamblers, and miners that would have ascended these stairs. The staircase rose up the middle with rooms on both sides. A wrought iron crossbar structure was laid between the spaces that separated the balcony floors. I guess that was to prevent someone (drunk) from falling off the balcony onto the lower floor. The rooms were small and well kept. We were delighted to have the opportunity to step back in time. Later that day, found us drinking a beer in the "Bucket of Blood" saloon. Nope, there were no buckets of blood, only t-shirts and pins.

Mark Twain lived and worked in Virginia City for two years, from 1862 to 1864 in the basement of the Territorial Enterprise newspaper. Open to the public, an excellent exhibit showed his writing desk, the cases where the type was set and the printing press that was run by a water wheel. Next to his desk was a large portrait of Mark Twain and in the shelves that lined the room were old copies of the newspaper. One copy's front page told of the San Francisco earthquake. Its headlines read, "San Francisco Doomed. Hundred Die In Ruins!". By late afternoon, it was time to continue our journey to Truckee while the sun was still shining. Virginia City was, to us, the west at its best.

By 4 p.m., we arrived at our friend's cabin at Donner Lake, California. Just like last year, the pop-up fit nicely between the two cabins. Our plans were to leave the camper there for the July 4th celebration and drive the truck to San Francisco. Our friends were going out of town and they asked us to house sit their cat. Can life get any better?

Chapter Six

A Bad Day

Without a doubt, San Francisco is one of the loveliest, friendliest cities in the world, so I am sure that I was just having a "bad" day.

It started when we drove into the city with Julia. Leaving her office, we walked seven blocks to the Visitor's Center for brochures of all the sights and tastes that makes San Francisco so charming. It was a brisk walk on a sunny day. Having never been to Coit Tower, we checked the bus schedule to take us there. At the bus stop, we asked a Chinese man if this was the right bus. Using hand signals, he motioned "three blocks up the hill and five minutes". He made this motion several times, so we headed up the hill. A half hour later, all uphill, we still hadn't reached Coit Tower. Instead, we found ourselves in North Beach, where the beat generation was born. In the "City Lights Bookstore", Jack Kerouac and Alan Ginsburg denounced society and expressed their left-wing political views through poetry and prose. Upstairs in the poetry reading room, a whole section was dedicated to Jack Kerouac. Across the street from the bookstore was the "Bohemia Hotel". A guidebook said it was a "must" for their photographs of the 1940's and 50's. Some of the hotel's more famous guests were Janis Joplin, the Jefferson Airplane and the Grateful Dead. The guidebook was right. After ringing the bell, we were let into a narrow stairwell. The gentleman at the front desk said we were welcome to view the gallery. Large black and white photos portrayed stirring street scenes, which reflected the changing mood of that generation. The music, the fashion, the heart of North Beach jumped out at us. One picture was of a well-dressed musician sitting in a dark stairway, with his trumpet across his lap, as if waiting for the light of day. Another picture was of a couple, holding hands, strolling down the dimly lit street. Striking was their 50's attire. She had on a fur collar and he wore a suit with a short brimmed hat. In a large frame was a picture of a tall statue of Christ, with outstretched arms, standing on the steps of a church. In front of him was a large Chevy convertible. The photograph seemed to be questioning the opulence of youth.

Heading to Chinatown to meet Julia for lunch, again we couldn't connect with the right mode of transportation. We had been walking for about four hours, albeit a very interesting four hours. After a while, my butt started to hurt from all the hilly walking and we both were getting tired. Part of the walk was on Stockton Street, which paralleled Grant Street. This is the heart of Chinatown. Peking Duck hung from the butcher shops, live fish jumped around in tubs, and several kinds of dried mushrooms were piled high in crates along with lots of vegetables that were unfamiliar to me. The colors and smells were intriguing. I wanted to take pictures, but the clerk clearly gestured "no pictures". Finally, I was glad to be walking downhill.

We met Julia at the "Gate to Chinatown". She wanted to take us for dim sum and to get to the restaurant we had to walk up another long hill. It almost killed me. Charles and Julia laughed as I couldn't talk and walk at the same time. It was too tiring. After lunch, we left Julia near her office and again tried to connect with public transportation, but when we wanted a bus, none were to be found.

Out of the corner of my eye, I saw an old fashioned trolley car. It brought back memories of getting around Philly in the 50's when we didn't have a car. The trolley I saw was just like the kind I used to ride, with my parents. We would visit relatives and shop downtown, all for 12 cents. So we walked down to Market Street just to ride the trolleys and rest. Ironically, most of the trolleys were from Philly and dated back to the 1940's. However, a few were imported from countries as far away as Milan, Italy. We couldn't resist the Milan trolley with its wide windows and comfortable red velvet seats. The end of the line was the Castro district, a primarily gay area where huge rainbow flags lined the main street and small cafés offered espresso. For the ride back, we boarded a trolley made in Philly. San Francisco's trolley drivers are notorious for *kibitzing* (joking) and today was no exception. I asked if the trolley we were on was from Philadelphia. His reply was that the city had to raise the ex-mayor Frank Rizzo from the dead, to get the trolleys. That led him to kid with me all the way back to Julia's office. Everyone in the trolley car laughed as we discussed the merits of bagels. The driver couldn't understand what the big deal was about the New York bagel. He thought that given all the New Yorkers in San Francisco, at least one of them would have smuggled in the recipe. The lady next to me said there was nothing like a New York Bagel and suggested the water had something to do with the taste. A guy across the aisle said he had traveled the world tasting bagels and couldn't really tell the difference. The lady next to me just shook her head. Charles sat on the bench to my right and pretended not to know me. The driver then asked what I was doing in the city. When I told him I was house sitting, he wanted to get his "bros" together for a "house party". He said he hadn't been to a good house party since the 80's. To show he wasn't cheap, he said he would bring a six-pack of beer. I told him he better bring a keg! It felt good to be tempted by trouble, and I was flattered. However, I know that Julia would have killed me if she came home and found out that the "bros" had been partying in her house.

The following day was a down day as we recovered from all the walking. We both suffered from a lot of back and butt aches.

Julia left us her car, so we thought we would drive around Golden Gate Park. However, once in the park, we couldn't find any of the wonderful things there. Every turn led us to an exit. Not to be deterred, we went around in circles in the north section, seeing nothing. Charles even commented, "Is this all there is?". Frustrated, we found a nice gardener who showed us the way. It seemed like we were led through a portal. Soon, the Rose Garden, the Conservatory, and the Falls were directly in front of us. Because of an afternoon luncheon engagement, we only had time to see the Conservatory of Flowers. It is one of the finest examples of Victorian architecture in San Francisco. Encompassing over 12,000 square feet and 16,000 panes of glass, it is the oldest existing glass and wood greenhouse in the United States. It arrived in San Francisco in crates from Europe, having traveled around Cape Horn. Civil engineers of the time had the daunting task to assemble it for a public opening in 1879. The Observatory barely survived the earthquake of 1906, but was lovingly restored. In 1955, a severe windstorm closed the Observatory and major repairs were needed. Those repairs took eight years. We were glad to be there shortly after it re-opened.

Driving through the hilly neighborhoods to the California Culinary School was fun. That was, until we found ourselves navigating the same streets more than twice. We tried parking in a garage, but the "Public" sign turned out to be valet parking. Charles was on a steep incline when the parker refused to move the car in front of us so we could turn around. It was a nasty situation and I did have a few words with the attendant who quickly ignored me. Charles was able to back up the truck while I watched apprehensively. Remembering some free "on street" parking, we drove around the block again and finally parked. Lunch service ended at 1 p.m. and it was 12:50 p.m. A quick four block walk uphill brought us to the first door with the name of the school on it, but that was the registration area. The restaurant was around the corner. Hurriedly, we made it there with a few seconds to spare.

The California Culinary Institute is located in a circa 1929 building that once was a German retreat. The dining area was in the large ballroom, and had white linen covered tables and hardwood floors. Along one wall was a glass-enclosed classroom. This was so the diner could observe the cooking. Above our heads, in what was once a balcony, was another glass-enclosed classroom. Students could be seen presenting papers to their peers while being graded by their instructors. Tired from the rushing (did I say "uphill"), we sat down and were greeted by our waiter. The first thing he did was spill the flower vase, fortunately, away from us. After some apologies, he set it upright and walked away. There we sat, with a wet tablecloth and a dying flower. Our order was taken and a short while later, another person approached our table. He was carrying bread and seeing that we had none, placed some on our table. Then another person came over to fill our water glasses. Everything seemed disjointed. An instructor is usually present, like at other restaurant schools we have dined in. Here, we did not see any instructors other than the one in the overhead classroom.

For an appetizer we ordered *Asparagus and Goat Cheese Fritters*, which was very good. After a long wait, our second course of *Ragout of Morels* arrived. That too, was very tasty. I asked about the ingredients of the Ragout and was surprised that our waiter didn't know how it was made. The staff is usually prepped for the upcoming meal before the restaurant opens. Our waiter then went back into the kitchen and returned to tell us "it was nothing special. Just long grain rice made into a pattie and fried". Nothing special? That was why we were there. To observe students learning their craft, taste their accomplishments and enjoy good service while they tried to impress their Professors. Through the window, we could see our dessert being made and there was our waiter, flirting with a young lady and he was the only one in the kitchen without a hat. He then disappeared for about five minutes and came through another door with our dessert in hand.

The dinner ended with a smell of burnt food coming from the kitchen. Guess we weren't the only one having a bad day.

Chapter Seven

A Joyous July

It was time to rejoin our camper and the party that was about to start at Donner Lake. Friends and family brought this year's count to fourteen people. Bill and Julia bought the cabin over twenty years ago when it used for fishing. Over the years, they have lovingly restored it and the July 4th party has been going on for about as long as they have had the cabin. Special guests this year were Bill's mom and dad, from Boise, Idaho. Seeing everyone again induced lots of warm and happy feelings.

Every day flowed into the next with lots of lounging, visiting, shopping and wine. Jeannette and Julia were wonderful cooks and Doug made breakfast every morning. To minimize the cooking responsibility, each couple made a dinner and appetizer. Lunches were foraging in the refrigerator for leftovers. Bill and Jeannette's daughter Andrea, surprised us one night, with recipes from the cover of "Redbook's" Easter feast. Pork tenderloin was prepared on the grill accompanied by fancy asparagus and potatoes.

One day, Charles and I decided to take a day trip around Lake Tahoe. The drive took us through the quaint town of Tahoe City and passed the remnants of the Olympic Village in Squaw Valley. Our friends told us to look for "Fanny Bridge" which crossed the Truckee River. The trout under the bridge were so large that people hung over to see them, thus exposing their "fannies".

The first thing we noticed about Lake Tahoe was its immense size. The Indians called it "Lake in the Sky" because it sits at 6,200 feet in elevation. Lake Tahoe is over 22 miles long and 12 miles across and straddles the Nevada and California state lines. From the Emerald Bay overlook we could see Fannette Island, the only one on the lake. The day was bright and clear and we were excited to be exploring this natural wonder. At the Visitor's Center, we found out that one of the nearby attractions was the *Ponderosa* movie set. Another attraction was the Cal Neva Hotel, which interested us more.

A well-paved road circled the lake. The California side was winding and undeveloped. In contrast, the Nevada side had casinos, an active harbor at Zephyr Cove and beautiful beaches. Our destination was the Cal Neva, once owned by Frank Sinatra. It got its name because it was built on the state line where this distinction was made by a black line that ran down the center of the pool with "Cal" on one side and "Neva" on the other. In the early 60's, this was the playground for the "rat pack" and the Kennedys. The hotel offered a tour of the underground tunnel, but that was only available at night. One can only imagine the celebrities who came this way to perform in the *Celebrity Room*. Today, center stage and next to the silent piano, is a life size photograph of Frank Sinatra. The scene was reminiscent of the clubbing days of the 50's. The hall that led up to the *Celebrity Room* was lined with photographs from this bygone era. One was of Sinatra celebrating a birthday with pals that included Marilyn Monroe, Sammy Davis Jr., Peter Lawford and Dean Martin.

Back at Donner Lake, everyone's thoughts turned to decorating, as it was the day before Independence Day. Neighbors of all ages got into the spirit. With wine in one hand and red, white, and blue decorations in the other, the merriment began. Everyone brought a dish for a potluck lunch, which was served at the neighbor's cabin. July 4th dawned sunny and cool. The fun and games started around noon. A scoreboard was hung on a tree and everyone put a quarter in the hat. Teams were drawn up and games began. A lot of friendly competition went into the bocce ball and bean toss, while Bloody Marys and Gin and Tonics fortified the teams. Dinner was then served on two long folding tables. Dishes of potato salad, hot dogs and beans, macaroni and cheese, barbeque meatballs are just of few of the delicious dishes that the neighbor's brought to the table along with apple pie and fudge brownies for desert. The grand finale of the afternoon's party was a form of baseball where the girls competed against the guys. A board with holes for "strike", "out", 1st, 2nd, 3rd base and "home run" was propped up. Each team member tossed four beanbags trying for a homerun. It was great fun but the boys won. The evening ended with a parade to the beach for fireworks and patriotic songs. There was a sense of gratitude for our men and women who are fighting for freedom abroad. The next day was the annual sand castle contest. Our team's design was of a great big shark whose teeth were cleverly made from pinecone parts. Our team proudly finished first in their age group, just like the year before.

A few days after July 4th, people started leaving and the neighborhood returned to a sleepy fishing camp. We stayed a few extra days with Bill and Julia to relish in the week's memories and drink our last glass of California wine together. Upon leaving, we stopped to watch reinactors portray what life was like when the Donner party passed that way. In the center of Donner Memorial State Park is a statue showing how deep the snow was when they wintered there during the winter of 1846.

Heading for the California coast, Highway 20 was going to take us around Clear Lake. Anxious to reach the coast, we decided to take a short cut. However, the shortcut turned out to be a 12-hour, 340-mile mountainous ordeal. The mistake was navigator error by taking the first Rt. 175 instead of the second one. When the compass showed a heading of south instead of west, we knew we were in trouble. Thirty miles of curvy and steep roads traversed Boggs Mountain State Forest and there was no place to turn around. Finally, at the bottom was civilization and the town of Middletown. We looked for several people with "local" knowledge for a road to the coast, but it seemed that everyone was from someplace else. In desperation, I stood at the front counter of a pizza shop and asked out loud, "Is anyone from around here?" A nice man offered his assistance and showed us a less mountainous and more scenic route to Clear Lake where we discovered a lot of nice campgrounds on the lake and vowed to come back and make sure to take the right road.

As we reached the Pacific coast, wineries started appearing on the hillsides. Highway 128 led us through the Navarro River Redwoods State Park. Tall green trees and the sounds of rippling water from the river followed us to the coast. After a long day of rough travel, the sound soothed our souls. The smell of the ocean was in the air. As the river grew larger, we had a sense that the coast was fast approaching. Over the last hill, the fog that is indigenous to the west coast, greeted us with a cool blast of ocean breeze. Van Damme State Park was recommended so we went to check it out. Besides the campground being "full", there was nothing there but primitive camping. All for $20 a night. We were told we could stay in the empty parking lot, but we didn't want to dry camp so close to the road. Besides, the bathrooms were smelly. Given that we had such a hard day, we rewarded ourselves with a night at the "Little River Inn" near the lovely town of Mendocino. The room was large and filled with antiques. An antique rocker in front of the window invited us to sit and watch the ocean. Through our binoculars we could see the seals playing on a nearby rock. As we were checking in, the host said they had lots of videos and someone had just returned Sea Biscuit, which we had wanted to see. Our day ended with a cup of hot tea, a great movie, and the sound of the waves was our lullaby to sleep.

The next morning, feeling very refreshed, we headed out to explore the village of Mendocino. Most of the quaint buildings dated from the late 1800's and it was here that Angela Landsbury solved many mysteries in *Murder She Wrote* (and we thought it was on the Maine coast!). It was difficult getting Charles off the rocks that lined the shore. Each nook and cranny held something for the curious. Wonderful shops were abundant, and we could have easily spent a week exploring. Most inviting were the tide pools, the river's headwaters, wineries and restaurants. Coastal temperatures were in the mid 60's during the day and low 50's at night.

One could stop a thousand times to explore the beaches and vineyards along Highway 101. The wildflowers alone were worth a stop. The road was hilly and windy, but being a major highway, the curves were a lot smoother than what we had previously experienced. One hundred and fifty miles later, we arrived at Patrick's Point State Park. With luck on our side, we were able to get a campsite, but only because they were doing renovations to some of the sites. This park had water and electricity, so we made ourselves at home and enjoyed hiking to the overlook and exploring Agate beach. Agates are small, smooth, semi-precious stones that take a lot of patience to find. We didn't find any, but did find (as we discovered later) jasper and jade.

Our map showed a 31-mile route that led through the "Avenue of the Giants" which ran through large stands of majestic redwoods. Several stops had to be made to stand in awe of these 1,000 year old giants. Tree hugs were in order, although we could only reach around a small part of the tree, and a bow in reverence to their age and beauty. The campgrounds tempted us to stop and camp amongst the trees, but we were anxious to see our friends in Salem, Oregon.

The last town in California that we visited was Crescent City. In 1964, a tsunami, which originated in Alaska erupted, and demolished the city. Fully recovered, it has a large information center for the city, state, and surrounding forest, which provided us with lots of good information for future trips.

It was mid-July when we entered Oregon. We were welcomed with fields of Easter lilies, which are grown here for distribution to supermarkets and florist across the country. Oregon must be the most prolific flower garden in the United States. That night we camped, perched high on a bluff, at Cape Blanco. The bluff was 200 feet above the sea and the view extended for miles. The hike to the lighthouse was beautiful and the beaches were littered with driftwood. Unlike California, the Oregon coast is accessible as the highway runs along it and has many places to stop and explore. Also, the campgrounds were a lot less expensive than California, making it even more inviting.

The next morning our truck wouldn't start. Nothing we did seemed to help. A call to AAA RV Plus brought a big flatbed truck. The truck and camper had towing insurance good for up to 100 miles.

When the driver asked where we wanted to be towed, I said that we did not know and asked where he would take his mother if she were having car problems. He towed us to the Ford dealer in Coo's Bay, which was on our way to Salem. Having telephoned the garage ahead to let them know of our situation, they had a bay ready and with the expert maneuvering of the tow truck, our truck was safely in the mechanic's bay. Fifteen minutes later, the loose starter wire was tightened and we were on our way again.

The garage mechanic was impressed that we drove all the way from Florida and recommended we take a side trip to see the herd of elk. *The Dean Creek Elk Viewing Area* was located off of Highway 101. At first, all we saw were antlers sticking out of the tall grass. A closer look revealed huge elk resting in the marshes. From a truck repair to seeing the awesome elk, was there a connection?

Chapter Eight

From Tillamook to Seattle

After spending a week in Salem with friends, it was the end of July and Tillamook, Oregon, was our next destination. Tillamook may sound familiar because they export cheese all over the country. Our mission was to get six, five-gallon ice cream buckets for our friends in Tacoma. At fifty cents apiece, this was a great deal and so was the free samples of cheese.

A local map showed the way to the coastal town of Pacific City, which is part of the Three Capes loop. We had great difficulty locating Pacific City as there were no signs and it was not in our atlas. The reason for our search was that we heard they had a large dory fleet worth seeing. As we approached the beach, we saw a huge rock just offshore. To the right of the rock, was a large sand dune where people climbed up and ran down the dunes. Chitchatting with our parking lot neighbor, he said, "we must" climb the sand dunes and explore the top. So up we went to see the spectacular view of rocks, caves, and pools being filled with the awesome power of the Pacific

Ocean. It was mesmerizing. A little further across the dunes we were able to look down and see outgoing waves crashing with incoming waves sending spray 100 feet into the air. We could have stayed there for hours watching the tide change. Carefully, we made our way down the dunes as a crescent bay stretched out before us. Our parking lot neighbors were happy to hear the details of our exciting exploration and recommended we check out the campground across the highway. That is where the famous "dory" fleet calls home. Early in the morning, these large boats launch from the shore to go fishing for salmon. The launch is said to be a great sight.

Heading back to our campsite, we stopped at the "Blue French Cheese Factory" where they had several bars set up with free pretzels, sauces, dips and chips. It made a great appetizer to our dinner, which was fresh caught salmon we bought at a local market.

The next day we explored the other side of the loop. We noticed several folks walking along the banks during low tide. Of course, we had to check it out and found out they were crabbing and catching Dungeness crabs. At a nearby stand, a steaming pot to cook the crabs was waiting at a cost of $5 a batch. We took all the information and put it on our "Must Do List" for our next trip.

Proceeding up the coast, we thought Cannon Beach would be a good place to camp, but found it to be too crowded. Further north was camping at Fort Clatsop, but it too was full because of the 100th anniversary of the Lewis and Clark Expedition. There was a long line for a campsite. Not wanting to wait, we moved on. Across the bridge from Astoria, Oregon, we found the village of Chinook, Washington. Following camping signs, we turned down Washington Street. At the end of the street was a small campground with a big welcome. It felt very homey and we were immediately invited to cocktail hour. The campground overlooked the Columbia River and at night, we could see the lights from Astoria. One of the campers was from Louisiana and when she saw my "I ♥ Zydeco Music" bumper sticker, she treated us to some down-home Zydeco music.

The Chinook Country Store was as backcountry as I cared to get. On the walls were several moose heads and large fish of various kinds mounted on wooden boards. Old photos showed the men who caught them.

The town north of Chinook was the fishing village if Ilwaco. That seemed to be the main fishing port and was very picturesque. Many signs advertised "oyster shooters" and I had to have one. They were the freshest oysters with the most delicious cocktail sauce I had ever had. From there we headed east towards Tacoma and the Pacific Northwest.

While visiting friends in Tacoma, they suggested we visit the Olympia Farmers Market. Olympia is the capital of Washington State and is located on the southern tip of the Hood Canal and the Puget Sound. Lots of foods were displayed that I did not know existed. Yellow cherries and yellow plums were intriguing and tasty. Of course, the pastry and ice cream was to die for.

One of the loveliest places in the United States, in my humble opinion, is the Pacific Northwest. The weather in the summer is cool, with a fresh ocean breeze caressing one's face. The vegetation is lush because of all the rain. I can only imagine what the fields must be like in the spring as the tulips, daffodils, irises and lavender start to bloom. Late July is the cherry and blueberry season. These fruits are sold at many roadside markets. One campground's privacy hedge was filled with blackberries while another campground had yellow plum trees lining the entrance. Everywhere we looked was water. Many campgrounds dotted the Puget Sound and Hood Canal with its numerous bays. The Strait of Juan de Fuca was just over the mountain ridge of Olympic National Forest and beyond that was the Pacific Ocean. When the sun shined, which, so far, had been often, the blue sky was dotted with puffy white clouds that complimented the sparkling blue water. Perfect for an artist's canvas.

Seattle is the gateway to the Pacific Northwest and has a very interesting history. A friend from Seattle said we must go on the tour of Seattle's underground. Below its streets was a shopping district that had been vacant since 1907. The tour began at Doc Maynard's restored 1890 public house, which is in the oldest section of Seattle known as "Pioneer Square". Thanks to "Doc" this area has been preserved for all to see. I would like to share with you an abbreviated story of how Seattle grew.

Arthur Denny and his family took four months to travel across the country in a wagon train. They met several unfriendly Indians along the way, but were not deterred. Eventually they settled in Elliot Bay. At first, Seattle was called "New York" because that was a well-known name from the east coast, but it didn't catch on. Then the name was changed to "Dowumps", but that name didn't fly either. Finally, it was changed to honor Chief Seattle, whose tribe had lived in the area for over 1,000 years.

After many land negotiations, a city was built. The main industry was logging and after the San Francisco fires, wood became an important commodity for rebuilding. The term "skid row" came from this time, as trees slid down the street from the mountains above, to the water front and awaiting boats. A man in England by the name of Thomas A. Crapper invented the first flush toilet and a boatload of crappers were purchased and shipped to Seattle. However, the sewer system wasn't in place to handle the sewage. A big problem for this emerging town was what to do with the sewer as the expanding town was built on a tidal plain. One unfortunate day, the outgoing tide took the "crap" out into Puget Sound and on the returning tide, the pressure was so strong that it blew the tops off the crappers. The local papers reported a 4 to 6 foot burst all over town, or so we were told.

Despite many difficulties, the town flourished, as did the garment industry, which doubled as the prostitution district. Miners and lumbermen would visit the garment industry to have their clothes repaired along with other matters of pleasure. This meant that the area hotels, bars, and general stores flourished. Miners from as far away as San Francisco came to be "mended". The taxes levied on the "garment industry" sustained the city for the next four years making up 87 percent of Seattle's budget. The city flourished, supplying the miners of the "Klondike Gold Rush of 1897" era with supplies.

In 1889, a great fire swept through Seattle. To make matters worse, the local hardware store had just received a shipment of dynamite for the miners. Due to shoddy construction of the town's infrastructure and a low tide, 33 square blocks were destroyed by fire in just 12 hours. When the city was rebuilt, the streets were raised, but the stores remained on the first level. Unbelievably, ladders connected the streets to the stores. Many men fell to their deaths trying to navigate the bars and ladders while inebriated.

All these stories were told as we traveled the alleyways of the old city and disappeared into unassuming doors to walk down a flight of stairs into the underground. "Crappers", old signs, logs that were the original water pipes, a bank with a teller's window and vault, and old photos showed what the streets looked like. Broken street lamps and boarded up shop windows where just some of the interesting sites in the underground. It was a wonderful tour. The grand finale was the bathroom in the gift shop. Ornate porcelain crappers and sinks that were recovered from the underground continued the mystique of that time. Shadow boxes lined the walls with novelty items from this bygone era.

Chapter Nine

Old Friends, New Friends

On August 1, we boarded the ferry to Port Townsend and traveled across the Strait of Juan de Fuca to Whidbey Island. Friends we made last year asked us to join them at the county campground in Oak Harbor, on Friday Island. The campground was lovely with wide, green, spacious lawns and clean bathrooms. Not far from our window was a view of Oak Harbor. On an easy walk around the park, we passed the pool, a fighter plane display and nice beaches with lots of driftwood. Continuing past the park, we could walk into downtown and visit the shops and restaurants. The island itself is only 64 miles from tip to tip. As heavy rain was bombarding Seattle, the rain shadow of the Olympic Mountain Range kept us dry.

One day we drove around the island to see the many quaint villages. In Coupeville, we met friends for lunch at "Toby's", which is famous for their fabulous mussel stew. Also in Coupeville is a pier where the largest starfish I have ever seen, clung to the pilings underneath the pier. The scenery of the surrounding islands was spectacular and we hoped to tour them in a few days.

The map showed a lighthouse at Bush Point, which looked inviting because it overlooked Admiralty Bay. Trying to find it we got into a neighborhood of many dead end streets, but we were not deterred. The UPS man showed us the way. Once there, a "no trespassing sign" crossed the path to the lighthouse. Since no one was around, we decided to ignore it and proceeded to the waterfront. There we were able to see the Olympic Mountain Range stretching out across Admiralty Bay. This is where the Bay of Juan De Fuca met the Puget Sound.

Another day trip we made was to Anacortes, a small town located on the easternmost part of the San Juan Islands. To get there from Whidbey Island, we crossed the much photographed "Deception Pass Bridge". Deception Pass got its name when early explorers thought they were entering a bay, as marked on an old Spanish map. Instead, they found turbulent waters separating two islands and felt deceived. When one views this bridge they see a marvel of steel. Beautifully constructed in 1934, it was the handiwork of the Corps of Engineers and at that time was considered an engineering feat. It spans two islands for a total of 1,487 feet. Hiking trails abound both on the hills and down by the water where I hear the tide pools lead to great exploring. The week we were there was the same week as the Anacortes Craft Fair. Since it was a rainy Friday, we didn't think it would be crowded and it wasn't. A highlight for me was a drumming circle where an energetic lady welcomed us into the circle and demonstrated drumming techniques. Charles watched and was amused from a distance.

After a few days of exploring, we needed a down day as the next few days were going to be hectic with our plans to visit the San Juan Islands. On Sunday, we deciphered the ferry schedule, which was very exacerbating. Ferries don't travel in a straight route and to complicate matters, some doubled back, so it paid to ask a lot of questions. From Anacortes, we took the ferry that stopped at Lopez and Shaw Island before it landed on Orcas Island. Like a beacon greeting visitors, the Orcas Island Hotel was 100 years old. It was the perfect place for a cup of coffee before changing to the Friday Harbor ferry. Our mission was to find a boat to go whale watching. Most boats were full, but we found the "Odyssey" which promised whale spotting or they would refund our money. Within an hour, we were in the middle of a pod of Orcas. The Captain and mate pointed out their behavioral patterns and how they recognized several members in the pod. On the way out, we could see Mount Baker's snowy peak and a panoramic view of the Olympic and Cascade mountain range. The day was sunny and warm and lovely.

We thought about staying for dinner, but a new friend at the campground was leaving the next day and we wanted to get back to say goodbye. The ferry ride back was very crowded, but we didn't care, as the day's adventure was fresh in our minds.

Our last day on Friday Harbor was very special as old camping friends and new camping friends got together for a sail aboard a 50-foot Cutty Sark sailboat. I saw an advertisement in the local paper and thought it would be a fine farewell as our old friends and ourselves were sailors in previous lives. A caravan of cars brought us to the boat where the Captain greeted us. After all were on board, we undid the dock lines and the sails filled with a light wind. We floated past a mussel factory, which produces 90 percent of mussels sold in the United States and watched the men harvest and re-seeded the mussel traps. Seals lounged on the platforms sunning themselves. We all took turns at the helm and it was sad when the day came to an end.

Our farewell was tearful. We enjoyed seeing our old friends and making new ones. Spending a week with a group of very nice people becomes a special gathering. Even the mechanic, located on the corner, became a friend. He helped us check out a used diesel truck we were considering buying. It seems everything happens for a reason. The dealer wanted too much money and I learned a valuable lesson. Always get a price before engaging an inspection. While chatting with the mechanic, he offered to check out our truck (at no charge) and found a problem with the axle. It was a simple fix, but could have been costly had it not been identified. It seemed like everyone was a friend for that moment in time.

Chapter Ten

The Road To Yellowstone

The tears faded with the miles and thoughts of the adventures that lay ahead. The scenery became more mountainous and within 80 miles we were in the North Cascades. The Cascades have the highest concentration of glaciers in the lower 48 states and they form the backbone of the Pacific Northwest. The range starts in California and traverses north through Oregon, Washington and British Columbia. It encompasses such impressive volcanoes at Mount Lassen, Hood, Adams, St. Helens and the queen of the range, at a height of 14, 410 feet, Mt. Rainier. Broad, lush valleys exist on the rainy west side. The east side has the opposite weather, arid and hot. Regardless of what side of the range one was on, the area is rich in produce. On the west side of the Cascades is the fertile soil of Napa Valley. On the east side are the irrigated orchards that produce numerous varieties of apples, peaches, pears, cherries, and blueberries.

At an altitude of around 4,000 feet, the glacier-topped mountains greeted us with cool weather and fair breezes. The Skagit River traveled with us along Highway 20. To fully appreciate the Cascades, we first stopped at the Visitor's Center. A video showed how man tried to exploit the Cascades, but the country proved too rugged. As the age-old story goes, the white man came along with his axes and tried to harvest the lumber, but the mountains were too steep. Then he tried to extract gold, but there wasn't much of it. In contrast, the Indians knew how to live within the boundaries of its wilderness and took only what they needed and preserved the rest. Eventually the land won and today it remains a pristine wilderness.

It was the second week of August when we arrived at the Colonel Creek campsite along the Skagit River. The river's color was a surprisingly brilliant turquoise, like the waters of the Caribbean. The turquoise color comes from rock that is ground super fine as the glacier expands from the earth's movements. Rains carry the sediment down into the streams and lakes, thus giving it the color. A short walk from our campsite was an area designated for tents. We were curious to see what their sites looked like, and were surprised to find the area almost washed out. Picnic tables were buried under debris and fire rings were turned over and filled with rocks. Streams of water and rocks were everywhere. Charles thought that a boulder might have obstructed the river, which changed it course. I didn't have a clue but knew that the force was tremendous.

A young couple was playing at the river's edge so we asked them if they knew what happened. It was then that we were introduced to the term "active alluvial fan". The lady told us that the mountain ranges of the Cascades are very active, including volcanic Mt. Baker, which wasn't very far. Last October, this area experienced an unusual amount of rain. Since it wasn't cold enough for the water to freeze on the glaciers, the water rushed down the mountain, picking up rocks that the glacier had been grinding below the surface. The result was an avalanche. As rocks and debris tumbled down the mountain, the force fanned out the debris. Here at Colonial Creek, it changed the course of the river by a quarter of a mile. Where there was once a sandy beach and campgrounds was now a river. Lots of granite rock came from the glacier, 13,000 feet up the mountain. I asked if this made headline news in Bellevue, Washington (which was where they were from), and she said this was the way of life in the Cascade

Mountain Range. We found out later that 52 campsites were washed out and that the river reverted back to its original course that existed before the campground was built. The Park Service was going to try to build a road over the river to connect the few remaining campsites with those that weren't destroyed by the avalanche. It was exciting walking over a large fallen tree that lay across the torrential river below.

The overlook at Diablo Lake showed glacier mountains that were once covered by an ocean. At the bottom of these massive mountains, the turquoise waters of Diablo Lake glistened. Further along Rt. 20 we encountered smoke from fires around Rainy Pass. White clouds rose high over the ridge and road signs warned of smoky conditions on the road ahead and a reduced speed limit. Our surroundings became visibly hazy. Firemen watched along the roadside as planes dumped buckets of water. This fire was called the "Freeze Out" and was started by lightning on June 24. It was now only 17 percent contained. Very scary! We later found out that these fires were getting close to the Canadian border and that Canada had asked the United States to help with its containment. News bulletins and warnings of the danger were posted on bulletin boards at every gas station and grocery store in this region.

About 20 miles down the road we reached Washington Pass, and the fire threat was gone. From an overlook, we could see the road as it descended into the valley. The Indians believe that these mountains contain many spirits. In fact, I felt the spirit from my parents. As we walked to the overlook, a bird seemed to be trying to get my attention. It went from tree to tree making a loud chirping sound. As I took in the scenery, two birds sat on a fence, on both sides of me. Charles said they both were looking in my direction. Just that morning I was thanking my Dad for teaching me to appreciate nature and wished he could be with me to see these incredible sights. That day, I felt he was.

As we dropped in altitude, the temperature started to rise. Soon it was in the 90's and made us wish for the Pacific Ocean or the Cascade Mountains. But we knew that in a few days we would be in Yellowstone and it would be cool again.

The arid land started to yield lots of fruit orchards. It is here where we could see that apples are the main crop of Washington State. Orchards were everywhere and wooden crates were being filled with apples getting ready for markets all over the world. Along with apple orchards, we saw peach and pear orchards. Our campsite was on the Alta Lake and it didn't take long to set up and jump in the lake's cool and refreshing waters.

Not far from Alta Lake State Park was Lake Chelan. Huge fires were being reported in the nearby mountains, and the town and lake had a grey look to it. The "Lady of the Lake" boat ride took people into the heart of the Cascades and the villages of Stehekin and Holden. These villages were accessible only by boat and came highly recommended. What they failed to tell us was the boat left at 8:30 in the morning. We reached town around noon and missed the boat. So instead, we drove along the lake and marveled at all the orchards and how big the lake was. A sign for seafood attracted us, so we stopped. We figured we might get lucky and get some Dungeness Crabs for a good price since Seattle was only three hours away. But that didn't happen as the price was eight dollars a pound and the smallest package was two pounds. However, we did have a nice chat with the farmer. He was growing "Delicious" and "Granny Smiths" apples on the hillside that meandered down to the lake. He then picked us some apples right off the tree. They were the best we have ever eaten. He also gave us some corn that he had grown. The farmer recommended basting the corn with maple syrup before grilling. We did that for that night's dinner and it was delicious.

Driving home, we got in an argument about directions. This has been an on-going problem. It seemed when Charles retired, that part of his brain died. He use to be very good with directions and now everything is opposite. If we were supposed to go right, he wanted to go left. In disgust, he told me to drive. No problem, I said and got behind the wheel. It was at night and we were on a major highway. He grimaced when I pulled out into traffic. Not being use to the truck, I almost rammed a car when I tried to change lanes. This had Charles clinging to the handlebars. My driving adventure was capped off when I jumped the curve going into the campground. I guess he won't be asking me to drive any time soon.

At night, the stars were awesome. A picnic table by the lake was the perfect place to star gaze. After about twenty "falling stars" we ran out of wishes and realized that this was a special night. We later found out that August Perseid meteor showers filled the night's sky and folks up and down the lake were lying on their docks watching the show.

As the weekend approached (a difficult time to secure reservations), we were very lucky to get a spot at Steamboat Rock State Park. It was the last reservation with hookups. Baker and Roosevelt Lakes surrounded Steamboat Rock State Park, located five miles from the Grand Coulee Dam. This is a fisherman's paradise and many fisher-families were camped at Steamboat.

Eleven dams stretch across the Columbia and Grand Coulee Rivers that irrigated the land. A brochure said that Coulee means a "steep sided ravine". This ravine was left after the Ice Age receded. Built in 1933, the *Grand Coulee Dam* was the brainchild of Franklin D. Roosevelt as part of the Depression Era Public Works effort. This area was known for rich farmland, but flooding was a big problem. President Roosevelt had a vision of taming the Columbia River (the second largest river in the United States) to irrigate the fields it borders. The Grand Coulee Dam was his solution and it brought water to the fields, which produced the luscious fruits at our markets and aided in flood control. This dam was the largest hydroelectric plant of its time. Our tour of the turbines was cancelled due to the 110 degree heat. By evening, it had cooled down for the nighttime laser show. On the walls of the dam, a colorful presentation depicted the history and accomplishments of the men and woman who built this impressive dam.

On another day, we took a trip to "Dry Falls" where we learned that about "about 17 million years ago, this area experienced the largest lava flow ever to appear on the face of the earth. About one million years ago, the Ice Age began and formed an ice dam that blocked the Columbia River. This sent torrents of water cascading over cliffs, which was 3 ½ miles wide and dropped over 400 feet. Comparatively, Niagara Falls is one mile wide and drops 165 feet. The glaciers then moved south into Washington, Idaho and Montana leaving Dry Falls a skeleton of what was once the world's largest waterfall. Now, all that exists is sheer lava walls devoid of water." It was amazing to see and understand the geology of this area.

Steamboat Rock State Park lay 60 miles northwest of the city of Spokane (pronounced Spoke-CAN') and on the way, all the eye could see were rolling wheat fields. A rich brown soil appeared where the wheat was plowed. The fields were in the middle of their harvest, but no one was working, as it was Sunday.

Not far from Spokane was the Idaho border and the quaint town of Coeur d'Alene. The golf course there is well known and Charles couldn't wait to see it. Tucked off the main street of Coeur d'Alene is Riverwalk RV Park. Being a member of "Passport America", we were able to camp at half price. After setting up, we headed into town. The lady at the Visitor's Center told us of a bluegrass festival going on in the city park. The park was located at one end of Lake Coeur d'Alene and had some very nice beaches with lifeguards. It was great sitting with the locals and listening to live music. After the concert, we went for a walk around town. There were many cute shops along the tree-lined street. One was a candy store that featured over 375 different candies from over 20 countries. Do you remember "wild cherry Scotties" or "Walnetto's"? They were all here, colorfully displayed in glass candy jars with big, metal lids. On the wall hung tin advertisement signs and the display counters were all made of wood and glass. It was nice to see remnants from a bygone era that was my childhood.

The best way to find out what's happening in town is to check with the concierge at the best hotel. In this case, it was the Coeur D'Alene Resort. As we walked through the lobby, its elegance greeted us. Through glass etched doors, we saw the crisp blue awnings shading various boats at the marina. Upon further investigation, we discovered they were 1991 Chris Craft look-a-likes. These boats were taking guests to the Coeur D'Alene Resort Golf Course. Not being shy, we asked the captain if he would take us over to the golf course. He asked if we were staying at the hotel, and without hesitation, we said yes. Off we went, in this beautiful cruiser, across the lake, to an incredible manicured course. What makes it so famous, besides the exceptional greens, is that the 14th hole is a floating island. Golfers are ferried to and from it in a pontoon boat. The gift shop was expensive and classy, but the scorecards were free. We took a few to send to our golfing friends. The average cost to play eighteen holes was $200, but the boat ride was free.

Enroute, leaving Idaho, a sign led us to the oldest building in the State. The Coeur D'Alene Indians built the "Old Mission" with wood from the surrounding area. They numbered around 3,000 and were a peaceful, intelligent, spiritual people who lived in teepees and fished along the banks of the lake. The Indians found their beliefs similar to the preaching of the Jesuit priests whom they called Blackrobes. They both believed in a supreme being, doing penitence and being thankful for the bountiful year. Neighboring tribes had powerful medicine men with great magic and the Coeur D'Alene Indians wanted magic also. The Jesuits seemed to be the answer. They settled in this area in 1842 and taught the Indians many things. Blends of beliefs led to a peaceful existence. When the white man wanted land for the settlers, the priest intervened and made sure that the Coeur D' Alene Indians had a place to live. It was nice to hear a story about Indians that had a happy ending.

A short ride across the tip of Idaho was Montana's "Big Sky Country". We stopped at the Visitor's Center, and got a few campground brochures. There were lots of exciting brochures on hot springs, horseback riding, ghost towns and sapphire and opal mines, (where you can pick your own gems) but Yellowstone was our destination. Knowing how fast the weather can change, we didn't want to get caught in Yellowstone when winter arrived.

The first campground the Visitor's Center recommended sounded interesting, but it was booked. That owner recommended another one down the road. It was getting late in the day, so we couldn't be too choosey. That night we stayed at Ekstrom's Stage Station for a cost of $25 a night. We considered that high, but we didn't have many options.

The registration area used to be a stagecoach stop welcoming travelers and a sign on the door read "Enter Travelers & be Replenished." Log buildings dating back around 150 years were moved here from the surrounding territory. They were original homestead and frontier buildings. A chuck wagon and stagecoach sat nearby. The area looked like it might be used for large gatherings and maybe even a pow-wow. Several teepees were scattered about. A short walk from our campsite took us to "Clarks Fork", which was named by Meriwether Lewis for William Clark during the Corps of Discovery expedition.

There was only one problem at Ekstroms. The bathrooms were deplorable. Useable, but not very clean. The dumpster was overflowing with trash and, not surprisingly, they were having problems with bears. We didn't sleep very well that night, and left the next morning. Rumors were the place was for sale.

As we left Ekstroms, we saw a sign that read "Rock Creek Lodge Testicle Festival, Welcome Hustlers. Have a Ball". Under that read "Montana's Original Since 1982 TESTYFESTY.com". We couldn't believe our eyes. In the parking lot were two big RV rigs and it was there we met Anita and Larry. They spent the night in the parking lot. When traveling in something that big, owners don't have to worry about finding a campsite. They gave us a tour of their rig and it looked like a luxurious condo equipped with a living room, dining room, bedroom, kitchen and bath. The night before, they checked out the bar where the festival was held and said it was a hoot, especially a video of the "Testicle Festival".

From chitchatting in the parking lot, they told us about a lot of neat places to visit and things to do. It was an amazing meeting out in the middle of nowhere. One never knows what's around the next turn.

Chapter Eleven

Buffalos, Bears and Dinosaurs, Oh My!

Entering Yellowstone was one of the highlights of our travels. We had tried to come this way last year, but the weather wasn't cooperating. It was the middle of August and about two weeks ahead of last year's try. What a difference that time made. It seemed this year the timing was right because it wasn't very crowded and temperatures were still warm. Many kids had returned to school, so that left just the retirees and a few young couples. From the mountains and lakes to the geysers and meadows, all the scenery was breathtaking. The land supported herds of buffalo, elk and occasionally, a bear or eagle. There is only one word to describe it. Magnificent!

Yellowstone was established in 1872, but for thousands of years, the Shoshone and Ute Indians used to hunt buffalo, collect medicinal plants, and camp here.

There are two loops in Yellowstone that make a figure eight. Our first day out, we tried to cover the lower loop and only got a quarter of the way around. The vistas change constantly. One minute a forest surrounded us, and then the landscape starts to smoke from the steam vents. There were several lookouts and boardwalks to go exploring. It was a wonder to see the hot springs flow into Lake Yellowstone, which has an average water temperature of 45 degrees. The mountains rose to sharp pinnacles and the valleys were a rich, yellow color. Two fires devastated a lot of the park. In 1988, a fire burnt over 36 percent of the land. More recently, in 2003, another fire broke out. I was happy to see Mother Nature renewing the growth cycle as witnessed by new evergreens, five-feet high.

The most amazing part of Yellowstone was the large animals you meet along the way. A familiar scene was cars pulled over along side of the road and congregations of picture takers armed and ready. For our first sighting, no one was getting out of their cars. We knew why when a huge buffalo came toward us. It passed the window on my side of the truck and I could see right into his eye. It left me shocked and I couldn't stop saying "unbelievable".

The next day, we left early in the morning to check out the "Norris Geyser Basin" campground. It was a huge expanse of "the hottest and most dynamic of Yellowstone's hydrothermal areas. Many hot springs and fumaroles have temperatures above boiling (199°F) and features change daily because of water fluctuations and seismic activity" (from the National Park Trail Guide). A few cars were pulled over because in the field could be seen antlers from the herd of sleeping elk. One elk was waking up and munching on grass. We hurried down the hill to a stream that separated us from the elk. I was able to get within 25 yards of him. Then the elk decided to get a drink of water, right in front of us! Slowly backing off, we watched in sheer amazement. A few more elk started waking up and walking towards the stream. The crowd started to get thicker, so we figured it was time to go. We were so surprised we could get so close.

Old Faithful Inn was celebrating its 100-year anniversary and being fond of old hotels, it was a "must see". A lobby sign listed times of various geysers gushing and Old Faithful was going to blow in about 30 minutes. The blow was usually several hours apart, so lucky us. This gave us time to walk around the Inn.

The first guest checked in at the Inn on June 1, 1904. Since then it has survived a 7.5 earthquake, severe winter weather and still keeps its beauty and charm. Lodge Pole Pines and stone pillars blended in with the outside surroundings. The lobby spans four floors with a veranda for looking down. A huge fireplace reminded us of how cold winter can get. In the meantime, we were enjoying lovely weather.

At the approximate time, Old Faithful blew. It sent plumes 50 feet into the sky. The erruption lasted for about ten minutes and then it returned to a small, bubbling pond. The crowd applauded.

After three days of mind-blowing beauty and close encounters with the animals, we wanted to visit the town of West Yellowstone. In the camping store, a woman came in and said that day was free fly-fishing day at the "International Fly Fishing Show". The registration area was in a Holiday Inn that was not like any Holiday Inn I had seen. It was once the "Oregon Short Line's Yellowstone Special" Terminal designed by the Union Pacific for its wealthy passengers. The bar called "The Iron Horse Saloon" was decorated with animal heads like bear, elk and moose. It had a rugged, manly feel. The beautiful stone fireplace had more animal heads. Above the reception desk, a mounted mountain goat was perched high on a rock. After a day's hunt in Yellowstone, this would be the meeting place for men (and some women) to share tall tales and have a few drinks.

Exploring further, we entered the private railroad car of E. H. Harriman, President of the Union Pacific Railroad. In 1905, he made a special trip to Yellowstone to see if it was feasible to extend the Oregon Short Line and determined it was. Images of the movie, *Orient Express,* flashed in front of us. Narrow, dark wood hallways, private coach sections with plush velvet seats (that turned into beds), ceilings of ornate gold filigree and stained glass windows were part of the decor. In Mr. Harriman's boudoir, the linens were a rich beige silk pin stripe; the coverlet was red velvet and the walls and wardrobes were sumptuous rosewood. Brass fixtures and a porcelain washstand finished his cabin. We left with our mouths agape.

Across the street, the fly-fishing demonstrations were underway. Long ponds were laid out on the lawn and several teachers and free rods invited on-lookers to try the sport. As we were observing the instruction, a man asked if we would take a picture of his wife and her instructor who was a world-renowned fly fisherman. There was great admiration around this man, so I felt the importance of the moment and tried to capture it.

A very cute guy asked if I was from a trade publication because I was taking pictures. I said no. While the picture requestor went to get paper and pen to give me his address, the cute guy took me over to a practice area and gave me a few pointers. He agreed that "Mel Krieger" (the fisherman's guru) was the best. At that moment, I was very close to this gorgeous guy, who had his arms around me as he showed me how to cast. All I could do was smell his cologne and feel his closeness. That doesn't happen very often to a middle-aged, married woman. I hoped that Charles would let me enjoy the moment and he did. Off in the distance, I could see Charles taking my picture. The picture guy then joined us with his e-mail address and introduced us to another instructor who began to show us the basics. I looked around, but cute guy had disappeared. It was a nice moment. We listened to the instructions and Charles picked up casting right away. Me – well, I need a lot of practice. If a tree were near, my line would get tangled in it.

Later in the day, we saw an Imax movie of the Lewis and Clark expedition. It was 100 years ago that they set out from St. Louis in 1804 to explore the Missouri and Columbia Rivers as a passage to the Pacific Ocean. Little did they know that the Rocky Mountains lay in their way. It took them two years and 8,000 miles to accomplish their goal. I was reading an epic novel about Sacagawea, the Indian Squaw, who accompanied them and the book helped bring a deeper perspective to what we were seeing.

We decided to do a day or two trip to Cody, Wyoming, eating out and spending the night in the truck. It made sense to keep the camper at the Lion RV Park in West Yellowstone because we liked it and being members of "Passport of America" made it very affordable. We unpacked a lot of what was in the truck and moved it to the camper to lighten our load. With gas at $2.25 a gallon, every pound less we needed to carry helped our mileage.

Taking our time leaving Yellowstone led us to explore Mammoth Hot Springs in the northern area of the park. It had a massive rock formation of terraces with pockets of boiling blue water and lots of steam. This was also the home to Fort Yellowstone where the barracks are open to visitors. The post office is a large concrete building built in the 30's with stone bear figures guarding the entrance. I asked where the original post office was and discovered a one-room log cabin. It was fun trying to imagine what it was like during the 30's, when folks came here by train and then stagecoach. Some of the grand hotels have burnt down, but luckily a few still remain like the Mammoth Hot Springs Hotel which dates from the late 1800's.

As we approached the park's exit, the familiar bunches of cars were pulled over to the side of the road. This time it was to watch a brown bear. The guard tried to wave us on, but seeing folks knelt with binoculars, we knew it was big. Through our binoculars, we saw the bear lying beside a log with her sleeping cub. We saw the same familiar cars pulling off the road on our way to Cody, Wyoming. This time it was for a big moose that was having lunch by the Shoshone River.

About 15 miles outside of Cody we found another campground listed in the "Passport America" directory called the "Yellowstone RV". For $12 a night, we had clean rest rooms and a plug for our electric blanket. After checking in, we were off to discover downtown Cody. A five-lane highway wasn't what we expected to be going through Main Street of this historic town. It just didn't have that Wild West feel. However, the *Irma Hotel*, built in 1902 by Buffalo Bill, did feel like the Wild West. This was Buffalo Bill Cody's showcase and he named it after one of his daughters. When the Burlington Railroad completed a spur line to Cody, the hotel became a stopping off point for people traveling to Yellowstone. Buffalo Bill had his offices here as well as a private stateroom. The cherry wood bar was imported from France with a carving of a buffalo head at its apex. The rooms were nicely furnished and we could feel the hospitality that was extended by Buffalo Bill to his guests. Many pictures showed him with international dignitaries, including Queen Victoria, who gave him an audience when he took his Wild West Show on European tour. The Grand Duke Alexis of Russia stayed at the hotel before going on a hunting trip. Auditions for his Wild West Show were held down the block. Cody was very proud of his hotel and it showed. At 6 p.m., locals staged a gunfight in the street in front of the hotel and a Buffalo Bill look-a-like stole the show. He fired his pearl-handled guns and brought justice to the town.

We ended the day at the famous Cody Stampede Rodeo. A parade started the show followed by cowboys on bucking broncos, and cowboys rustling cattle. Young-uns raced their horses around barrels as fast as they could ride and the clowns were hilarious. It was a great way to end the day in the Wild West.

A "must do" was the Buffalo Bill Historical Center. It consisted of three wings. One wing was devoted to Wild West art, another to the Plains Indians, and the third to Buffalo Bill himself. The art wing had many paintings and sculptures by Frederic Remington and his protégés. Pictures showed Indian encampments, covered wagons being raided by Indians and Indians being killed by the white man. The whole story was told from many different perspectives. Frederic Remington's studio, imported from New Rochelle, showed his talent as an artist as well as a sculptor. I was surprised to see a group of paintings by N.C. Wyeth, father of Andrew Wyeth. His paintings showed cowboys rustling herds of cattle and what family life was like in the late 1800's. Remington and Wyeth were personal friends of Buffalo Bill and painted him in several of their paintings.

The Plains Indian Room had life-size mannequins of Indians on horses. They showed them migrating to different hunting grounds. Also displayed were the tools they used and the clothes they wore. Several buffalo headdresses were showcased. The Indians believed that if they were wearing a headdress with buffalo horns, they would be protected - that was, till the white man came with their guns.

The last room was a tribute to Buffalo Bill. Born William Frederick Cody, he lived from 1846 to 1917. Many heirlooms had been saved which was a real treat. The original living and dining room from his home showed where he would have greeted his eagerly awaiting guests. Buffalo Bill and his wife's clothes and jewelry were also on display along with several diamond pieces that were gifts from royalty for his expertise in the hunt. Most exciting for me was a movie that showed his Wild West Show. It was filmed at the end of the 19th century in an arena in Chicago. The film was a slightly deteriorated, early black and white film called Kinetocope. It started with Indians setting up their teepees. The story began with the Indians capturing two white women in revenge for a previous atrocity. The grand finale was Buffalo Bill and his cowboys riding in to save the day. The *Wild West Show* was a big hit in the states as well as abroad and toured for close to 30 years. Besides putting on the *Wild West Show*, Buffalo Bill was a famous scout riding for the Pony Express. He also took a keen interest in children and the "Boy Scouts" are named after his scouting abilities. Besides being a scout, Buffalo Bill was a rancher, miner and a Colonel in the U. S. Army. After spending two days in Cody, it really felt like we visited with the legendary Buffalo Bill.

Before leaving Cody, we had to say one last good-bye to Bill's Irma Hotel. The manager let us go upstairs and look into unoccupied rooms where his guests might have stayed. Three floors rose around a magnificent mahogany curving staircase. All the rooms were named after Buffalo Bill's closest friends.

The ride back to Yellowstone took about two hours. There were many tempting National Forest campgrounds along the Shoshone River. Some even had electricity and water, and we heard that the fly-fishing was very good. It started to rain as we entered the East Gate of Yellowstone. A huge buffalo came out into the middle of the road and walked in front of the traffic. It seemed to be an omen to slow down. That night it got very cold and we knew it was time to go. Old Man's winter's breath was in the wind.

The next morning, in a light drizzle, the camper quickly came down. The plan was to have breakfast at McDonalds, but they were charging $1.80 for the $1 meal because they were the only fast food joint in town. Remembering a local bakery from around the corner, we went to Ernie's Deli and Bakery and wished we had discovered it sooner. Even though we spent more money, it was nice patronizing the local businesses. For $3 we split a large, home made bagel with a cheese omelet on top. They also had wonderful, fresh baked cookies.

The road led south to the Grand Tetons and onward to Jackson Hole, Wyoming. The beauty seemed endless with peak after peak jutting up towards the blue sky. A light dusting of snow covered the highest peaks confirming the coming of winter. When the early trappers saw these inspiring peaks, they named them the "Tetons" which means "three breasts". Somewhere, I remembered hearing a "must do" was to take the boat ride across Jenny Lake to the base of the Tetons. For a minimal cost, the boat left us off at a dock across the lake. We found a sign pointing to Hidden Falls, which cascaded down the mountainside, and Inspiration Point, which looked out over the valley. Deep in the rock, a marmot (woodchuck) poised for pictures or food, but we didn't feed it. We barely made it back to the dock to catch the last boat out, which was 6 p.m.

About 30 miles south of the Grand Tetons National Forest was Jackson Hole, Wyoming. In the old days, a cowboy called a valley between mountains a "hole", hence Jackson Hole. We heard it was going to be expensive, but was shocked when a campground in town wanted $40 for a cramped spot. Instead, we opted for a $90 room with a fabulous bathroom, lots of heat (which came in handy for drying out our wet towels from the previous night's rain), cable TV, and a Jacuzzi. That night it got down into the low 30's. The next day, we heard that the east entrance to Yellowstone was shut down for three hours because of snow and they were expecting several more inches that day.

The morning was bright and sunny as we walked around. The nearby entrance to the town's square has arches made from antlers. This was to commemorate the nearby National Elk refuge, which accommodated over 7,500 elk. During the winter, the Boy Scouts would feed the elk and in the spring they collect their shedded antlers and have an auction to raise money for their activities. A sign invited us to have breakfast with the cowboys and sure enough, three booths away, was a rugged-looking man in a cowboy hat and wearing worn buckskins. A closer (discreet) look revealed he was a real cowboy. High on a beam was the American Flag sharing space with the head of a buffalo wearing a top hat. Both the restaurant and town had a lot of character.

As we wandered through town, checking out the old buildings, and peering down alleyways, we spotted the "Jackson Hole Playhouse". It caught my eye and begged to be visited. The sign over the door said it was built in 1918. Certain places have certain spirits. Buffalo Bill's spirit was certainly at the Irma Hotel and here we could feel the jolly saloon crowd getting ready for dinner and a floorshow. The bar stools were saddles, the waitresses were dressed in saloon costumes and a red velvet circular couch graced the lobby. Several kids were milling about and all at once they ran backstage. Of course, I followed. It turned out that the Children's Theatre Academy had weekly programs for aspiring actors. This Wednesday's matinee was entitled "Unfinished Fairytales". The director invited us to stay for the dress rehearsal and we were honored. Inside, the theatre was very authentic and the production lots of fun. Being the only ones in the audience, we provided the ahhaahs, boo's (when the cue card came across the stage) and the laughter. At the end, we gave them a standing ovation. Of course, I took flashless pictures throughout. As we were leaving, the director asked me to send him some pictures.

We searched the map for the most scenic and direct route to Frisco, Colorado, where friends asked if we would cat sit for a week at the end of August. We were happy to oblige. On the way we went through Flaming Gorge to a campground right off Highway 191. All alone with not another car in sight, we drove and drove. The road lead into a gorge and it was getting dark and scary, but the road was good and the weather fair. As darkness approached, a campground came into view. It was called "Firehole Canyon" and was located at the headwaters of the Green River. A fellow camper pointed out the *Alpenglow* sunset on the distant mountains. The campground host was very helpful in making us feel comfortable and warned us not to leave food out, (which we never did). However, I forgot the popcorn bag and in the middle of the night we had a visitor – a mouse. It kept Charles up most of the night trying to find it. When morning came, the mouse left and so did we.

South of Flaming Gorge, near Vernal, Utah, was the "Douglas Quarry Visitor's Center". In 1909, Earl Douglas discovered the first of thousands of dinosaur bones that have been unearthed in the surrounding mountains. The Visitor's Center was a three-story building built into the side of the mountain. There, visitors could view a wall of bones just like the archeologist who found them. A large window showed a slice into the rock and a peek into prehistoric times. That night we camped by the "Green River", in a valley where these giants had once roamed.

The North Cascades, Coeur d' Alene, Yellowstone, Cody, The Grand Tetons, Jackson Hole and Flaming Gorge. It was mind boggling how much there is to see.

Chapter Twelve

A Rocky Mountain High

There is something very special about Colorado. The air seems cleaner and the mountain ranges more inviting. Route 70 follows the Colorado River through the canyons of the vast White River National Forest. It took 12 years to build this scenic highway while respecting the landscape. The highway twists and rises to blend in with the surrounding beauty. On our way to Frisco, we passed the ski resort of Vail and saw the large, mineral swimming pool at Glenwood Springs. The scenery was awesome.

We arrived at our friend's house to be greeted by a neighbor who gave us a key. Another neighbor came over and invited us to join them for a round of golf at the Raven Golf Club at Three Peaks. Charles was in his glory as this fit in with his dream of playing a variety of courses. The course lived up to its name as the three peaks vista was pleasantly distracting. I don't play golf, but enjoyed riding in the golf cart and taking pictures.

Frisco's elevation of 10,000 feet makes it a pretty high place. It is a lovely, small town that has kept its charm while others around it were building and developing around ski slopes. Wherever our eyes looked, the mountains and blue sky came sharply into view. The main street still had a lot of the old buildings from its earlier mining days. A walk down the side streets brought us to small log cabins mixed with new houses. The historical society had purchased ten old log buildings and built a park to preserve their history. The one-room schoolhouse, a trapper cabin and jailhouse were brought back to life. Also, the park is surrounded by sculptures that highlighted Frisco's story. Nearby, Lake Dillon provides both summer and winter sports. Main Street, with its casual restaurants and small boutiques, was a leisurely two blocks walk from our friend's house. How did we get so lucky to have friends here?

A few days of down time allowed me to process pictures and write. Charles cleaned out the camper and truck and got caught up on finances. Since we knew we would be staying in Frisco for a while, we asked our kids to hold our mail until we arrived. We touched base with the local post office and let them know we were expecting a "General Delivery" package. The next day, a thick "Priority Mail" envelope was received. Since most of our finances are setup for automatic transfer that we check on the Internet, there were no surprises.

Once caught up, it was time to do some sightseeing. Someone had told us of hot springs located deep in the mountains. The Visitor's Center at Steamboat Springs gave us directions to "Strawberry Park Natural Hot Springs". After several wrong turns, we were about to give up when the blacktop ended. At the top of a mountain we saw that a few cars were parked, so we went to check it out. Down a narrow, stone staircase we came to a series of hot tubs flowing like a waterfall. On several levels were flagstone patios with wooden chaise lounges. Five waterfalls provided a unique experience to bathe in a variety of temperatures. Because of the difficulty getting to Strawberry Park, I was glad that we wouldn't be driving home in the dark.

Marty and Carol arrived home from their Alaska vacation and were happy to see that their cat had survived their absence. Marty, being an avid fisherman was amused at my interest in fly-fishing and invited us to go fishing with him. Carol went along for the ride and probably the amusement of watching me fish. On the way we stopped in the old town of Leadville and saw the 1880 Jewish cemetery. Gold was discovered here in the 1860, followed by discovery of silver in 1877. What made this town so interesting to me was that a lot of the miners were Jews from Central and Eastern Europe. When one thinks of the Wild West, synagogues are not what comes to mind, but here in Leadville, there were two. Leadville was also known as the training ground for the famed "Soldiers of the Summit". They fought valiantly in World War II and helped defeat the Germans in the Swiss Alps. Once a vibrant mining town, the architecture of the houses was impressive. Some of its wealthy citizens were the notably Meyer Guggenheim and the "Unsinkable Molly Brown".

The lake that Marty took us to was out in the middle of nowhere. He fitted me up in a pair of his waders and into the water we went. The lake had a grassy bottom and I was afraid that I would fall. Taking my time and making sure of my footing, I was able to wade out, waist deep. To my surprise, the "waders" didn't let any water in and were very comfortable. On my first cast, our lines got tangled. Marty shook his head, undid the lines and moved farther away from me. What a thrill to be standing waist deep in a lake surrounded by mountains. Marty caught several fish, but they weren't biting for Charles or me. It didn't matter because the day was a lot of fun.

Another day we all drove to Denver taking a side trip to the "Red Rocks Amphitheater". Two 300-foot columns of red sandstone encircled the stage making it a perfect place for concerts, both acoustically and visually. A band was setting up for that night's performance and I could hear "rap". At the gift shop, I asked what band was playing and was told it was the "Beasty Boys". This happened to be my son's favorite band. I left a message on his cell phone of where I was and held the phone close to the stage, so he could hear their crew setting up. We didn't see much of Denver because the end of season sales got our attention. We all got lucky at Eddie Bauer's sale.

There was so much to do that every day was an adventure. One night, it snowed and left a dusting on the mountains behind the house. It was beautiful. Breckinridge, a nearby town, was having a crafts fair and people seemed excited about the prospects of snow. The fair took up a good portion of the town and had many interesting items for sale, all at good prices. I could have bought a lot, but then Charles asked, "Where are you going to put it?". Since I didn't have an answer, we just shopped and admired with our eyes.

Rocky Mountain National Park was our next destination, but before entering the park a big sign on the front porch of the Grand Lakes Lodge said "End of Season Sale". How could I resist? Inside was a large lobby with comfortable chairs inviting everyone to sit a while. It was a very busy lobby and the guests seemed genuinely happy. The gift shop was off the lobby and it gave me a thrill because the jewelry was unique and everything was 50% off. Charles bought me a beautiful turquoise and lapis necklace that I will treasure forever.

It was an easy ride to the peaks of the Rocky Mountains. Slowly, the forest gave way as we rose above the tree line, which encompassed about one third of the park. From the Visitor's Center, we followed the "Trail Ridge Road" and along the way, admired the snow covered peaks that were on the horizon and the emerald colored glacier lakes that sparkled in the mountain's crevices. At Long's Peak we reached 14,259 feet. This was the highest point we had ever been. The wind blew fiercely and it was difficult getting out of the truck. In fact, it felt like the wind was going to blow the truck off the road. At an overlook, we watched as a brave soul attempted to stand. She had to lean into the wind to be kept from being swept away. Along the edge of the road, six-foot high sticks reminded us of how high the snow gets in the winter. Returning to the valley floor, it was nice to see the green of large Ponderosa pines, the mighty Douglas firs, the glistening blue spruces and stout Lodge Pole pines.

Wanting to see more high peaks in Colorado, Pike's Peak was our next day's trip. Images of early settler's wagons with signs reading "Pike's Peak or Bust" played in our minds. From an overlook, we could see where the Great Plains ended and the mountains began. The Ute Indians would pass this way going to and from their winter quarters. They probably would climb these mountains to set traps for eagles and other prey. The eagle was especially important because its feathers were treasures and used in headdresses and ceremonies.

We passed a road that lead up to the summit of Pike's Peak and were reminded about an automobile race I had heard of. A brochure noted that the "Pike's Peak Hill Climb" was the second oldest, continuous automobile race in the country which was run in 1917. The oldest automobile race was the Indianapolis 500 that dates back to 1911. Not wanting the difficult task of driving up the mountain, we opted out for the "Manitou & Pikes Peak Cog Railway". Mr. Zalmon Simmons, owner of the Simmons Mattress Company, was so taken with the beauty of this land that he organized and funded a company to build a cog railroad. A sign at the train station read, "Built in 1891. This railway was able to overcome the exceptional steep grades of Pike's Peak – up 25 percent - by employing the ingenious propulsion system of Roman art." The cog railroad's tracks are smaller than that of a regular railroad, and a rack-and-pinion mechanism help pull the trains up the hill. It was a very exciting ride, one that I know we will take again. At the summit, was a huge sign that said we were at 14,110 feet.

It seemed that Pike's Peak and The Broadmoor Hotel complimented each other. The Broadmoor was originally built as a casino in 1891. With the advent of tourists coming to see Pike's Peak, it flourished into a grand hotel. With the mountain backdrop, the striking pink stucco exterior stood out like a precious jewel, and the interior of the hotel was one of the most opulent I had ever seen. Charles and I wandered around this five-star hotel with our eyes wide open in wonderment. Crystal chandeliers hung in the ballrooms from the Wedgwood embossed ceiling and the bathrooms were a decorator's delight done in gold and black. Each sink had a bottle of luxurious hand cream and several hand towels were stacked neatly under gold-embossed sconces. One of the most amazing sights of The Broadmoor is the pool. Large cabanas with curtains of bright yellow and white stripes give the guests privacy. Since there was no one around, Charles and I had to sit down on the navy blue pillows and pretend that we were one of the fortunate to be able to afford this wonderful hotel. I heard that on Valentine's Day, the Broadmoor has a $99 special. I wondered how high the snow would be.

Rosh Hashanah, the Jewish New Year, was the middle of September and was fast approaching. I was looking forward to going to services with Marty and Carol. Marty and I use to go to services when he shared a house with me many years ago, back in Maryland. It was a very special feeling spending the holiday with them and their friends at the appropriately named "Synagogue on the Summit (SOS)". It was a small service put together by members of the congregations and their commitment was very spiritual. Sadly, we had to say goodbye to our dear friends as we headed south.

Chapter Thirteen

Going Home to the Aftermath of "Hurricane Charley"

Traveling quickly, with one night stays, we made our way from Colorado through the northeast corner of New Mexico to arrive in Houston, Texas. This trip took four days. From the cable TV at our Houston campground, we watched hurricanes bombarding Florida and we were getting anxious. One after another they blew through - Frances, a category two, Jeanne, a category three, and Charley scaring us the most at a category four. Even more frightening was that Charley came close to our condo. That was when I felt I had to go home.

Just before Hurricane Charley threatened the west coast of Florida, it was the Jewish Holiday of Yom Kippur. This is the "Day of Atonement" and it was important for me to be in synagogue. Having previously attended services in Houston, I called and asked if I could worship there. They were happy to have me. Yom Kippur is the holiest of days in the Jewish religion and we spend the day fasting for sins and praying for a good, peaceful new year. Our friends in Houston weren't home, so we found a "Passport of America" campground just outside Houston. It was clean and comfortable. Trying to comply with various aspects of religion can be challenging while traveling, but it can also be very rewarding. The woman I sat next to during services invited us back to her home to break the fast.

The year 2004 will be remembered as having the most hurricanes to hit Florida. We heard that Highway 10 near Pensacola had been washed out. A call to my neighbor in the condo downstairs confirmed the horror that was gripping Floridians. Laverne said all was safe, but the winds were terrible. It was after that conversation that I booked a flight home. It was easy to get an inexpensive flight out of Houston and make arrangements for a friend to meet me at the airport. Charles said he didn't mind bringing the camper home himself.

On the drive from the Tampa airport, I saw debris everywhere. It was a relief to see our complex fairly untouched, although a few trees were down. Knowing that humidity was a problem in Florida, it was with much trepidation that I opened the door to see if mold had formed on the walls. I was grateful for my friend's company. We went from room to room, sniffing like hound dogs, trying to detect any smell of mildew. Ah! Everything was as it should be, that is until we opened the refrigerator. Yikes! Mold was everywhere, as this was the only appliance not left open. We had disconnected the electric and never thought to leave the door open. My friend quickly showed me how to clean it with "Fantastic", a cleaning solution that I had under the sink. Since we were planning on buying a new refrigerator, I was lucky this wasn't a costly mistake.

And so ended a two-year journey. They say nothing stays the same and that change is inevitable. In our case, it was a whirlwind. I look back with great memories and I hope this book will encourage you to travel the road of adventure or at least enjoy the trip from your favorite reading spot. There is so much out there to see and experience. In school, I wasn't a very good student, but seeing, feeling, and tasting has made me realize how special our country is. Each turn in the road had a story and it was these stories that I shared with friends. I really surprised myself in researching details to make these stories more interesting. Unintentionally, I pushed my envelope beyond my imagination, and did it all while *Popping Up Across America.*

Afterward

What a difference a year or two makes. When we first traveled along the Florida coast, who would have thought Florida would experience three hurricanes. In 2004, Hurricane Ivan did the most damage, submerging Big Lagoon State Park's office under four feet of water. In 2006, I called Big Lagoon State Park and was assured that the park was on the mend. They said they had rebuilt the observation tower as well as most of the walkways. However, the beach suffered a lot of erosion and downed trees were still a problem. Fortunately, Big Lagoon is open for business with 90 percent of the campsites operational.

As if that wasn't bad enough, in 2005 Hurricane Katrina devastated New Orleans as well as the Gulf Coast. The Jefferson Davis Library was severely damaged as was most of the Gulf coast that runs from Biloxi to New Orleans, especially along Beach Boulevard. It will take a long time to recover.

Bayou Segnette State Park, near New Orleans, was damaged and the park is closed to house victims from that terrible storm. Sadly, no date has been set for it to open to campers.

The towns of Jean Lafitte and the Barataria will take a long time to recover. However a call to the Barataria Preserve of Jean Lafitte Historical National Park assured me that most of the trails are open as well as the Visitor's Center in the town of Jean Lafitte. Jeannette from the Victoria Inn in Jean Lafitte (1-800-689-4797) describes the bayou as brown. She said the grass and trees suffered major damage, but regrowth is visible.

Tried and True Travel Tips

CAMPER LAYOUT

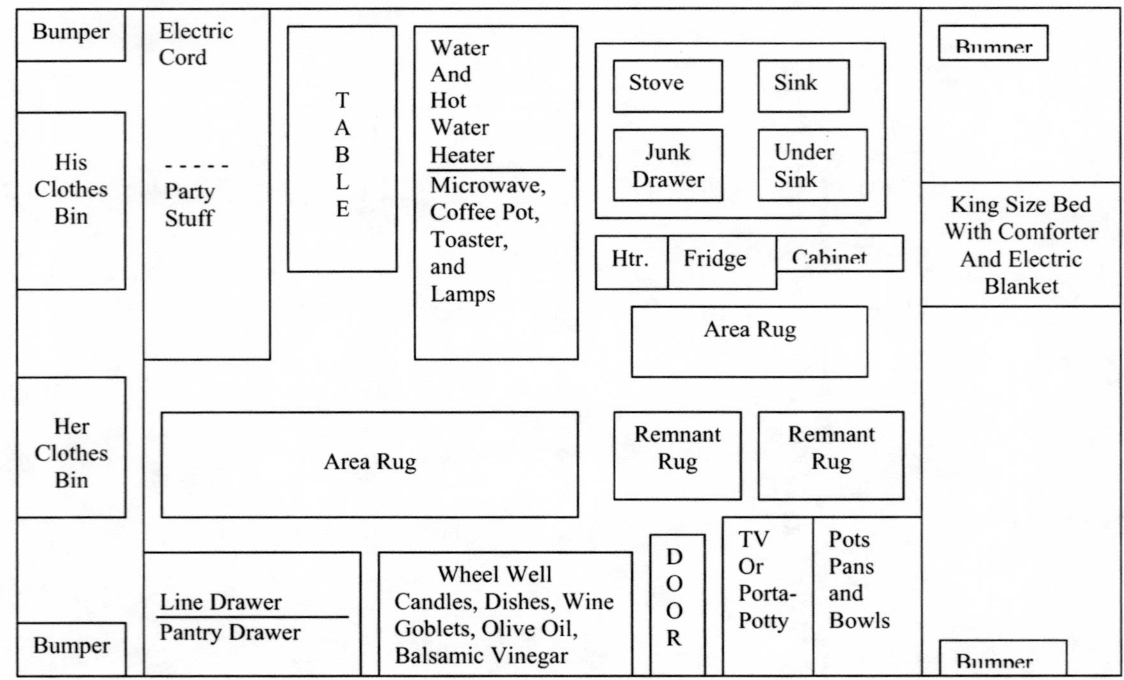

Preparing to Leave Home

This can be a very stressful time. If you plan well, then you can leave with a clear mind. This is just a model for you to plan your departure for an extended trip.

Before you go, make sure to give a neighbor and/or relative a key to your home and car along with the number of your cell phone. Our neighbor said he used the car key once when the alarm went off. He was able to shut it off, thus saving us a dead battery when we return home.

Change the filter in your air conditioner/heater and any water filters (e.g. sink and refrigerator). That way, it is one less thing to do when you come home. If you have a battery powered smoke detector, now would be a good time to change the battery.

We leave our air thermostat at 78 degrees. If you live in a hot climate, where your air conditioner might be running a lot, have a neighbor change the filter for you while you are away. We live in central Florida so our neighbor changes ours every three months.

Turn off main water valve and turn off the electric to the hot water heater.

We turn our refrigerator to medium-low and fill it with water jugs so less space needs to be chilled. Another choice is to turn off the refrigerator, cleaned out, and prop open the door so air can circulate inside and prevent mold.

Vacuum behind the refrigerator to remove any dust particles that might ignite.

We unplug all appliances except refrigerator but turn off the icemaker.

Leave a copy of the "Personal Spreadsheet" (see Spreadsheets at the end of this chapter) with a close relative or friend, along with instructions as what to do in case of an emergency.

Call your credit card company before you go and let them know you will be traveling. They will appreciate it and understand why charges from around the country are being made.

If you have an extra car that you are leaving behind, keep the tank three quarters filled with gas. That way, if it is hot and the gas expands, it won't drip out. Check with your car insurance company, as you may be able to get a deep discount because the car is not being used.

We cover our car and secure the cover with bungee cords. When we return, the car is taken in for a check-up, as tires tend to deflate when the car is sitting still.

Lock all windows and doors.

Make copies of items in your wallet or purse such as credit cards, driver's licenses, passports, vehicle and medical insurance cards, vehicle and camper registration. If your wallet or purse is stolen, these copies should be easily retrievable for quick action to contact the appropriate authorities.

Truck Maintenance Before You Leave

Change oil, oil filter, power steering, and brake fluid.
Change transmission oil and filter.
Check front wheel bearings and brake pads.
Check radiator and anti-freeze.
Check tires including your spare and inflate to recommended pressure.
Check batteries. Make sure you have your warranty with you.
Have a supply of motor oil.
Always log your maintenance into the "Vehicle Maintenance Log" (found at the end of this chapter).
Have some kind of road insurance for emergency situations.

Camper Maintenance Before You Leave

It is advisable to do a dry run before an extended trip to check for the following:
Check and fill propane tank.
Check lights and brakes.
Make sure furnace, water heater and air conditioning are working properly.
Take along any specialty tools you may need.
Take along all maintenance books for vehicle and camper.

Have wheel bearings repacked every 12,000 miles of camper use. Confirm this figure with you owner's manual, as each camper may be different. We have our wheel bearings examined every 6,000 miles. Have the camper checked out by a certified dealer who will look at the lift system, the hitch and tire inflation including the spare.

Husband's Handy Tools

Leather Gloves
Rags (cheap wash clothes work well)
Digital tire pressure gauge
Voltage meter to check battery, 12V lights, and incoming current from the campsite's electrical box.
Gorilla and Elmer's Glue
Flashlights and batteries
Duct tape, electrical tape and measuring tape
Toolbox (pliers, flat and Phillips head screwdrivers, wrenches, hammer, saw, assortment of nuts, bolts, screws and nails)
Fifty feet cable wire and 50 feet heavy-duty power cord. This is used for the ceramic heater because it takes a lot of volts. It is also used as an extension if the 30-amp cord is not long enough to connect to the electrical box.
Flares, reflective warning signals and jumper cables
Extra drive belt and fuses

Mail

We have been fortunate to have our kids handle our mail. An "Official Change of Address Kit" was filled out at the post office, which forwarded our mail to them. You can also go on line at *www.usps.com* or call 1-800-ASK-USPS. It is a good idea to follow-up with the post office in a few days to make sure that the form has been processed which should be done in 24 hours. One year, the form fell between the cracks and the lesson learned is to always follow-up.

If you'd rather not bother your kids, mail services exist. For a nominal fee, they will give you a post office box and all your mail can be forwarded there. A simple phone call from the road will have your mail forwarded to you "General Delivery" at the nearest post office. You can call 1-800-ASK-USPS for zip codes or any post office will be able to help you. All you need to do is estimate where you will be and find out the zip code of that post office. The post office will hold your mail up to 30 days before returning it to sender.

Check with your Yellow Pages for a service in your town. Here are some useful numbers and web sites for mail forwarding services, to help you receive you're mail while on the road.
Escapees at - www.escapees.com - 1-800-231-9896
Good Sam's Club at - www.goodsamsclub.com - 1-800-234-3450
America's Mailbox - www.Americas-Mailbox.com - 1-866-747-3700
Mailroom - www.mailroom@atlantic.net - 1-800-921-9328
Fast Forward Remail - www.FastForwardRemail.com - 1-866-624-5523
Mail Call USA - www.mailcallusa.com - 1-877-447-2758
Snow Bird Mail - www.snowbirdmail.com - 1-800-800-0710

The Camper

Putting Up the Camper

Before entering a site, we both get out the truck and walk around checking for rocks, protruding tree roots, low lying or fallen branches, discuss where the most level place is to put the camper and look for anthills. We learned this the hard way when we found ants in the camper that traced back to one foot being on an anthill. Charles then backs the camper into the spot with me giving him hand directions. We never yell. Our signal for a problem is holding our hands crossed in front of our chest with clenched fist. Since Charles always has me in his sight, he can stop immediately. We then discuss and resolve the problems. Sometimes, I need to walk away and let him do his thing, as long as there is no danger.

Four levelers are attached to the outside of the camper. Two are on the centerline of both sides and one is centerline in the front, and one is centerline in the back. A quick look at them will tell if the camper is balanced. If it is determined that we are not level, then before detaching the camper, we put several one-half inch, pressurized boards under the back of the camper's tires. We use the truck to drive up on them. The chocks are then put in place. Most of the time, this is effective and perfect balance is achieved. After making sure that the chocks are set around the wheels, Charles disconnects the truck and I drive it a few feet from the camper. This is a good time to take off the air conditioning cover, if you plan on using it. The camper is raised and the stabilizer legs are lowered. If the ground is sand or soft grass, a brick about 2 inches thick, is put under the stabilizer legs to keep them from sinking into the ground. Having a level camper will prevent back problems because you will be walking on a flat surface.

Charles starts attaching the water, water filter and electric. It takes me about fifty-seven cranks to raise the camper. I think it is important that the same person crank and count. That way, you can hear and feel the gears in motion and know when to stop.

Once the camper is raised, we extend the bed platforms, connect the bungee cords that keep it taut and connect the poles under the bed boards. Carefully, we walk the door down, secure it in its groove and we are home. After the water is connected, it is run through the lines to get any air out. Turning on the air conditioner also checks the electric current connection. The total process takes about 10 minutes.

Taking Down the Camper

First, we make sure everything is put away and there are no obstructions. The throw rugs are always shaken out and the floor swept. I drizzle liquid Clorox into the sink to sanitize it. The microwave, coffee maker and toaster are put away under the settee. If there is time, I'll wipe down the cabinets and floor with a mild detergent. The clothing and paper bins are placed on the floor and the extra blankets are laid on the flat area of the collapsed dining table. The paper towel holder is dismantled and put in the clean plastic trash bucket.

Once Charles disconnects the water, we turn the faucet on to take the air out of the lines. A quick wipe with a paper towel removes any moisture in the sink. I also like to polish around the handles and spigot, as it is nice to see it shinning and clean when setting up. The door in then dismantled. Charles detaches the inside bed poles and goes outside to wipe down the canvas with a damp rag.

Charles then disconnects the electric. The electric cord is fed back into the camper, under the settee. I neatly coil it to keep it from tangling. The water hose is drained and joins the filter in a bucket. This is stored in the camper, next to the clothes bins.

That completes the inside process. Now I join Charles outside to undo the cords under the bedding, disconnect the poles and push the beds in. I begin to crank down. At the halfway point, both Charles and I walk around the camper tucking in all the sides. We pay particular attention to make sure that the clips are fastened as they have a tendency to get caught. We fold the screen into the camper as if it were an envelope. I have to stand on the front tongue and back bumper to reach in and make sure there is nothing sticking up. At three-quarters of the way down, we walk around the camper again; running our hands along the fold, making sure everything is tucked in with as few creases as possible. The door is closed and locked. If this is done properly, the reward is an easy closure. If not, the top is raised and redone until closure is easy.

A final walk around the camper checks that the water and electric hook-ups are covered. The stabilizer legs are then raised and the camper is ready to be connected to the truck. With chocks still in place, the front of the camper is lifted to accommodate the connection to the truck.

I back the truck up and Charles uses hand signals to direct me to the camper. The first thing I do when I get in the truck is put down the windows so as not to lock the keys in the ignition. If there is a problem, he comes to the truck window and explains what he is seeing. There is never any yelling. It is important not to hurt yourself when connecting the camper. Don't try to push it or pull it to the ball, just drive forward and start over again. With a little patience and good directions, it can easily be achieved. It has become a game to see how close to the connection we can get it. Charles connects the sway bar and secures the electric cord to the truck with a bungee. He locks the tongue with a sturdy combination lock, checks that the back lights and signals are operational and puts his full weight on the back of the camper to make sure the hitch is hitched. We take off the chocks and if necessary, drive it off the platform. The bricks and chocks are retrieved and stored. Lastly, we walk around the campsite, picking up any trash. The camper's creed is "*take only photos and leave only footprints*". We then take a moment to say "thank you" for a wonderful stay.

Making The Camper a Home

Throw rugs add a lot of warmth to the camper. The floors are kept clean by a quick sweep and shaking the rugs out. A small hand vacuum helps get into corners and hard to reach places.

Chotchkies (stuff) such as a "dream catcher" dangle from the bar above our bed. Mobiles, purchased at special places, hang on the snaps for the door. Another great spot to hang things is the door wire near the entrance. We even screwed a small eyehook in the ceiling for a porcelain balloon picked up at the Albuquerque Balloon Fest. A "welcome" sign is attached to the front of the camper and a frog holds a red disc to show us where the curb is. A shoe brush and an outdoor rug completes our "home" and helps clean our shoes off before entering.

We carry two small electric lamps, like the ones you may have on your nightstand at home. At night they add a nice glow in the camper for watching TV or reading.

Another household item we love is the electric blanket. We turn it on an hour or so before we go to bed to warm up the sheets. The blanket thermostat is kept in between our pillows so we can easily turn it off, during the night, when it gets too hot.

To ward off the chill, when relaxing in the evening, we have a ceramic electric heater. Do be very diligent about where the cord is and do not leave it on if you leave the camper. If it gets really cold, the camper's thermostat controlled propane heater works like a charm.

Since it is just the two of us, we close the curtain on the extra bed with clothespins. This minimizes the area being heated

Suggestions and Ideas

We found the Wal-Mart atlas to be very helpful because it clearly show campgrounds as well as the closest Wal-Mart, which sometimes is the only store around. On the first page of the atlas, we mark the date we left and the odometer reading. A highlighter diligently marks our route. We make other notations such as *spectacular scenery, a good motel, cheap gas* etc. on each state's page. Yellow highlighters fade so use another color.

Placing wine bottles in socks helps to prevent them from breaking. If they do break (which has happened), the glass is contained and wine is not splattered all about. As an added precaution, if we have extra wine, we keep the bottles in a bucket. Beer is kept in its original box, which also prevents breakage.

Unwrapped peppermint gum left on the picnic table helps keep mosquitoes and flies away.

Camping stores have a laundry bin that folds up into a disc. It fits perfectly in between our two clothing bins that reside on the opposite bed. When traveling, it stores under the table.

Travel with two soft suitcases, in case you need to fly home or spend a few nights visiting friends.

A bungee cord, fitted from the pole latches underneath the rear of the camper makes a great place to dry towels or bathing suits. If we need to leave and the towels are still damp, they are laid over the food and medical bins in the cap of the truck.

Having a compass in the truck has proven invaluable. It keeps us on track. On the dashboard is the GPS that assists in navigation. It lets us know how much further to go to connect with a road and identifies our exact location.

In the truck, we have a CB for weather updates and listening to the truckers when there are accidents on the road or detours. The truckers are helpful in telling us where cheap fuel can be found, what the problem is, and alternate routes.

We keep our shoes in an open plastic tray in the cap of the truck. That way, if they are wet or muddy, they don't mess up the truck or the camper.

If the hitch lock gets stuck (which happened once) a handy hacksaw blade will cut it. We found that the park service is likely to have such a tool.

Large pinecones are great fire starters. Take four pinecones and place them so that the tips are touching. The tips are filled with sap that is collected when they hang down from the tree. Sap is highly flammable, so be careful. Then add wood and you will have a great fire. When we find large pinecones, like the ones from the Pacific Northwest, we keep a supply, double bagged, in the back of the truck.

Line kitchen drawers and cabinets with wallpaper remnants found at Goodwill. Not the sticky stuff, which is hard to get off. The wallpaper has some weight to it and by putting a lip around the edges will keep dirt in. For yearly housekeeping, it is easy just to throw the liner away and replace with a new one.

On the sink shelf, next to the bed, is a clock When you touch it, it lights up and gives the time, day, date and temperature. Accompanying the clock is a night mask, which I use when there is an irritating light outside, like one that might be near the bathhouse.

No-see-um bugs hate air conditioning and fans. If they are out, we use the air conditioner before 10 p.m. and switch to a fan for the rest of the night. Most campgrounds have "quiet" hour from 10 p.m. till 7 a.m.

If the sticker falls off the cranking mechanism that shows which way to crank, re-mark it with a *Sharpie* indelible pen to show which way is open.

I take family pictures that are dear to me. To keep them safe, they are wrapped in bubble wrap and then put into a zip-lock bag. These are stored under the settee.

It seems I accumulate a lot of paper when we travel. Many magazines have helpful articles. While waiting in the laundromat for the clothes to be finished, or waiting in a doctor's office, I will tear articles out of old magazine. Then there are the brochures that are picked up at Visitor's Centers. I keep organized by separating paper into categories and storing them in gallon-size freezer strength Ziploc bags. Some of the categories are: File for articles on health, travel, camping information; Read general articles from magazines, and Computer for items that need to be input like recipes and travel information. An accordion file could also work.

Have you ever lost a screw from your glasses? To prevent this from happening, apply a small drop of crystal clear nail polish to the threads of the screws before tightening them.

When putting the camper away after a trip, or if there is no food in the refrigerator, it is turned off, left open by the specially designed locking mechanism. This is to prevent mildew. As an added precaution, we wedge a pillow in the door.

Dumb Things Worth Remembering

Use a heavy-duty household electric cord to power the ceramic electric heater. We went out visiting for a few hours with the heater unattended on a household cord. We came back to find that the mattress was burnt. Fortunately, the material was fire retardant and all we got was the impression of the wire, but it could have been a lot worse. We quickly changed to a dedicated, heavy-duty extension cord, lead from the 120-amp plug on the outside electrical box and always turn the heater off when we are out.

When taking down the camper, never force it to close. On time we left the paper towel holder in place and the camper wouldn't close. After opening it up, we found our mistake. There is always a good reason. You just have to find it.

One day, when it was really hot, we turned on the air conditioner and nothing happened. We scratched our heads in wonderment. Then the light bulb went off as we remembered we forgot to take off the air conditioner cover.

In hot weather, always drink plenty of water and slow down. We had the unfortunate experience, in Lake Powell, of Charles passing out because he was dehydrated.

Don't be surprised if you set off the alarm in the camper when spraying bug spray with Deet. You may want to do this outside. It is very toxic, but does keep the mosquitoes away.

Make sure you have a spare handle to open the camper and put down the legs. Somehow, I lost one. Fortunately we had a spare. If not, we would not have been able to set up the camper.

Very important: Whether putting the camper up or taking it down, before you step out of the truck, make sure a window is down. Once, I locked the keys in the truck, while it was running. We were lucky to have a spare key to open the door. We recommend that you do not use the magnetic key boxes for storage of an extra key. They can fall off or you can forget where you put them. Both incidences happened to us.

Also important is to make sure the chocks around the camper wheels are in place before the truck is disengaged. This should be the first thing done when setting up and the last thing done after the camper is attached to the truck. After all, you don't want the camper roll away.

Husband's Tips

To connect to water, Charles uses a two-foot long hose from the campsite's main water spigot that is attached to a Cullegan RFV-10 water filter. From the filter, a 25-foot hose connects to the camper. The water filter is supported in a three gallon bucket with two indentations where the water hoses rest. Holes in the bottom are for drainage. Underneath the camper's outside water drain is a 5-gallon bucket to collect gray water from the sink. When we are ready to leave, all this water apparatus goes into the bucket and is stored in the camper along with a pressure gauge and Y valve, in case we need to share the water with another campsite.

An anti-sway bar attached to the truck hitch and trailer tongue prevents the camper from swaying.

RV stores carry rubberized, black covers for the ball hitch. The ball is greased so that the camper is easily lowered onto it. The black covers keep the grease off our clothes, legs and hands.

Put Comet cleanser around tires and jacks to prevent ants from climbing into the camper.

Use Silicone spray sparingly, to lubricate the external lift system and swing down stabilizers.

Check tire pressure before leaving, and visually inspect tires at each stop.

Periodically, the front of the camper body and the front of the truck are wiped down with an oil base "Orange" cleaner. This helps keep bugs from sticking to the exterior

To wash the canvas, fill a 5-gallon bucket with water and mix one-quarter cup concentrated car-washing soap with 1 cup Clorox. Apply with a soft brush and wipe off with clean water.

It is most important to read and re-read the Owner's manual and understand it. If you have any questions, call your dealer.

Bins and Canvas Bags

In the truck are 3 bins, which house the medicine cabinet, food overflow and Charles's tools. In the camper are his and her clothes bins and a paper bin. In addition are:

Computer and Printer

The computer is stored in a black computer case, which is on the back seat's floor. It is covered with our sweatshirts and rain jackets. Sometimes I use the computer, when traveling, to compose e-mails, write stories and read travel files. The printer is kept in the back of the truck, which we use to print correspondence, envelopes and business cards.

Also under the back seat is a container of office supplies, described under "Office Supplies".

Munchies

A canvas snack bag, in the back seat, satisfies on the road munchies. Granola bars and road side market fruit is always delicious. Sometimes, before we leave a site, I will cut up slices of cheese and bag it. My favorite snack, besides cookies, it to pour some almonds and raisins in a zip-lock bag. Beef jerky, pretzels, and Dove chocolate squares (bagged) have all found their way into the snack bag. Also, in a gallon Ziploc bag are napkins, hand wipes, plastic utensils and small pocketknife. Bring on the impromptu picnic.

Rags and Ropes

A separate canvas bag contains rags and another canvas bag is for rope and bungee cords. These are tucked into the back of the truck.

Laundry

A large box of powder detergent is kept in the truck. Small amounts are transferred into a small bucket with a lid for easier carrying. In a canvas bag goes a bleach stick (for whites only), Shout stain remover stick and fabric softener sheets.

Fishing Poles, Walking Sticks and Beach Umbrellas

These are stored in a golf bag bought at the thrift store for $5.00. The reels are in the side pockets of the golf bag. It rests on the wheel well in the back of the truck secured by a bungee cord.

Clothing Bins

His and her clothes bins are kept in the camper. It keeps our clothes easily accessible. Below is a list of the clothes we take.

An extra pair of glasses and extra sunglasses are kept in these bins.

When camping, the his and her bins are kept on the opposite bed from where we sleep. In front of the bins are our waterproof satchels for toiletries.

His:

1 pair nice dress slacks
2 nice short sleeve dress shirts
4 "golf" shirts
3 pairs of shorts
1 "work" shirt
2 bathing suits
2 baseball type hats
Underwear and socks

1 pair of sandals for showers
1 pair of sneakers
1 hooded sweatshirt and sweat bottoms (to sleep in on cold nights)
1 Suede Jacket
1 Lightweight all-weather jacket kept in the back of the truck.
1 Sweatshirt also kept in the back of the truck
Foul Weather Boots kept under the back seat

Hers:

I keep a plastic bag in the corner of my bin for underwear, as I tend to change them the most. Next to the plastic bag are my socks. I found wearing white socks wicks away moisture and keeps my feet dry and clean.
1 Dress Pants Outfit with Jacket. Jacket can also be worn with jeans to dress them up.
1 Hooded Sweatshirt to sleep in. If you keep your head warm, then your body will be warm.
3 Short Sleeve Blouses
3 T-Shirts – you will probably buy more on the road
5 Tank Tops (I live in these)
3 Long Sleeve Tops
3 pairs of shorts
2 bathing suites
1 pr of jeans
Underwear and socks
1 pair of sandals for showers
Sneakers
Flip-flops for showers
Beach wader

Office Supplies

Office supplies are kept in two places - in a container under the back seat of the truck. Larger items, such as brown padded envelopes and writing tablets are kept under the settee. The container under the seat has:

Legal envelops
Thank you note cards
Pre-printed return labels
Disc's to back up the computer
Music disc's to record friends CD's
Pencils and Pens
Highlighters – various colors and Sharpies to permanently mark things
Velcro
A small scissors
A small stapler with extra staples
Rubber bands
Paper clips (large and small)
Black clips (various sizes)
Scotch tape
3 x 4 post-its

Business cards come in handy when exchanging information with new friends you meet along the way. They can be printed on the computer.

I always keep a few pens and the 3x4 post-its in the front next to me, to jot down notes.

Bedding

We take two pairs of sheets, flannel for cold weather (like on the west coast) and cotton for warm climates (like the desert). The higher the thread count of cotton, the softer the sheets. Over the mattress and under the sheet is an egg carton mattress cover, which keeps the mattress clean and is comfortable to sleep on.

Four large beach towels are put on the long sides of the beds where the tenting is hooked underneath the bed boards. The towels are rolled up as bumpers to keep insects out and it helps insulate the bed area. The towels are folded in half and laid on the bunks for easy storage when closing.

A nice bedspread, two pillows, the electric blanket and a throw blanket make up the bedroom.

The Kitchen

With limited space, here is how I arrange our kitchen.

I prefer silverware to plastic and bought place settings at Goodwill. They have a nice selection along with other houseware items. Most of the time, paper plates, bowls and napkins are used. When we are settled for a while, the bulk of these are kept in a bin, stored outside of the camper, underneath the back bunk. When traveling, this bin is stored on the floor of the camper and fits between the settee and drawers.

We store plastic wine glasses in a canvas bag in the cabinet near the wheel well. Also in this area are large candles stored in heavy-duty Ziploc bags, Corelle dishes (for special occasions) and to the right, near the drawer, stand olive oil, balsamic vinegar and a bottle of wine. This is the center of the camper, which is the most stable place. Bottles are kept in an old pair of clean socks. Tall plastic containers of cereal are kept here, along with a food grinder. The bulk cereal is kept in the "food" bin, stored in the truck.

In preparing meals, good knives are a girls (or guys) best friend. They are stored in the "junk" drawer, under the sink. Cardboard sleeves keep the blades covered to avoid being cut. A sharp knife for slicing and cutting meat, a bread knife, and a smaller knife for cutting vegetables are essential. For a dinner with meat, we carry four steak knives.

Items in Our Junk Drawer

Spatulas and whisks
Bag of clips
Leveler
Fire sticks
Fuses
Scissors
Quarters for washing clothes
Can opener
Masher
Ice pick

Sink stopper
Net for over dishes when dining outside
Tongs and basting brush
Grater and garlic press
Wine bottle caps
Plastic scraper for removing dried food from pots
Measuring spoons on an O-ring
Clear Nail Polish to repair any pin holes in the canvas

Cabinets

The cabinet directly under the sink is extra sponges along with a small plastic bottle of dish detergent, measuring cup, and plastic coffee mugs. Ziploc Freezer bags (pint, quart, gallon & 2 gallon) are also kept there. These are taken out of their boxes and rubber banded for storage with a label telling their size. That way, insects cannot get into the cardboard boxes and they store more compactly.

Also in this area is aluminum foil, plastic wrap and wax paper (for microwave cooking).

In the cabinets under the sink and next to the refrigerator are stored glass bottles and cleaning supplies. A heavy duty Ziploc bag holds liquid Clorox for the sink and Pine Sol for washing the floors. A small plastic bucket has a clean, dry cloth, rubber gloves and a sponge, which is used to clean the inside of the camper. A gardener's foam pad really helps the knees when washing the floor.

Across from the sink is another large cabinet. In there we keep two, three, and five quart pots, two different sized frying pans, glass bowls for mixing and serving salads, strainer, 4 cup measurer, cutting boards, electric food processor and flashlights. A three-tiered wired basket is kept there and when set up, hangs from a "handle/hanger" above the cabinet for fruit and snacks.

We found a removable paper towel holder at a camping store, which is very convenient. When we take the camper down, the paper towel holder goes into the wastepaper bucket along with toilet paper (which is used instead of tissues because it is more compact).

Food Staples:

*Indicates item bought in bulk, taking advantage of coupons and stores such as Costco's. These are kept in a large plastic "food" bin, which is found next to the "medicine" bin in the back of the truck. Indigenous foods found along the way, bought in bulk, like Community Coffee in Louisiana, canned oysters from the Oregon Coast, and Chinese foods from Chinatown in San Francisco are also kept in the food bin.

Spice Racks:

We have three spice racks. In the cabinet next to the bed, are installed two spice racks. Another spice rack is on the door, under the sink. Spices include:
Garlic
Sea Salt in a grinder
Pepper in a grinder
Cinnamon Sugar
Ground Ginger
Paprika
Dried Oregano
Dried Basil
Dried Thyme
Dried Tarragon
Gumbo File

What's In The Fridge?

Even though the refrigerator has a travel lock, as an added precaution a pillow is put in between the door of the refrigerator and the back of the sink, when the sink is lowered. This will avoid a costly repair should the fridge door come open. This happened once, and we were lucky that all we had to do was reset the system by turning the refrigerator off and then on. Make sure the refrigerator is kept at 40 degrees. An inexpensive thermometer, purchased at a local hardware store, lets you see the temperature.

Thick carpet remnant placed in front of the fridge helps the knees when kneeling to get food out. Try not to keep the door open too long, as this quickly raises the temperature in the refrigerator.

Put a shallow plastic tray on the bottom of the refrigerator (like the ones that produce comes in). It helps keep food dry from condensation.

While traveling, we keep the refrigerator full, which keeps bottles and containers from bouncing around and breaking. When the refrigerator is not full, plastic milk jugs are filled half way with water. This fills the void and helps keep the fridge cold.

Items kept in the fridge are:
Mayo
Garlic (minced)
Salad Dressing
Peanut Butter and Jelly
Honey Mustard
Marinades for barbeques
Hot Dogs
Beer
Milk
Cheese
Hot Sauce
Flax Seed
Lunch Meats

A flask of raspberry liquor, mixed with lemon, makes for a great cup of tea on a cold night.

Tomatoes, Onion and Lettuce. Keep lettuce towards front of fridge so it won't freeze.

Lettuce and other veggies, such as green beans, broccoli, carrots, are kept in plastic bags with a paper towel to absorb moisture. They will last longer.

There are two long drawers next to the wheel well. I call one the **"Pantry"** drawer and the other the **"Linen"** drawer.

Items Found In Our Pantry:

Tuna fish*
A can of pineapple cubes in natural juice, to dress up many dishes
Three cans of hearty soups*. Add hot dogs and serve over rice or pasta, for dinner
Two cans of chicken soup with matzo balls
A small container of Nestlé's Quik for hot chocolate
Pasta* and Long Grain Rice transferred to a glass jar
Almonds*, Pecans* and Sunflower Seeds (kept in medium size glass jars)
Coffee * and a variety of teas (including Chamomile for restless nights, Smooth Move for constipation, Echinacea for the beginnings of a cold and Lipton's Green Tea with Jasmine because it tastes good.)
Macaroni and Cheese *
Small cans of corn, green beans, spinach and mushrooms*
Apple Sauce* – sold in small cups, six to a package and needs no refrigeration.
Olive and Canola Oil *
Parmalat* (This milk has a long shelf life. It comes in handy when we run out of milk)
Packets of mustard, ketchup, relish and lemon juice (kept in small, glass jars)
Chopped Clams
Brown Sugar* kept in a glass jar
Crystallized ginger in glass jar – great for upset stomachs
Small packets of Splenda for guests who prefer it in coffee
Microwavable Popcorn
Oatmeal* and Raisin Bran Cereal*

Recipes

I have a file on the computer for recipes collected over the years. When I want to cook something, I just turn on the computer.

It is fun to be creative. Recipes can be found almost anywhere. Inspiration can come from reading food packages and cans. You can be creative by adding whatever you have in the pantry drawer or in the "Food" bin.

Recipes from magazines are always challenging. Magazines can be found in Doctor's offices, Laundromats, campground family center or the checkout line at the food store. If we like a recipe, it gets added to the file on the computer.

I find that I cook more on the road and eat healthier because the ingredients vary from one state to the next. Also, the markets are fun to shop in, which provide local flavor and a taste of the culture.

I also look for cookbooks of the region in used bookstores or garage sales with simple recipes that I can make either in the Microwave, grill or stovetop. Libraries have "book sale" shelves where books can be purchased for a dollar. I also like to make up my own recipes. Here is a sample of my creativity.

Breakfast

We usually have cereal, toast and coffee or green tea. A banana is added for extra potassium. Sometimes I will make an omelet using fresh vegetables.

Appetizers

Slice a banana. Put a dollop of peanut butter on it. To make a dessert, add chocolate syrup or sprinkles.

Marinate orange slices, strawberries or other fruit in raspberry liquor. Serve over Angel Food cake with whip cream.

On the Road Snacks

Orange and/or apple slices with peanut butter and cheese slices are a staple for lunch. If we find a bakery, we buy fresh sourdough bread or something interesting and have it with cheese and fruit, like the French do. Sandwiches made with fresh bread, lettuce, tomato, mayo and cold cuts are prepared in the morning before we leave. I put the tomato in plastic wrap to be added to the sandwich later. That way the bread isn't soggy.

A jar of almonds, and raisins, are very tasty.

Granola bars are kept in the glove compartment and are great for a quick hunger pain fix.

Peanut Butter and Jelly on fresh bread is our favorite. If you put the peanut butter on both sides and the jelly in the middle, the bread won't get soggy.

Dinner

Steamed vegetables done in the microwave. On the grill we cook pork loin, steaks, hot dogs, ham steak, hamburger, and fish. That way, there is little clean up.

Husked corn can be cooked in the microwave for about 4 minutes and then rotate and cooked for an additional 3 minutes. Baste with Maple syrup and finish off with 3 minutes on the grill. Yum!

Canned vegetables are high in sodium and used only when I can't get fresh.

Corn in salsa along with ground meet or hot dogs, served over rice or pasta makes a good dinner.

Sweet peas and tuna added to macaroni & cheese is a healthy meal in itself.

Small cans of mushrooms add flavor to many dishes.

Spinach is a healthy vegetable to go with chicken or steak.

Campbell's Select and Chunky Soups are great for adding veggies and meats for a meal.

Cans of claims added to garlic butter with a twist of lemon. Served over pasta, it is great for serving company.

Imported Can Hams (1 lb.) can be grilled and leftovers used for Shiskabobs

To Compliment A Meal

Apple Sauce – in the small cups is easy to serve.

Marinades for meats that are cooked on the grill are done before hand kept in a plastic Ziploc bag.

Nuts added to salads and vegetables give the dish an extra crunch

Linen Drawer

Bath Towels (3)
Wash Cloths (2)
Dish Towels (4)
Pot Holders and oven mitts (2 each)
Hot mats (2)
Placemats and Napkins (4 each)
A Deck of Cards
Wine Glass Trinkets
Sewing Kit
A Night Light – for guests

The Medicine Cabinet

Indicates items bought in bulk. Items are kept in a plastic "Medical" bin stored in the cap of the truck. I don't like to run out so I have back-up items in this bin. Personal items are transferred to smaller containers to make it easier to handle when using in campground bathrooms.
Ibuprofen for Inflammation
Tinactin Antifungal Spray for Athletes Foot
Preparation H and Tucks
Di-Delamine – Antihistamine for bites and sunburn
Cough Medicine
Excedrin for Migraine Headaches
Antiseptic Wipes
Epson Salts for Foot Baths (For tired feet, put in a bucket of cool water)
Aloe & Natural Body Lotion*
Body Splash
Shampoo*
Cotton Swabs
Bug Spray with SPF 30 and Deet
Vaseline
Vick's Chest Rub

Sun Tan Lotion SP15 and 30
Therma Care Ice Packs
Toothpaste *
Dental Floss*
Mouthwash *
Extra Sonicare Toothbrushes*. Brush heads are changed every four months.
Brown Soap (Phels Naphtha). A ranger once told me that a cold shower (using brown soap) would remove poison ivy oil and it does!
Extra Empty Plastic Bottles of Various Sizes
A Baggie Containing Plastic Gloves and Face Masks
Hand wipes

Things that leak are kept in Ziploc bags. Surprisingly, lip balm is very messy if not stored in plastic. It tends to melt and leak in a hot truck. You can buy small baggies at the craft store to hold small items.

A First Aid kit is kept under the back seat in the truck, which contains:
Bandages
Neosporin
Tweezers with a small
Magnifying glass
Refresh Eye Drops
Ibuprofen
Alcohol Swabs
Tums
Chapstick (in a small baggie)
Sinus Tabs
Ambesol – for toothaches
Moleskin

Personal Products

Astringent*
AM Face Moisturizer with SP15*
PM Face Moisturizer*
Cotton Balls*

Panty Liners*
Make-up
Face Scrub*
Shaver Replacements*
Deodorant*
Vitamins*

Vitamins are bought in bulk, because it is a lot cheaper. I have 31 film canisters, which I fill with vitamins. I double the amount in each canister, so I know there is a 2 month supply. The canisters are kept in a plastic bag. One bag is for full canisters and another is for empty canisters. Seven canisters give me a two-week supply and are kept in a small cloth bag in the camper. Also in the cloth bag is a small jar with my husband's vitamins. That way I can make sure he takes them. The big plastic bags are kept in the medicine bin.

Health Notes:

Washing your hands constantly is a sure way to fight infections. It is amazing how dirty our hands get. When washing, I say the alphabet. This ensures the scrubbing lasts for at least 20 seconds, which is recommended for clean hands. We try to not use our hands to flush the toilet. Instead, our feet do the job. If this isn't possible, then we use toilet paper on the flush handle. Once our hands are clean, we shut the water off either with a paper towel or if the handles are long, with our elbows. If at all possible, we use a paper towel to open the bathroom door. You can also use the hem of your shirt.

Prescriptions. Having a good relationship with your doctor and letting him know that you will be traveling is important. Carry prescriptions for your medicine with you so that they may be refilled. Once filed with a major drug stores (including Wal-Mart, CVS, Walgreen's, etc.) will make it easier to have them filled.

Replace electrolytes during physical activity, especially when the temperatures are above 80 degrees. Drink Gatorade or other electrolyte replacement drinks or eat foods high in potassium and sodium such as dried fruits and beef jerky.

Never, ever, take a shower without medium-soled flip-flops or some kind of protection on your feet. "Athletes foot" and "Staph" can last up to two months and be very uncomfortable (personal experience speaking here).

As a woman, the most important item I carry, are panty liners. I keep them in the pocket of my shorts, in my pocketbook and in my shower case.

Medical Tips That Work

Change plastic water bottles every few months to avoid bacteria builds up.

Did you know that scratching a mosquito bite with a bar of soap (similar to those you get in a hotel) helps take the sting out? We keep a small bar in the glove compartment and in the camper. It has come in handy many times.

Treatment for Poison Ivy Cactus Thorns, and Splinters

Poison Ivy – "Shiny leaves of three, let them be".

Learn to recognize these plants. Check out poisonous plants on the web site at *www.poisonivy.org* for good photos . This site has valuable information and will help you recognize poisonous plants.

When hiking in the woods, wear long pants and a long sleeve shirt. Change your clothes right after the hike to prevent lingering residues from coming in contact with your skin.

Take a cool shower, using a hard brown soap (Phels Naphtha) as soon as possible after contact. Use plenty of soap and water. I am very allergic to poison ivy and have learned to use brown soap when showering. It works amazingly well.

Avoid inhalation of smoke from fire that may contain these plants, which can cause a painful and dangerous reaction in the throat and lungs.

Do not scratch the rash, as it may become infected. Use a spray such as Calamine lotion or hydrocortisone, according to directions on the package. Take an over-the-counter antihistamine, such as Benadryl, following directions, which can ease symptoms.

If you experience difficulty in breathing, swallowing, or if the rash is particularly severe, see a doctor. When traveling, do not hesitate to visit a clinic or emergency room. (One time my face swelled up from poison ivy and I went to the emergency room and another time the rash was so bad, I went to a clinic. Medication was prescribed and I felt better within two days.)

Cactus Thorns

A plant called cholla (pronounced "CHOH'-ya") is found in the Southwest. If you've strayed too close, its stickers will jump on you. That is why it is nicknamed "jumping cholla". These stickers are the spines that help the cactus reproduce. Sticking to you helps them travel to new locations to grow. Use a tweezers to remove the cactus spines. A comb or credit card can also be helpful in cactus country to pull off stickers that attach to you.

Splinters

If you have a splinter and are having a hard time removing it, put a drop of glue or clear nail polish on it and let it dry. Once it is dry, peel it off the skin and the splinter will come off with it. If there is no time to let glue dry or nail polish dry, try duct tape. It's strong, and will pull the splinter out.

Apply alcohol or other antibacterial ointment to punctured wounds. Bandage if necessary, but take bandage off at night, so the wound can get air and dry up. I keep alcohol swipes in the glove compartment for such emergencies.

Flu Remedies

At first sign of cold or flu, we take Vitamin C three times a day.

Echinacea tea is good to drink along with plenty of water.

Zinc tablets are taken the first few days follow package instructions.

"Airborne" can be found in the drugstore. I have taken Airborne and my symptoms were not as severe as others who did not take it.

"Vernor's" Ginger Ale, made in Michigan, is great when heated. Drinking a cup of hot ginger ale just before bedtime helps us to feel better in the morning.

Recipe for Jewish Chicken Soup. Cut 4 lb chicken into quarters and place in a big pot, on the stove. Pour in enough water to cover chicken. Bring to boil. Add 1 onion, 1 carrot, 1 parsnip, and 2 celery stalks. In a garni bag, place parsley, dill and garlic. Let simmer for about 30 minutes or until the chicken is tender. Occasionally skim fat off top. Enjoy and be well.

Entertainment on the Road

I do not like to drive, although will do so if the situation warrants it. I see my job as the navigator and providing entertainment. Music, reading books out loud, planning snacks, and preparing information for discussion on sites to see at our next destination, are ways to make the trip interesting.

Spirituality

I really miss the congregation at home, and try to compensate by reading my prayer book at the same time as they do for the service in Frederick. Believe it or not, I do feel the connection.

Be Weather Wise

It is important to understand weather systems and how they move across the country.

We use a citizen band (CB) radio in the truck to hear the National Oceanic and Atmospheric Administration (NOAA) weather forecasts along with a portable AM/FM that we listen to in the camper. You will find that on most state maps, there is a number for the highway department to call and check road conditions.

Never leave your awning open when high winds are expected. It will be torn.

If you are not able to see the road due to fog or heavy rain, pull off and try to find a safe place to wait until the condition improves.

The website we found most useful to find weather conditions, both immediate and long range, is www.weather.com.

A weather radio can be purchased at Radio Shack that will give you an audible forecast from NOAA. The unit will emit a signal alerting you to specific warnings for high winds, dust storms, sever thunderstorms and flash floods.

To prepare for bad weather, make sure your headlights are clean, know where your foul weather jackets and boots are and make sure your cellular phone is charged. If we are camping and bad weather is expected, we put everything away in case we have to take the camper down in a hurry. Our back-up plan is to sleep in the truck, motel or a bed and breakfast.

Be extra careful when picking a sight at a campground. You don't want to be near creek bed or under dead tree limbs when bad weather is forecasted.

If Your Credit Card is Stolen

Immediately file a report with the police and keep a copy of the report for your files. Alert your bank and credit card companies. Call the following major companies: TeleCheck at 800-710-9898, Certegy at 800-437-5120, International Check Services at 800-824-6117. The goal is to create as many roadblocks as possible.

Notify Trans Union at 800-493-2392, Equifax at 888-766-0008 and Experion at 800-397-3742 about your status and complete a fraud affidavit. Request a base line credit report, which will show you how your credit rating has been affected. Ask that your file be red-flagged with a fraud statement, which will prevent a thief from illegally signing up for credit in your name.

Be organized. Keep meticulous records of whom you talk with, what institution they are with, the date of the discussion and what was discussed.

As an extra precaution, make sure that when you use your credit card, your name is on the credit card that is handed back to you. Scams are around every corner. Be careful.

Recommended Reading

<u>**Blue Highways: A Journey Into America**</u>
By William Least Heat Moon
Little Browan and Company, 1982

<u>**Travels with Charlie: In Search of America**</u>
By John Steinbeck
Viking, 1962

<u>**On the Road**</u>
By Jack Kerouac
Viking, 1957

Magazines and Organizations

AARP - American Association of Retired Persons

AAA - If you are a member, they can help plan your trip and have great roadside service.

Good Sam's Club. They also offer camping discounts and assistance.

Trailer Life Magazine

Camping Life

Country Discoveries

<u>Trailer Life RV Parks, Campgrounds & Services Directory</u>. This is the Bible for researching campgrounds. The rating system is a good guide in finding a clean, well-kept campground. The directory includes national, state and private campgrounds.

Suggestions on How to Buy a Camper

Your camper may qualify as a second home. Therefore, any interest on a loan could be deductible from your federal taxes. IRS Publication 936 states, "For you to take a home mortgage interest deduction, your debt must be a secured debt on a qualified home. A home includes a house, condominium, mobile home, house trailers, boat or similar property that has sleeping, cooking and toilet facilities." Toilet facilities could be a porta-potti. Visit www.irs.gov.

First decide on the type of camper that suites your family. Decide on what you want to do with your camper and what options are important to you. Below is a list of manufacturer's web sites. You can also look in magazines listed in the "Magazines and Organizations" section of this book. I make a spreadsheet to compare features. Once the camper of your dreams has been decided upon, call or visit a number of dealers to compare options and prices.

Know your credit score. To find your credit score, go to www.FreeCreditReport.com. If your credit score is high, then you should be able to get the best interest rates. If you credit score is low, then check out several lending agencies. A credit union may be able to help you. Offices can be found by searching www.cuna.org or by calling 1-800-356-8010. Also, Essex Credit can help. Go to web site www.rvloans.com or call 866-377-3948. Essex Credit's website has a calculator to determine how much you may be able to afford in monthly payment. To see what the lowest interest rates are, go to www.bankrate.com.

Being well informed is the key to successful negotiations

RV Manufacturers

Fleetwood Folding Trailers – www.fleetwoodrv.com
Jayco RV – www.jayco.com
Palomino – www.palominorv.com
Starcraft – www.starcraftrv.com
Viking – www.vikingrv.com
Rockwood – www.forestriverinc.com

Campgrounds We Stayed At

2003 Campgrounds

March 2003 - Feb. 2004

<Index 15>								
Miles	**Park Name**	**State**	**Notes**	**Cost**	**Fm**	**To**	**Nts**	**Total Cost**
240	Da Greggs	Virginia Beach, VA	Friend	Free	3/10/2003	3/12/2003	2	Free
180	Goose Creek SP	S. of Washington, NC	Dry Camping	2.50	3/12/2003	3/13/2003	1	$2.50
380	Skidaway SP	Savannah, GA		14.00	3/13/2003	3/26/2003	13	$182.00
325	Family	Dothan, AL		Free	3/26/2003	4/2/2003	7	Free
160	Big Lagoon SP	Pedidio Key, FL	Beaches	14.00	4/2/2003	4/9/2003	7	$98.00
350	Bayou Segnette SP	Westwego, LA	New N.O.	6.00	4/9/2003	4/11/2003	2	$12.00
205	Chicot SP	Ville Platte, LA	Cajun Praire	6.00	4/9/2003	4/13/2003	4	$24.00
100	Sam Houston SP	Lake Charles, LA		6.00	4/13/2003	4/16/2003	3	$18.00
150	Galveston SP	Galveston, TX	Beach	17.00	4/16/2003	4/20/2003	4	$68.00
195	Palmetto SP	Luling, TX		17.00	4/20/2003	4/24/2003	4	$68.00
120	Guadeloupe SP	New Braunfel, TX	Fiesta	17.00	4/24/2003	5/4/2003	10	$170.00
220	Seminole Canyon SP	Comstock, TX	Desert	14.00	5/4/2003	5/6/2003	2	$28.00
380	Ft. Davis SP	Fort Davis, TX	Mountains	14.00	5/6/2003	5/9/2003	3	$42.00
	Drove to the center of Big Bend NP, but it was too hot for our liking							
230	Marriott	El Paso, TX	Near Mexico	Rewards	5/9/2003	5/11/2003	2	Free
115	Caballo SP	N. of Las Cruces, NM	South of T&C	14.00	5/11/2003	5/17/2003	6	$84.00
220	Valley of Fire Nat'l Rec.	Carrizozo, NM	BLM	7.00	5/17/2003	5/21/2003	4	$28.00
155	Monzano NF	Los Lunas, NM		14.00	5/21/2003	5/22/2003	1	$14.00
140	Patricia and Paul	Albuquerque, NM	Friend	Free	5/22/2003	5/26/2003	4	Free
115	Abiquiu Reservoir	Abiquiu, NM	BLM	7.00	5/26/2003	6/2/2003	7	$147.00
110	Pagosa Springs	Pagosa Springs, CO	Private	21.00	6/2/2003	6/3/2003	1	$21.00
130	McPhee Reservoir	Delores, CO	BLM Desert	10.00	6/3/2003	6/4/2003	1	$10.00
80	McPhee Reservoir	Cortez, CO	BLM - Mesa Verde	9.00	6/4/2003	6/9/2003	5	$45.00
	Drove a loop that went Ridgeway, Ouray, Silverton, and Durango							
90	Devils Canyon	N. of Blanding, UT	Arches	2.50	6/9/2003	6/10/2003	1	$2.50
90	Hite	Lake Powell, UT		Free	6/10/2003	6/11/2003	1	Free
95	Thousand Lake RV	Torrey, UT	Private	15.75	6/11/2003	6/14/2003	3	$47.25
115	Red Canyon NF	Panguitch, UT	N. of Bryce	5.50	6/14/2003	6/16/2003	2	$11.00
150	Virgin River	Mesquite, NV	Hotel	20.00	6/16/2003	6/17/2003	1	$20.00
60	Circus, Circus	Las Vegas, NV	Hotel	39.99	6/17/2003	6/20/2003	3	$119.97
330	Mono Vista RV Park	Lee Vining, CA	Private-Mono Lake	25.00	6/20/2003	6/22/2003	2	$50.00
65	Tamarock Flats	Yosemite NP, CA	Yosemite	Free	6/22/2003	6/23/2003	1	Free
75	49's Ranch	Columbia, CA	Private	25.00	6/23/2003	6/24/2003	1	$25.00
160	Half Moon Bay SP	Half Moon Bay, CA	Beach	Free	6/24/2003	6/26/2003	2	Free
	Bill and Julias	San Francisco, CA	Friend	Free	6/26/2003	7/1/2003	5	Free
185	Bill and Julias	Donner Lake, CA	Friend	Free	7/1/2003	7/8/2003	7	Free
150	McArthur Burney Fall SP	Burney, CA	N of Lassen Vol NP	14.00	7/8/2003	7/10/2003	2	$28.00
160	Crater Lake NP	OR		8.00	7/10/2003	7/12/2003	2	$16.00
255	Heltons	Salem, OR	Friend	Free	7/12/2003	7/21/2003	9	Free
200	Grants	Tacoma, WA	Friend	Free	7/21/2003	7/29/2003	8	Free
	Rics	Annapolis, MD	Friend	Free	7/29/2003	8/17/2003	19	Free
	Grants	Tacoma, WA	Friend	Free	8/17/2003	8/20/2003	3	Free
115	Dungeness Spit SP	Port Angeles, WA		14.00	8/20/2003	8/24/2003	4	$56.00
100	Lake Ozette NP	Olympic NP, WA	Dry Camping	5.00	8/24/2003	8/25/2003	1	$5.00
110	Sul Doc NP	Olympic NP, WA	Dry Camping	6.00	8/25/2003	9/2/2003	8	$48.00
	Did a lot of exploring from Sol Doc, including trips to Cape Flaterry, La Push, Hoh and Lake Crescent							
80	Victoria	British Columbia	B&B	70.00	9/2/2003	9/3/2003	1	$70.00
50	Dungeness Spit SP	Olympic NP, WA	Dry Camping	14.00	9/3/2003	9/4/2003	1	$14.00
40	Heart of the Hills NP	Olympic NP, WA	Dry Camping	6.00	9/4/2003	9/7/2003	3	$18.00
450	Grants and Heltons - Bye	Tacoma, and Salem	Friends	Free	9/7/2003	9/11/2003	4	Free

2003 Campgrounds

March 2003 - Feb. 2004

Miles	Park Name	State	Notes	Cost	Fm	To	Nts	Total Cost
155	John Day Dam	La Page, OR	Army Corp	8.00	9/11/2003	9/12/2003	1	$8.00
280	Boise	Boise, ID	Hotel - Car Repair	45.00	9/12/2003	9/13/2003	1	$45.00
100	Culvert	Hailey, ID	Little Wood River	Free	9/13/2003	9/14/2003		Free
230	Challis Hot Springs	Challis, ID	Private	25.00	9/14/2003	9/15/2003	1	$25.00
5	Challis Mtn Lodge	Challis, ID	Hotel - Weather	50.00	9/15/2003	9/16/2003	1	$50.00
165	Lava Springs Cottonwood	Arimo, ID	Private	25.00	9/16/2003	9/17/2003	1	$25.00
173	Best Western	Provo, UT	Hotel - Weather	45.00	9/17/2003	9/18/2003	1	$45.00
165	Piute Reservoir	N of Kingston, UT		Free	9/18/2003	9/19/2003	1	Free
225	Zion NP	Zion, NP, UT		7.00	9/19/2003	9/21/2003	2	$14.00
250	Grand Canyon NP	Grand Canyon NP, AZ	North Rim	7.50	9/21/2003	9/22/2003	1	$7.50
220	Outside Petrified Forest NI	Petrified Forest, AZ	Dry Camping	Free	9/22/2003	9/23/2003	1	Free
280	Santa Fe RV Park	Santa Fe, NM	Private	25.00	9/23/2003	9/28/2003	5	$125.00
60	Cochiti	Cochiti, NM	BLM	5.50	9/28/2003	10/13/2003	15	$82.50
200	Valley of Fire	Carrizozo, NM	BLM	5.00	10/13/2003	10/14/2003	1	$5.00
160	Brantley Lake SP	Brantley, NM	S of Roswell	14.00	10/14/2003	10/19/2003	5	$70.00
210	San Angelo SP	San Angelo, TX		12.00	10/19/2003	10/20/2003	1	$12.00
260	McKinney Falls SP	McKinney, TX	Near Austin	14.00	10/20/2003	10/21/2003	1	$14.00
165	Sharon	Houston, TX	Friend	Free	10/21/2003	10/23/2003	2	Free
225	Lake Fausse Sp	E of New Iberia, LA	On the Levee	6.00	10/23/2003	10/28/2003	5	$30.00
160	Bayou Signettee SP	Westwego, LA	Near New Orleans	6.00	10/28/2003	11/6/2003	9	$54.00
90	Fox's	Biloxi, MS	Private - Awful	9.50	11/6/2003	11/8/2003	2	$19.00
150	Big Lagoon SP	Pedidio Key, FL	Near Pensacola	14.00	11/8/2003	11/14/2003	6	$84.00
60	Grayton Beach SP	E of Fort Walton, FL	Beach	10.00	11/14/2003	11/15/2003	1	$10.00
125	Family	Dothan, AL	Family	Free	11/15/2003	11/17/2003	2	Free
200	Laura S. Walker SP	Waycross, GA	Okefenokee Swamp	13.50	11/17/2003	11/21/2003	4	$54.00
60	Crooked River SP	St. Mary's, GA	On River	13.30	11/21/2003	11/28/2003	7	$93.10
40	Jennings	Jekyll Island, GA	Friends	Free	11/28/2003	12/2/2003	4	Free
70	Crooked River SP	St. Mary's, GA		13.50	12/2/2003	12/3/2003	1	$13.50
60	Anastasia SP	St. Augustine, FL	Old City	19.50	12/3/2003	12/10/2003	7	$136.50
70	Sebastian SP	Sebastian, FL	Near Melbourne/Ver	19.50	12/10/2003	12/17/2003	7	$136.50
60	Jonathan Dickson SP	Jupiter Island, FL		7.28	12/17/2003	12/24/2003	7	$50.96
180	Bob and Susan	Ft. Lauderdale, FL	Friends	Free	12/24/2003	1/4/2004	11	Free
115	Koresham SP	Ft. Meyers, FL	E. of Sanibel	9.25	1/4/2004	1/8/2004	4	$37.00
75	Oscar Scherer SP	Osprey, FL	S. of Sarasota	9.07	1/8/2004	1/13/2004	5	$45.35
110	Hillsborough SP	Lakeland, FL		7.28	1/13/2004	1/16/2004	3	$21.84
85	Rainbow Springs SP	Dunnellon, FL	Near River	10.16	1/16/2004	1/19/2004	3	$30.48
90	Manatee Springs SP	Chiefland, FL	Saw Manatee	5.99	1/19/2004	1/23/2004	4	$23.96
150	3 World RV Resort	Kissimmee, FL	Private	14.00	1/23/2004	2/1/2004	9	$126.00
	Drove to both coasts several times and Disneyworld twice							
156	Myakka River SP	Chiefland, FL		12.00	2/1/2004	2/5/2004	4	$48.00
150	3 World RV Resort	Kissimmee, FL	Private	24.00	2/5/2004	2/10/2004	5	$120.00
125	Anastasia SP	St. Augustine, FL		12.00	2/10/2004	2/14/2004	4	$48.00
160	Dan and Jane Jennings	Jekyll Island, GA	Friends	Free	2/14/2004	2/17/2004	3	Free
175	Mariott (Twn & Country)	GA	Going Home	Pts	2/17/2004	2/18/2004	1	Free
20	Skidaway SP	Savannah, GA		19.00	2/18/2004	2/21/2004	3	$57.00
170	Oak Plantation	Outside Charleston, SC	Private	24.00	2/21/2004	2/23/2004	2	$48.00
220	Fairfield Inn	Fayetteville, NC	Hotel	Pts	2/23/2004	2/24/2004	1	Free
120	Fairfield Inn	Franklin, VA	Hotel	Pts	2/24/2004	2/25/2004	1	Free
274	Annapolis	MD	Friend	Free	2/25/2004	2/27/2004	2	Free
75	Frederick	MD	Friend	Free	2/27/2004	2/29/2004	2	Free

2003 Campgrounds

March 2003 - Feb. 2004

Miles	Park Name	State	Notes	Cost	Fm	To	Nts	Total Cost
14,548	Point to Point						357	$3,407.41
18,392	Touring, especially in Florida and the Pacific Northwest							
33,000	Total							

2004 Campgrounds

May 2004 - October 2004

Miles	Park Name	State	Notes	Cost	Date	Nts	Total
							Cost
125	Manatee Springs SP	Chiefland, FL	Springs	$10.00	5/23/04	1	$10.00
200	Port St. Joseph SP	Port St. Joe, FL	Beaches	$10.00	May 24-25	2	$20.00
206	Big Lagoon SP	Pedidio, FL	Beaches	$10.00	5/26/04	1	$10.00
240	Bayou Segnette SP	Westwego, LA	Near N.O.	$6.00	May 27-29	3	$18.00
250	Sam Houston SP	Lake Charles, LA		$6.00	5/30/04	1	$6.00
158	Sharon	Houston, TX	Friend	Friend	5/31/04	1	Free
250	Lady Bird Municipal Park	Fredericksburg, TX	County Park. Great Golf	$18.00	June 1-2	3	$54.00
245	Big Springs SP	Big Springs, TX	Comfort Inn. CG too windy	$54.00	6/3/04	1	$54.00
245	Bottomless Lake SP	Roswell, NM	Near Carlsbad Caves	$14.00	June 4-5	2	$28.00
176	Santa Rosa SP	Santa Rosa, NM	To Far Fm Anywhere	$14.00	6/6/04	1	$14.00
175	Ambassador Inn Motel	Albuquerque, NM	Needed to near the airport	$31.00	June 7-8	2	$62.00
2270	Sub Total of Miles Went						
	Albuquerque Airport	NM	Left Camper and Truck at Airport	Friend	Jun 9-15	6	Free
	Ambassador Inn Motel	Albuquerque, NM	Flight got in late	$31.00	6/15/04	1	$31.00
300	Sundance RV Park - Private	Cortez, CO	Cortez, CO - Fab w/e/c	$25.00	Jun 16-17	2	$50.00
265	1,000 Lakes Private CG	Torrey, UT	Capital Reef.	$17.00	June 18-19	2	$34.00
265	Great Basin BakerNF CG	Great Basin, NP, NV	Near CO and NV Boarder.	$5.00	6/20/04	1	$5.00
220	Private	Austin, NV	Baptist Church Pking Lot with w/e	$15.00	6/21/04	1	$15.00
	(next time camp at the Holiday Inn in Ely for free and the next night try Coldprings)						
190	Ft. Churchill SP	Fallon, NV	Mesquitoes. Next time Latonnia SP	$12.00	6/22/04	1	$12.00
180	Truckee	Truckee, CA	Friend	Friend	Jun 22 - 24	3	Free
185	San Francisco	El Cerrito, CA	Friend	Friend	June 25 - July 1	7	Free
185	Truckee	Truckee, CA	Donner Lake	Friend	July 2 - 10	9	Free
300	Little River Inn	Little River, CA	Near Mendocino	$125.00	7/11/04	1	$125.00
180	Sounds of the Sea	Near Patrick's Pt,CA	Private. More for big rigs	$30.00	7/12/04	1	$30.00
50	Patrick's Point SP	N. of Eureka, CA	no hookups - Fab	$21.00	7/13/04	1	$21.00
150	Cape Blanco SP	Orford, OR	Oregon Coast - Fab w/e	$16.00	7/14/04	1	$16.00
210	Heltons	Salem, OR	Friend	Friend	July 15 -24	10	Free
100	Bayview Private CG	OR	Near Hwy, w/e, Bad Cable	$22.22	7/25/04	1	$22.22
80	Washington Street RV Park	Chinook, WA	Private - w/e/cable on water	$20.00	7/26/04	1	$20.00
160	The Grants	Tacoma, WA	Friend	Friend	Jul 27 - Aug 1	6	Friend
110	Oak Harbor Cty RV Park	Oak Harbor, WA	Whidbey Island - Fab/ w/e poor TV	$20.00	Aug 2 - 9	7	$140.00
80	Colonial Creek NF	Cascades NP, WA	Fab. No hookups	$6.00	8/10/04	1	$6.00
250	Alta Lake SP	Pateros Lake, WA	w/e	$21.00	Aug. 11 & 12	2	$42.00
80	Steamboat Rock SP	Electric City, WA	Coulee Dam, w/e	$21.00	Aug. 13 & 14	2	$42.00
130	River Lake RV - Private CG	Coeur D Alene, ID	w/e/c - Passport of America	$18.50	Aug. 15	1	$18.50
200	Ekstroms Station Private CG	Clinton, MT	Might be sold	$25.00	8/16/04	1	$25.00
280	Lion RV Park - Private CG	W. Yellowstone, MT	Nice. Passport of America	$13.00	Aug. 17 - 22	6	$78.00
80	Cody - Side Trip	Cody, WY	Yellowstone RV, lots of NP choices	$12.00	8/20/04	1	$12.00
80	Jackson Hole Hotel	Jackson Hole, WY	Nice but expensive	$95.00	8/23/04	1	$95.00
220	Firehole NP CG	Rock Springs, WY	Flaming Gorge	$6.50	8/24/04	1	$6.50
128	Green River NPCG	Vernal, UT	Dinosaur Fossil Park	$6.00	8/25/04	1	$6.00
280	Marty and Carol's	Frisco, CO	Friend	Friend	Aug 26 - Sep 16	22	Free
	One week housesitting while friends were in Alaska.						Free
246	Country Host Motel & RV Park	Walsenbert, CO	Private	$19.30	9/17/04	1	$19.30
290	Palo Duro RV Park	Canyon, TX	Private	$18.20	9/18/04	1	$18.20
240	Lady Bryd Johnson Cty Pk	Fredericksburg, TX	Great Golf	$18.00	Sep 19-20	2	$36.00
235	All Star RV Park	Houston, TX	Special Price for Week, Passport	$28.00	Sept 21 - 28	7	$196.00
	AC Flew Home to Florida to assess Hurricane Damage. $221.00 on SW. Fortunately, there was little damage						
360	Charles - Baton Rouge	LA	They forgot to charge him	N/C	9/29/04	1	Free
420	Dothan	AL	Family	Family	Sep 30 - Oct. 3	3	Free

2004 Campgrounds

May 2004 - October 2004

Miles	Park Name	State	Notes	Cost	Date	Nts	Total
							Cost
340	Tarpon Springs	FL	Home				
11609	Point to Point					134	$1,397.72
4049	Touring, especially California, San Juan Islands, Yellowstone and Colorado						
13398	Total						

Spreadsheets

Personal Information

Year

First Name	**Last Name**	**Address**	**City, State, Zip**	**Phone #'s**	**Other**	**Description**	**E-Mails**
The top part of this spreadsheet is for friends.							
The middle part of this spreadsheet is for Vendors.							
Name	Acct #	Address	City and State	800 #s			
I.e. - Banks, Credit Cards, Doctors, Lawyers, etc.							
The last part is names of new friends made along the way							
Name	Where we met		Adress	Phone			E-mail
This form is updated periodically and sent to my son for safe keeping.							
Just case something goes wrong, he has all the information to settle our affairs							

Financials For (Year)

	28-Jan	12-Feb	15-Mar	18-Apr	16-May	15-Jun	15-Jul	17-Aug	16-Sep	Oct. 15	Nov. 17	12-Dec
Gas												
Life Ins												
401K												
AC Ret.												
Retirement Total												
Credit Card												
Credit Card Awards												
Mortgage												
Savings												
Checking												
Electric												
Phone												
Notes:							Mony Tsf'd fm Savings					
							Amt.		Description			

Ford F150 Repair Records

Date	Garage	City, State	Work Done	Cost	Notes
Sold in January 2005					
9/?/04		Frisco, CO	Rotate Tires	$16.00	
8/28/2004	Express Lube	Frisco, CO	Oil Change	$43.00	
8/9/2004	Jakes Auto	Oak Harbor, WA	Replaced R Real Axil Seal	$111.01	
			PCV Valve OK		
			Greasted U Joints & Steering		
8/7/2004	Mike's Garage	Oak Harbor, WA	Checked Truck. Discovered Axil	n/c	
			Greased Camper Ball Bearings		
7/23/2004	Les Scwab	Salem, OR	Rotate Tires	n/c	
7/20/2004	Direct Auto	Salem, OR	Radiator Hose Replaces	$161.00	
			Oil and Oil Filter Changed		
6/16/2004	Pep Boys	Albuqueque, NM	Replace Oil Pressure Sender	$431.07	
			Oil and Oil Filter Changed		
			Replace Fuel Filter		
			A/C Recharged		
5/20/2004	Tire Kingdom	Tarpon Sp., FL	Upgrade Rear Suspension	$382.85	
			Change Auto Trans Fluid		
			Flush Transmission		
			Add Rear Load Levelers		
4/19/2004	Jiffy Lube	Tampa, FL	10W40 Oil Change and Filter	$27.00	
2/9/2004	Jiffy Lube	Kissimme, FL	15W40 Oil Change and Filter	$29.95	
2/2/2004	Rice Tires	Frederick, MD	Rotate Tires	n/c	
1/27/2004	B. Guillen	Haines City, FL	Replace Starter	$74.20	
1/21/2004		Chiefland, FL	Replace Serpentine Belt	$75.00	
1/2/2004	Good Year	Ft Lauderdale, FL	Brakes Worn	$682.00	
			Bleed and Flush Brake System		
And so on					

Medical Information

Date	Doctor's Name	Procedure	Cost	Ins. Status	Owe	Paid	Date
2003							
					Prepared:	Date	
On a separate page, is the names, addresses and phone numbers of all our doctors and labs.							
					Prepared:	Date	

Printed in the United States
97794LV00007B/61/A

9 781425 941727